BLUE SKIES FOR AFRIKANS

Life and Death Choices
for Afrikan Liberation

by

Paul Ifayomi Grant

Navig8or Press, Nottingham, United Kingdom

Published by Navig8or Press
58 Sunnydale Road
Nottingham
NG3 7GG
United Kingdom

Cover Layout by Jeremy Prince 3PD design

British Library Cataloguing in Publication Data
A catalogue record for this book is available from the British Library

ISBN 0-9545529-1-1

Printed and bound by Tandem Press
www.tandempress.com

This book is dedicated to

The Creator

My positive female Ancestors
My mother Orinthea Grant
My Wife Beverley Angela Grant
My sister Tracey Nicole Grant
My daughter Abiba Ashia Orinthea Grant

My positive male Ancestors
My Father Reuben Grant
My brother Nigel Anthony Grant
My son Jawanza Kwesi Grant

To all who struggle for justice

"I have not committed treason against my ancestors."

33rd principle of Ma'at from the
Kemetic 'Declarations of Innocence'

"The most dangerous of all dependencies is to depend on your powerful oppressor to free you and share power with you, because powerful people never train powerless people to take their power away from them."

John Henrik Clarke

"Now, I ask you, had you not rather be killed than to be a slave to a tyrant, who takes the life of your mother, wife, and dear little children? Look upon your mother, wife and children, and answer God Almighty; and believe this, that it is no more harm for you to kill a man, who is trying to kill you, than it is for you to take a drink of water when thirsty; in fact, the man who will stand still and let another murder him, is worse than an infidel, and, if he has common sense, ought not be pitied."

David Walker
David Walker's Appeal

Yaa Asantewa: Afrikan Shero

At the end of the 19th century, when the British attempted to colonise the Gold Coast, now known as Ghana, Yaa Asantewa became the motivating force behind the Ashanti. She is famous for her passionate address to some of the chiefs who were afraid to make war against the British.

She said;

"Is it true that the bravery of the Ashanti is no more?...if you men of Ashanti will not go forward, then we will. We the women will. I shall call upon my fellow women. We will fight the white men. We will fight till the last of us falls in the battlefields."

Her speech moved the chiefs so much that they immediately swore the Great Oath of Ashanti to fight the British until the Asantehene King Premph was set free from his exile.

Source: *Ligali, March 2005 African History Newsletter*

Voice of a Youth

There follows a poem sent to me by a young man who was going through hard times at the time of writing. This young man had attended a cultural summer school run by Nubian Link, a community education organisation of which I am a part, a few years earlier. The important thing is not that we agree with every sentiment expressed, but rather that we hear and engage with the voices of our youth.

Defiance

I will not be crushed by force
I will not succumb to stealth tactics of brainwashing
Attacking the vulnerable mind early in the morning
Name and Number
I am not a number
If you wish to describe me as a number
I am number one
What happens in the future is an endless possibility
What has happened before is a negative
I am odd
I refuse to be placed into your world or your rules
That's why I am here
I have my own outlook on the world in which I will reach the number one
I will gain success according to my rules and my lifestyle
Your success is not mine and I do not want it
Manipulate these words with your prejudice to fit a moulded stereotype which you can't crush me into
This is the life I have chosen to lead
This is how I roll!

By Andrew Thorpe

Thanks, Praise, Acknowledgements

The writing of a book is a solitary, sometimes lonely affair; however it is never accomplished alone. There are always a group of people, paid or unpaid, who contribute to the production of the finished article. For writers whose work is published through well established publishing houses most of these people will be employees of the publisher. For self-publishing authors like me, virtually all of the advisors and helpers are volunteers. Friends and family, who gladly give of their time because they believe in what the author is doing.

These people act as content readers, proof readers, confidants, graphic designers, publicists, events co-ordinators, guest speakers, contributing writers, sales and marketing agents and above all provide moral support. Without these people the task would be daunting and very difficult to accomplish. With these people it becomes manageable, even enjoyable.

No man (or woman) is an island, and writing, which seems the most individual and solitary of tasks reinforces this point.

I should start by giving thanks to the Creator for all the good things I have experienced in life and for my health and strength and all those wonderful people that have been placed around me. I remember the sacrifice of my ancestors whose blood, sweat and tears mark the path along which I walk.

In many ways the production of this new book is very much due to the feedback I have received from those people who have bought and read my first book 'Niggers Negroes, Black People and Afrikans'. Without a readership a writer has no purpose and therefore I would like to sincerely thank all of those people who purchased my first book for making this book possible.

My mother, Orinthea Grant, is always due praise. She is a wonderful woman, full of love and generosity and kindness. The good in me is a reflection of her. She is at the front of an army of unsung sheroes, Afrikan mothers who have carried a heavy load without complaint.

My wife, Beverley, is like my mother and I can give her no higher praise than that. She is the love of my life, the centre of my life, my reason and my inspiration. 1st October 1989 is the most important day of my life. This is the day I met Beverley.

My wife provides me with the time and space to do this work and other activities in the community. She is so often the unseen, unrecognised support at my side.

I must thank my father, Reuben Grant, for giving me boundaries, my brother Nigel for his example and encouragement and my sister Tracey for her questioning and support.

There are the usual stalwarts who have not only supported me in my writing but also many other aspects of my life. There is Jeremy Prince who has once again helped with the design of the front cover, promotional material and promotion of launch events. There is my compadre Kwabena Osayande of Hotep Communications. Kwabena has not only worked on marketing activity but has also helped with content reading and the organising of my Birmingham launch event. The other content/proof readers who all deserve thanks were Paul Obinna Wilson-Eme, Judith Cowan, Robert Green (who also wrote the foreword) and Salome Graham.

Writers need the advice, encouragement and support of other writers and special thanks must go to Martin Glynn who has been so supportive of my writing and inspirational to my journey as an Afrikan man. Also, Abdullah Uhuru, who has recently published his latest book 'Killing Us Softly', and who has provided me with so much food for thought and ideas to reflect upon which have consciously and unconsciously influenced my work.

Mwalimu Aina Anku Ra (George Ben Anthony) is an elder in a sea of older people. He has always been there for me over the past nine years, teaching and advising. Mwalimu Aina is 'The Afrikan' and demonstrates an extraordinary commitment to the struggle. His presence in my family's life has been a blessing and particularly so for our children who have had the opportunity to interact with an elder who truly knows the Afrikan way which is manifested in his great love for children.

Robert Green and Judith Cowan deserve a second big up. They are two of my best friends who have placed great trust in me which I hope I have justified. They are always there for me.

A big thank you to Mark Dunwell, a friend, founding member of Nubian Link and the ABDF and who has written one of the chapters in this book.

I should also remember the Brother II Brother Egbe. We have shared some special moments together and the best is yet to come. The Nottingham Black Families in Education group has provided me with the opportunity to give service to parents and children experiencing difficult times in the child's schooling and through that service I have learned a great deal in a very practical way about the education system and the pressures experienced by many of our parents.

Finally, to all those people who have shown me support in my life and my writing, even in the smallest way, and whom I have not named, I say thank you.

Glossary of Terms

Asafo – Afrikan warrior scholar or scholar warrior

Asili – Term used by Marimba Ani to describe the developmental germ/seed of a culture.

Epistemology – Philosophical term relating to the search for the nature of truth.

Joe Grind – Generalised Jamaican colloquial name for a promiscuous man.

Honeymoon – Term derived from the ancient Greek practice of sodomising boys and girls under the moonlight.

Maafa – A tragedy of indescribable horror. Term popularised in Afrocentric circles by Marimba Ani to describe the genocidal assault on Afrikans by Europeans (and Arabs) that is sometimes referred to as the Black Holocaust.

Mangalize – Professor Maulana Karenga has suggested that this term be used to describe the appalling genocidal assault upon Afrikan people by Caucasians, which is epitomised by – but goes far beyond - the European trade in enslaved Afrikans, and continues to this very day. He suggests that this word is more appropriate than the use of Maafa (see above) since it speaks to the intentional nature and not just the horrific nature of what was and still is being done to Afrikans.

Mentor – Mentor is a figure from ancient Greek mythology who was charged with caring for the son (Telemachus) of his friend Odysseus whilst he was away warring, raping and pillaging. Has become a term used to describe an adult who provides advice, support and guidance to a young person.

Modus Operandi – A person's characteristic Method of operating or working.

Nom-de-plume – writer's assumed name, pen name, pseudonym.

Ontology – Philosophical term relating to the exploration of the nature of existence.

Peccadillo – trivial fault or tendency.

Race – European social construct developed as a tool for colour based oppression. Fully developed as a pseudo-scientific concept during the 18th century CE by people such as Friedrich Blumbenbach of Gottingen University who in 1763 described five human 'races' White, Yellow, Red, Brown, Black in hierarchical terms. Has its origins deep in Indo-European/Caucasian culture first manifesting itself coherently in the Hindu caste system created by the Aryan invaders of India circa 1300 BCE.

Shibboleth – Petty or arbitrary test of social correctness; formula, tenet, attitude, custom etc enforced on all members of a group. (Penguin concise English Dictionary 1970).

Utamaroho – Kiswahili term used by Marimba Ani which describes the vital force or energy source of a culture set in motion by the Asili.

Utamawaza – Kiswahili term used by Marimba Ani to describe culturally structured thought. It describes the way in which cognition is determined by a cultural Asili.

Xenophilia – Friendliness, warmth and openness to strangers or foreigners.

Xenophobia – irrational dislike, hatred, fear of strangers or aliens.

Zeitgeist – Spirit of the times

Foreword

To be a conscious Afrikan human being in an unconscious, vacuous, self obsessed world must be a lonely place. If ever the phrase 'ignorance is bliss' was true then it would surely be now.

We look around ourselves and find we occupy an uncertain world. The war on terror is seen for what it is, a euphemism for anyone daring to have a different world view to the United States of Amerikkka and it's 'sorcerer's apprentice' the UK.

Disease and famine continue to decimate large swathes of indigenous (read Black) communities across the globe. Hurricanes wreak havoc on ever ravaged coastlines now being reclaimed by the sea and to cap it all (pun very much intended) the polar ice flows, here for millions of years, continue to melt at an alarming rate.

For many of us too much is happening. Our brains struggle hard to cope with what's going on around us. Buried by a heavy sense of helplessness, the 'real worlds' of soap-land, make for a nutrient free substitute. They ease the pressures and the worry of work, the uncertainty of raising healthy Afrikan children (particularly boys), the lonely absence of a partner (particularly for Afrikan women) and latterly the piffling worry of being able to get home in at least one piece. We are led to believe that if it isn't the supposedly wild gun toting 'hoodie' that's gonna get us, it's probably likely to be the 'Muslim' looking guy, wandering close by with the ticking backpack who is going to put us all out of our misery and blow us all to hell (like we weren't there already).

Then out pops this book, this gnawing, penetrating reminder that there are people out there who not only worked this shit out already but who are actively prepared to do something about it. It is apt then that I should write this foreword the same evening that Mother Rosa Parks passed on into ancestry.

She reminded us of the irony that sitting down was her only way of standing up to White supremacy. However, the greatest irony was that we also forgot to stand up.

I look back at all those newsreels (back in the day) and marvel at the thousands of faces I see. All Afrikan, with Afrikan features and skin so black it makes you weep with joy or shame (for that depends on your perspective). I look around now and wonder where did all those faces go. Then I read 'Six steps to Whiteness' (I won't tell you where it is in the book, read the book and find out – for this is our destiny) and I'm reminded that Afrikans have no place in any New World Order, whether set in Nottingham or any other place on this Earth. Rumours of our demise if we are not too careful will soon become fact.

We are tolerated, not venerated. I have no wish to be accepted because it would always be on someone else's terms. Why venerate? It means to hold in deep respect. Why? Simple. We were here first and have watched our seeds spread across the globe wreaking havoc, raping the earth of her resources, wiping out whole nations, replacing we for me, she for he, wisdom for science and humanity for barbarity. The simple fact is that the people who currently proclaim the right of guardian of our planet do not deserve it. If you want to know why, read this book very carefully. If you find the words of an Afrikan hard to stomach then buy this book first (give the brother your moola – he worked hard for it) then read Michael Moore, anything by Noam Chomsky or John Pilger, then come back to this and read it from cover to cover.

The truth isn't out there; it's here, in this book, in all its painful glory. And if you were wondering whether the book was a ramble by another demented Afrikan with a huge chip on his shoulder, don't worry he provides you with lots of evidence to the contrary. He also asks you to examine his own life. A living embodiment of 'Practice what you preach'. All that the book asks is that you begin to think for yourself.

The media is a powerful tool. It made us hate ourselves so much that a White guy from Essex is now more Black than any Black person I know. Ummm…Black like Beckham. Remember, we live in the world of the Sorcerer and his apprentice but boy what a con trick that was.

Central to this book is the notion of Relationships. Relationships shouldn't be thought of as Woman to Man and vice-versa. Relationships should be those we have with everyone. We should understand our relationship with every person we come into contact with, especially those from other ethnic groups. We should as a matter of course understand their cultural legacy and how that influences subtly or overtly our spoken and unspoken dialogue.

The fact that this book also looks at the 'Loveship' is a wonderful bonus but not one that should ever be underestimated. In fact I would say it is the most important chapter, that and the chapter looking at the Raising of Afrikan children. Don't forget it was the systematic separation of the Afrikan family that made enslavement such a lasting bonus for those who profited. Because if the family had been maintained, those things that make community; like language, music, politics and spiritual beliefs, soulful understanding would not have been eroded and it might have meant a far quicker recovery from the ravages of enslavement. As it is we pick up any culture that puts itself forward – even if it's evidently poisonous.

This book then is **not** intended to **educate**, for most of us can read. In truth many of the titles quoted in the book a few of us already have, gathering dust and dead flies on top of shelves or buried in our 'things to read before I die pile'.

This book is intended to **change** – fundamentally change the way we not only view the world but behave within it whether that be the 'safe' confines of our own homes or the live round assault course that is work or the street.

Blue Skies is rooted in optimism. Why? Because it says quite openly there are things that we can do. As an example, turn off the tell-lie-vision for a few hours. Go out. Brothers, check out your dark skinned sisters. Halle Berry is not going to call. Sisters, look down, there's a short brother looking up. Then, as Marvin Gaye would say, 'Let's get it on'. Love yourself first, then love each other, then love those around you, keep them close and model what you want your children to copy. Understand your relationships. USE THIS BOOK AS A GUIDE. Even if you don't agree with everything inside, take those things that will nurture you. Above all believe as Mother Rosa Parks believed, one act of defiance may be the one thing that finally sets you free.

Robert Green

CONTENTS

List of Tables, Photographs and Diagrams

3

Introduction

Life is all about Choices and so is this book. In my previous and first book, 'Niggers, Negroes, Black People and Afrikans', I began a process of articulating some of the crucial understandings that I thought must be developed by Afrikans in the UK and worldwide if a serious attempt at Afrikan social/cultural reconstruction was to be fully operationalised. I say fully operationalised in recognition of the many and ongoing efforts that Afrikans, great and unknown, have and are making in defence of our Land, Languages, People and Culture. My previous book used organisations and organising as a starting point for analysis whereas this book will have a slightly greater focus upon the individual and how the sum of our Afrikan choices can change our world for the better or worse.

I have adopted a similar approach to ordering the contents of this book to that used for my previous work. Most readers seemed to appreciate the idea of being able to dip in and out of a book, non-sequentially if they so desired, and still being able to pick up on the general themes running throughout the work. Now obviously I would recommend that the reader starts at the beginning and finishes at the end, however I hope that you will find each chapter a self-contained essay in and of itself, each section a story and the whole book a journey from where we have been, where we are, to where we need to be.

There are a greater number of longer chapters by necessity which gives me concern that some readers will avoid the longer more in-depth chapters as 'too heavy'. I sincerely hope this is not the case since it is these chapters that will fully equip the reader – particularly those relatively new to this type of material and viewpoint – to fully appreciate the ideas I have tried to convey. The longest chapter deals with the most fundamental of issues, our genetic and cultural survival, and of course if the issues in that chapter are not addressed (particularly with regard to Afrikans in the UK) then the rest of the book is of nothing more than academic interest. For those Afrikans for whom the choices contained within this book are too difficult and too fundamental, this work will of course simply provide material for intellectual gratification, for it is one thing to engage with challenging ideas with just the head and another to engage with the head, heart and spirit.

Most people would rather remain in 'The Matrix' eating sirloin steak and drinking fine wine even whilst in the back of their mind they know they are plugged into the system as a unit of production, a human 'battery hen'. Sometimes reality seems too daunting and ugly to face so we lower our gaze and keep on chewing and sipping.

Where are our Afrikan social warriors? Where has the spirit of self-help and reconstruction gone? Into the grave marked Diversity?

Whilst this book is understandably and noticeably written from an Afrikan British perspective and experience, I have done my best to project out to different parts of the world. Firstly, as a test for the credence of my ideas, and secondly to put into practice what I preach, namely the absolute necessity for the development of a worldwide Afrikan consciousness which does not attempt to gloss over the real differences resulting from time and place, but which pulls on the commonalities in the assertion of our oneness. I see this as in some senses similar to the Afrikan theosophical concept of 'polytheistic monotheism' i.e. a range of deities emanating from the One Supreme Creator. We have many cultural manifestations all emanating from the core original Afrikan cultural template or asili (cultural seed [Ani 1996]).

One of the most pleasing aspects of publishing my previous book has been the positive reaction from the many secret undercover Afrikan writers. Lots of brothers and sisters have approached me and asked me how did I go about writing and publishing my book, and how they felt encouraged by my example. It is perhaps that old adage of 'if he can do it so can I'. This is by no means meant negatively. For many of us, writers are distant figures who do not play a part in our daily lives. This absence of first hand knowledge seems to have created a mystique around the whole process of writing and publishing books. Many Afrikans, in the UK at least, seem to have imbued writers with a special quality that is quite frankly undeserved. Writing a book is relatively straightforward but definitely hard work. Writing is a lonely business and requires discipline and commitment. For every one hundred people who say they are going to write (and publish) a book probably only two or three accomplish it. The difference between the two groups is not intellect or wealth, it is focus and determination. So if you think you can do it, stop thinking and start doing.

There is a depressing lack of non-fiction politicised writing coming out of the Afrikan community in the UK. I know of only two other Afrikan writers (Abdullah Uhuru and Pitman Brown) in Nottingham producing similar work to myself and very few others across the country, and yet there is not a dearth of Afrikan people with opinions and good ideas. I hope that those many people with good ideas will step forward and put pen to paper and bring forth their ideas to a wider public. Perhaps it is the fear of criticism and scrutiny that deters some people, for we are terribly unforgiving of each other even whilst we gladly forgive the sins of others. Personally I have found a very positive response from most Afrikans to my first book, save a minority who condemned me for its front cover without reading what lay inside. This is not to say criticism of the front cover was invalid, rather that criticism of a book should encompass the whole thing and not just the front cover. In any case criticism comes with the territory and even the negativity can be strengthening. On the subject of the front cover of my previous book, I was sent a very interesting article that appeared on the UK Nation of Islam's website Final Call to power online and that highlighted part of the reason why I chose the images I did for the front cover.

Controversial Racist Book Returns

"White supremacy disguised in a children's story, has raised its ugly head again, with the re-launch of a book first published over one hundred years ago.

'The story of the little Black Sambo' tells of the adventures of a Black boy in the 'savage jungle' of India, supported by his parents 'Mumbo' and 'Jumbo'.

Despite the glossy, colorful re-packaging of the book, there is no disguising the 'British Empire' perspective underpinning the story, as seen by the language, story lines, and most clearly, the characters.

The return of a book that was once the benchmark of institutionalized racism in school material indicates a desire to perpetuate a particular view of Black people that has never gone away, but had gone underground."

Source: *Final Call to power online edition*

I had anticipated some form of Caucasian and/or Negro backlash in response to my first book. The only surprise was the length of time it took for the assault to arrive. The myth of freedom of speech and expression is just that. My first book took Caucasians – and some Afrikans for that matter – to places they would rather imagine did not exist.

This book may get me into further hot water; however I have published this work with my eyes wide open. For all of us, at some point we will reach a crucial crossroads on our life journey which is a point of no return. You have to go one way or t'other. I have chosen my path and my destiny. I will stand for those things I know to be true to the Afrikan way and engage in the battle for the hearts and minds of Afrikans, here and abroad. I invite you to consider your own personal journey and whether your current path will fulfil your stated purpose (assuming you have come to an understanding of your purpose).

Of course Afrikans face these dilemmas because we operate at home and abroad from a position of relative powerlessness in relation to our Caucasian conquerors. We are therefore plagued by difficult choices and struggle to act independently. One of the choices and questions I explore in this book relates to what is the appropriate type of relationship Afrikans as a group should have with Caucasians. This has been a question that has hung like a cloud over our attempts at group reconstruction since Europeans first began their slave raids off the West Coast of Afrika in the fifteenth century.

To demonstrate the longevity of this question and the fact that over five hundred years ago wise Afrikans had gained a sense of the need to keep this relationship at arms length – in our best interests if not theirs – I have reproduced below a speech by Nana Kwamena Ansa, a king of Ghana, in 1482 to Diego de Azambuia who was the commander of a Portuguese expedition that was looking to gain a military foothold in Ghana by building forts on the coast, which were of course to aid the full introduction of the slave trade.

"I am not insensible to the high honour which your great master the Chief of Portugal has this day conferred upon me. His friendship I have always endeavoured to merit by the strictness of my dealings

9

with the Portuguese and by my constant exertions to procure an immediate landing for the vessels. But never until this day did I observe such a difference in the appearance of his subjects; they have hitherto been meanly attired; were easily contented with the commodity they received; and so far from wishing to continue in this country were never happy until they could complete their landing and return. Now I remark a strange difference. A great number, richly dressed, are anxious to be allowed to build houses, and to continue among us. Men of such eminence, conducted by a commander who from his own account seems to have descended from the God who made day and night, can never bring themselves to endure the hardships of this climate nor would they here be able to procure any of the luxuries that abound in their own country. The passions that are common to us all men will therefore inevitably bring on disputes and it is preferable that both our nations should continue on the same footing as they hitherto have done, allowing your ships to come and go as usual; the desire of seeing each other occasionally will preserve peace between us. The sea and the land being always neighbors are continually at variance and contending who shall give way; the sea with great violence attempting to subdue the land, and the land with equal obstinacy resolving to oppose the sea." (Budu-Acquah 1960: 23-24)

Speaking from a position of military weakness and cloaked in the language of poetic diplomacy the King's message is very clear. He wanted to keep the relationship with the Portuguese on a limited and strictly business basis – which did not include the slave trade – and that is the only sensible and logical type of relationship that should prevail between Afrikans and Europeans based upon what history tells us about Europeans' intentions towards us as opposed to what some Afrikan utopians would like to believe is possible. Let's leave the miracles to the Creator whilst we deal with the practical.

Life is all about choices and so is this book.

I hope this book is of benefit to you and worthy of your time and money.

PART I

BREAKING THE
STRANGLEHOLD

Do You Remember 1804?

On the 1st January 1804, 200 years before the writing of this particular chapter in this text, one of the most important events in the last 500 years of Afrikan, and indeed World History, took place. Can you think what this event was? Did you notice any grand celebrations and detailed – or even scant – news coverage commemorating this event during the course of 2004? Do you recall intellectual analysis of the relative importance of this event?

The answer to most of these questions is probably a resounding no. The event in question is the Haitian Revolution of 1804, the first and only time that an enslaved people overthrew their enslavers to found a fully fledged independent Republic (there was the Palmares republic in Brazil and the Maroons gained independence in Jamaica; however these were not nation states). The Haitian revolution was a catalyst, springboard and inspiration for Afrikans across the Caribbean and USA to increase the intensity of their ongoing fight for freedom. And what has been the reward for the magnificent Haitians? 200 years of persecution, oppression, corruption and misery.

Why were most Afrikans oblivious to the 200 year anniversary of this unique event and yet were acutely aware of the 1992 500th anniversary of Columbus getting lost and bumping into the 'West Indies'? Well, I am sure you can answer this question for yourself. The control and dissemination of information is a deeply political process. The media is not some amorphous, invisible force, it is made up of organisations that are controlled by people and those people prioritise information for broadcast or publication in a manner that reflects the priorities of the dominant racial/cultural group within their nation and the world.

That is to say the productive output of the so-called Western media reflects the values and goals of Caucasian culture and hence in both an automatic and largely unconscious way presents Caucasians as

13

heroic, good and altruistic and non-Caucasians, and Afrikans most particularly, as violent, immoral and corrupt. Therefore the more difficult it is to shape a story to fit this cultural imperative, the less likely it is that this story will be broadcast by the 'mainstream' – which means Caucasian – broadcast media. Naturally, you will always find atypical stories presented in specialist magazines, books, cable TV, websites etc. and Caucasians use this as an example of the freedoms they claim to cherish so dearly and wish others to enjoy, however the obvious truth is that the majority of the media sated populations of the 'West', or anywhere else for that matter, get their information from a very limited range of media sources that are controlled by a small number of transnational corporations.

Most people are extremely ignorant of the background and context behind what is presented to them as news and even more so about the important things happening in the world that are deemed as not important enough to be presented as news.

Let's go back to Haiti. The 1804 Revolution could not have been given in-depth coverage by Caucasian media outlets without exposing the viciousness of Caucasian racism or telling such gross lies as to risk exposure. It is always important to remember that if you want to deceive people it is always better to tell a lie which contains an element of truth.

The backdrop to the Afrikan presence in Haiti was of course the decimation of the indigenous population. In his mini-classic 'Christopher Columbus and the Afrikan Holocaust' John Henrik Clarke tells us that "In a short 40 years, the entire race of people in Haiti, a half million native Americans, were wiped off the face of the earth by Columbus and the Spaniards that followed him." (Clarke 1998: 68)

The Haitian Revolution shows Caucasians at their vindictive worst. The revolution was sparked by Napoleon's attempt to reinstate slavery which had been abolished by the French Revolution. He sent 50 shiploads of soldiers to crush the uprising in Haiti and got a right royal arse kicking. The Afrikans inspired by Bookman Dutty a six foot six Vudon priest, Jean-Jacques Dessalines, and to a lesser extent than generally depicted, Toussaint L'Ouverture, won their freedom from French oppression. Now many ignorant voices would claim that the Afrikans have had 200 years to sort themselves out, however those voices are unaware – or conveniently forget – that after inheriting a land whose agricultural base was destroyed to make way for sugar plantations the poor Haitians were forced to pay off the 'French debt'. The French price for such Afrikan impertinence was 150 million gold francs, the equivalent of $21.7 billion in today's money. This is 44 times Haiti's current annual budget. It took Haiti 134 years, until 1938, to pay of this evil usurious 'debt'. The Caucasian countries refused to recognise the birth of Haiti and France only did so in return for 134 years of Haitian penury.

The closest contemporary parallels with the behaviour of the French towards Haiti are the 25 year trade embargo by the US against Vietnam in revenge for the military defeat of 'the most powerful country on Earth' by a so-called 'Third World' country. The other example once again involves the US, this time its vicious campaign against Cuba which not only includes an economic assault but also the use of chemical and biological weapons.

With regard to Vietnam, just to give you an example of how blatantly Caucasians will distort history, let us look at the comments of Max Hastings, the former Editor of the Daily Telegraph, a rightwing national newspaper in the UK. Writing in the Guardian, a supposedly liberal, left of centre, national newspaper – it just shows you that whatever their political differences they never forget they are one blood – Max Hastings says:

"Consider this proposition from Edward Luttwak, the maverick American strategy guru. In a recent speech to a British audience, he suggested that the US began to win the Vietnam War the day after its envoy was humiliatingly evacuated from the roof of the Saigon embassy in April 1975. The military conflict was lost – but, argued Luttwak, the US began to achieve victory culturally and economically. Vietnam may still profess a commitment to communism, but in reality capitalism is taking hold at every level. American values, represented by corporatism and schools of management studies, are gaining sway over Vietnam as surely as they are every other nation possessed of education and aspirations to prosperity.

Luttwak describes what is happening as the US acquiring a "virtual empire" founded upon cultural dominance..." (Hastings, Guardian Newspaper 19 Jan 2005: 24)

So you see the breathtaking arrogance and intellectual duplicity of these people. Luttwak makes no reference to the impact of the economic war waged against Vietnam by the US for 25 years in this process of gaining cultural dominance. The US elite are absolutely hell bent on ensuring that no viable alternative to capitalism in general, and their particular brand of corporate capitalism, arises anywhere in the world, which is why they spend so much time trying to destroy alternative approaches such as in Cuba and Nicaragua (under the Sandanistas). If their economic system was so great and beneficial to everyone why would they even bother with what is happening in other countries? Wouldn't everyone just see the economic light over a period of time? Why expend effort trying to impede an inferior system?

As Mwalimu Marcus Mosiah Garvey suggested in relation to why Caucasians try to impede the progress of a people (Afrikans) who they say are inferior. Could it be because they know we are not inferior? Similarly, could it be that the Caucasian elite know that whilst capitalism is undoubtedly the greatest system on Earth at making the world's richest richer, it is also the greatest system on Earth at making the world's poorest poorer. Since the rich can always look after themselves I prefer a system that will look after the poorest.

The lesson of Luttwak and Hastings is that Caucasians wage war at every level, military, economic, cultural, psychological, spiritual/religious and that the resistance must take place at every level. As Mwalimu K. Bomani Baruti notes "Europeans cannot allow anyone to separate themselves from their cultural or economic order. ....They cannot tolerate the development of a rival power in their midst, even if that rival power has no threatening intent." (Bomani 2004: 156)

Returning to Haiti, we see that the country was born in abject poverty and political isolation and yet its example was so powerful that Haitians travelled across the Caribbean spreading the word of Afrikan freedom and inspiring rebellion. It was Haiti that provided

16

shelter and respite to Simon Bolivar, founder of Bolivia, when he was defeated and provided him with guns, boats and troops in 1816 to pave the way for his successful war of independence. All the Haitians asked for in return was that he freed the Afrikan slaves, and apart from a commemorative sword that was all they got.

In 1915 the US Marines invaded Haiti and during their 19 year occupation brought more misery to Haitians including introducing the type of racial segregation that existed in the southern states of the US. Even the Afrikan President was barred from hotels and restaurants once the US took control. Just to emphasise who was in control the US exhibited the body of resistance leader Charlemagne Peralte in a public square, crucified on a door. This is the nature of the lovers of freedom and democracy. Since 1934 Haiti has been to hell and back several times. The Duvalier dictators, the torture and double overthrow of Jean Bertrand Aristide by US backed forces and in 2004 the death of over 2000 Haitians at the hands of Hurricane Jean. The US in accord with its customary practice as exhibited towards Nicaragua, Cuba, Venezuela, Grenada etc. will not allow any alternative developmental path in its 'backyard' and has always returned power to the lightskinned, landowning, Haitian business elite who are immune to the suffering of the predominantly dark skinned masses. The island of Espaniol, with the Light skinned more favoured Dominican Republic on one side and the Dark skinned, shunned Haiti on the other, is the geophysical materialisation of the slave mentality that is crushing the Afrikan capacity for resistance.

One of the key, but rarely articulated lessons of the Haitian revolution is what it tells us about the 'White Question' (Carruthers 1999). In his brilliant book 'Intellectual War' Jacob H. Carruthers argues that "no issue has obstructed the pan African project of liberation more than the "White Question." ...The term "White Question" is not intended as the reverse of "The Negro Question" ....It is rather an attempt to summarize the most historically divisive controversy among African leadership groups in the United States over the last two centuries." (Carruthers 1999: 156)

Carruthers goes on to suggest that "Nothing better illustrates the problem than the history of the Haitian Revolution. Throughout the

17

struggle, various group leaders argued among themselves over ways to deal with the whites. Indeed, the revolution was delayed more than once by the bitter conflict. The argument resurfaced after the victory of the Africans and has blighted Haiti's future ever since." (Carruthers 1999: 156) Carruthers sets out how the divisions ran along the by now familiar Afrikan philosophical lines. The separatists, integrationists and assimilationists. As indicated above the integrationists won out and in their desire for acceptance "traded Haiti's future for the prize of recognition by France at a cost of a $25,000,000 indemnity." (Carruthers 1999: 156)

Bookman Dutty was the most prominent author of the Haitian revolution and may accurately be described in contemporary terms as a full blown Afrikan nationalist. As such he rejected the offers of negotiations by the plantation owners who had been rocked onto the back foot by the brilliant and unrelenting military campaign of the Afrikans in Haiti. Dutty knew instinctively that Caucasians only negotiate with Afrikans when they are in a position of weakness and as a ploy to win time. The following quote by the Commander of the French forces in Haiti, LeClerk, was made in 1802 when the French were feeling the Afrikan heat. It gives you an idea of the mentality of the French barbarians that the Afrikans were fighting against.

"Since terror is the sole resource left to me, I employ it..... I shall have to wage a war of extermination."

Since they have never considered Afrikans as fully human they do not feel bound to uphold any agreements they enter into with Afrikans or other non-Caucasian people. Two good examples are the record of Caucasians in their genocidal campaign against the indigenous people of the USA and the Lancaster House negotiations to transfer **political** power (and nothing else) to Afrikans in Zimbabwe. In the first case the Caucasians broke every single treaty they signed with the various indigenous nations that they negotiated with. Along the way they showed their growing appetite for genocide and biological warfare by infecting the blankets of one conquered 'Indian' nation with small pox. Remember, this was done after they had conquered these people and had herded them within a prototype version of a concentration camp.

18

In the case of Zimbabwe, the British, who the Afrikans foolishly allowed to act as arbitrators, reneged on their promise to pay 'compensation' to Caucasian farmers as part of the land transfer process that should have taken place upon Zimbabwe gaining 'independence' but which has only started in the last couple of years. How can you have your oppressor acting as mediator in negotiations with your oppressor's brother?

If we return to Haiti we find that Bookman's view did not hold sway and the other leaders of the revolution opted to negotiate with the slavemasters. Not only that but these integrationists/assimilationists sold out Bookman, offering him up as a sacrificial lamb as a sign of good faith. Bookman was duly assassinated and then to add insult to injury the Caucasians then demanded the unconditional surrender of the Afrikans.

This difference over how to deal with Caucasians was always the major fault line running through the Afrikan camp. Toussaint L'Ouverture – whose name and role has been pushed to prominence ahead of Bookman's – was an ardent Francophile and wanted nothing more than Haiti to be considered the Black France (Carruthers 1999). To this end, even after the forces of Napoleon Bonaparte, who had launched a massive invasion of Haiti in 1802 with the express objective of reinstituting slavery, had been defeated, Toussaint L'Ouverture jumped at the offer of negotiations from the French General.

One of the heroes of the revolution Jean-Jacques Dessalines counselled strongly against any such move; however L'Ouverture proceeded with his misguided course of action and was kidnapped, imprisoned in France and starved to death.

Dessalines took over and continued the struggle leading the Afrikans to victory. In a highly symbolic move he removed the white from the red, white and blue tricolour which he later supplanted with a new Black and Red Haitian flag "signifying the union of people of Afrikan descent." (Carruthers 1999: 238).

It is extremely significant that the name the Afrikans chose for their newly formed independent republic, Haiti, was the name given to the island by the original indigenous people (Ayiti), sometimes referred to as Amerindians – which of course is a Caucasian label. This was an act which demonstrated the best of Afrikan humanism and a true solidarity of the oppressed that Caucasian leftists could only dream about. In their moment of triumph they remembered and recognised those earlier victims of White Supremacy who had trod the soil of Haiti before them.

There are so many important parallels between the Haitian revolution and the achievement of 'independence' in Zimbabwe and South Africa. Whereas Dessalines articulated the need for victory 'without compromise' both Zimbabwe and South Africa were founded upon compromise which has come back to haunt the respective leaderships and the Afrikan people of each country. I have alluded to the Zimbabwe 'negotiations' earlier and in South Africa a similar route was followed by the overtly integrationist ANC (African National Congress). Today, we see a South Africa in which precious little has changed for the majority of Afrikans and in which Caucasians still hold the economic handle whilst Afrikans hold the blade. The current ANC tactic of creating several dozen Black capitalist millionaires is supposed to represent their strategy for economic redistribution.

The battle between the Afrikan Nationalists and the integrationists/assimilationists was and is an ongoing struggle which has been played out in the writings, words and deeds of Afrikans for over two hundred years. Caucasians love to lionise those with integrationist/assimilationists tendencies which is why Frederick Douglas, Martin Luther King and Nelson Mandela are promoted by Caucasians as representing the best of our struggle as opposed to David Walker, Marcus Garvey, Malcolm X and Steve Biko.

Afrikans have always resisted White Supremacy and there is an oral as well as written tradition that underpins this. This oral tradition is usually reserved for exclusively Black settings. Jacob Carruthers cites a powerful, earthy example about an African seaman 'Shine' who "abandons the Titanic after warning the white captain of the impending danger. As Shine swims toward shore, various representatives of European power over Africans beg him to save them by offering the symbols of the treasured white world: wealth,

status, prestige, power and white sexuality. The last verse....went
something like this:

> The captain's daughter ran upon the deck
> Her dress in her hand and her drawers round her neck.
> She said Shine Shine please save me
> And all my good White___is yours for free.
> But Shine said there's___on land
> There's___on the sea,
> But the___in Harlem is
> Good enough for me
> And Shine swam on.

(Carruthers 1999: 210-211)

Carruthers notes that Shine's words and actions represent the
rejection of the White world's most valuable treasures. After warning
them of their impending doom he allows the White world to sink
without trace choosing his own independent course of action. The use
of the Caucasian woman as the representation of the most desirable
things that the white world has to offer is no doubt both
acknowledgement of the psycho-sexual obsession that many Afrikan
men have developed for Caucasian women since our physical and
mental enslavement by Caucasians (Grant 2003) and perhaps playing
upon the misogynistic Biblical tradition of woman as temptress
bringing about the 'fall of man', in this case the fall of Black man, as
exemplified by the biblical myths of Adam and Eve and Samson and
Delilah. The story of Shine is a call to reject Caucasian culture and
choose Ourstory.

Who will shed a tear for Haiti, raped and abused by a vengeful US
and Caucasian world. In order to understand the present misery you
need to understand the history and this is why you heard so little of
the 1804 Revolution during the year of its 200th anniversary.

To reinforce the points I have made throughout this chapter, it is
worth considering some of the commemorative events that have taken
place in the UK during 2005. Not only were there the usual plethora

of European World War II commemorations, including a huge VE Day (Victory in Europe) celebration attended by all the Royal Family and an estimated half a million spectators – the Police are never shy with the crowd estimates for these types of events – , but what was more informative were the huge Battle of Trafalgar 200th anniversary celebrations. Why was I interested in these, when from reading this book I am sure you would have gathered that I don't normally involve myself in the cultural celebrations of Caucasians?

Well, the Trafalgar Day anniversary celebrations blew the gaffe, so to speak, on their desire for, and explanation of; why we should forget the enslavement period. Their usual argument says that it is legitimate to remember and give prominence to events that occurred within a human lifespan i.e. 80-100 years; hence the two European World Wars which fall within this rule of thumb remain the subject of intense remembrance.

However upon closer examination their hypocrisy becomes all too apparent. For example one sees that events involving Afrikans, and particularly all those which cast Europeans in a bad light, which in effect are virtually all events involving Afrikans and Europeans, are skimmed over or totally ignored by Europeans.

So, in this vein, the 100th anniversary of the ending of the enslavement of Afrikans by Europeans, with the abolition of slavery in Brazil in 1888 received no press coverage in 1988. You would think this was a major landmark in Afrikan and European history, but no coverage. Similarly, the genocide carried out in the Congo between the mid 1880's and ending in the early years of the 20th century under the insane psychopathic rule of King Leopold of Belgium and which resulted in the Congolese population falling from around 30 million to around 10million received no European press coverage over the past twenty years despite being one of the worst acts of prolonged genocide the world has ever seen.

If we compare the above two examples to the massive news coverage in the UK press given to a war fought against one of their European neighbours 200 years ago for no higher principle than world hegemony one sees the apparently inexplicable contrast. Of course the contrast is not inexplicable; this is the rhetorical ethic (Ani

1996) in play. Huge flotillas of ships sailing the English Channel and preparations involving the Navy that they proudly boasted took over one year are indications of their refusal to forget their ancestors and heroes. They even went so far as to mint special commemorative £5 coins to celebrate Nelson's victory.

Let's be clear, the events of the Haitian revolution were of greater significance to us than the Battle of Trafalgar for the Caucasian British and indeed far greater significance for the world in terms of the enduring message the Haitian Revolution carries about the fight of the oppressed against injustice.

We listen to the rhetorical ethic of Caucasians at our peril whilst they remember their history, and our ancestors can only cuss their wotless progeny! We turn our collective faces from the struggle, suffering, but ultimate triumph of our ancestors and in doing so miss out on the answers to our oft repeated questions as to what should we do.

And for what?

So that we can remain acceptable in the sight of those who have no care for us.

When will we learn? By 2104?

What Now for Haiti?

An article by journalist Naomi Klein appeared in the Guardian newspaper on July 18 2005 highlighting the ever present interference of the US government in Haitian affairs and their unwavering willingness to support criminals and despotic regimes so long as those governments are willing to do their bidding, which always equates to creating a legislative and economic climate conducive to the rape of the client state's economic resources.

Klein sets the context by highlighting the differential reporting of the tragedy in Haiti by the 'western media', something I have also highlighted in this book.

"When terror strikes western capitals, it doesn't just blast bodies and buildings, it also blasts other sites of suffering off the media map. A massacre of Iraqi children, blown up while taking sweets from a market stall, is banished deep into the inside pages of our newspapers. The outpouring of compassion for the daily deaths of thousands from Aids in Africa is suddenly treated as a frivolous distraction. In this context, a massacre in Haiti alleged to have taken place the day before the London bombings never stood a chance. Well before July 7, Haiti couldn't compete in the suffering sweepstakes: the US-supported coup that ousted President Jean-Bertrand Aristide had the misfortune of taking place in late February 2004, just as the occupation of Iraq was reaching a new level of chaos and brutality. The crushing of Haiti's constitutional democracy made headlines for only a couple of weeks." (Klein Guardian Newspaper, 18 July 2005).

The UN have also been used as a tool of repression in Haiti and Klein notes that on "July 6 300 UN troops stormed the pro-Aristide slum of Cité Soleil. The UN admits that five were killed, but residents put the number of dead at no fewer than 20. A Reuters correspondent, Joseph Guyler Delva, says he

"saw seven bodies in one house alone, including two babies and one older woman in her 60s". Ali Besnaci, head of Médecins Sans Frontières in Haiti, confirmed that on the day of the siege an "unprecedented" 27 people came to the MSF clinic with gunshot wounds, three-quarters of them women and children." (Klein Guardian Newspaper, 18 July 2005)

The siege was largely unreported and where it did receive coverage the line taken was that it was an unfortunate but necessary measure to control Haiti's violent armed gangs. Of course these same impartial reporters did not take the time to speak to the residents of Cité Soleil who tell a very different story. They speak of political repression and say that they are targeted for murder because they dare to demand the return of their elected but now ousted President Jean Baptiste Aristide. As a mark of their loyalty to Aristide they place his photograph on the bodies of their dead friends and family members.

It is worth remembering that it was barely 10 years ago that President Bill Clinton celebrated Aristide's return to power as "the triumph of freedom over fear". A decade later what has turned this champion of democracy into the enemy? As you will see it is the usual story in relation to US foreign policy. If you dare to go against the US agenda – particularly their economic agenda – friends quickly become enemies irrespective of whether they are democratically elected or not. The driving force of US foreign policy has nothing to do with spreading democracy – as can be seen by their current treatment of President Chavez of Venezuela who has twice received massive endorsement from the (poor) Venezuelan people in two free elections. No, US foreign policy is all about the Benjamins!

Whilst there were allegations of repression in Haiti under Aristide's leadership these are as nothing compared to the "rap sheets of the convicted killers, drug smugglers and arms traders who ousted him. Turning Haiti over to this underworld gang out of concern for Aristide's lack of "good governance" is like escaping an annoying date by accepting a lift home from Charles Manson." (Klein Guardian 17 July 2005)

In late June Ms Klein visited Aristide in Pretoria, South Africa, where he lives in forced exile. She asked him about the reasons underlying his dramatic falling-out with Washington. The response was highly informative and one that I have never heard discussed in relation to his overthrow by 'mainstream' commentators on Haitian politics. He said it in one word, three times: "Privatisation, privatisation and privatisation."

Aristide informed Klein that the dispute dates back to a series of meetings with representatives of the Clinton administration in early 1994. At this time Haitians were living under the barbaric rule of Raoul Cédras, who overthrew Aristide in a 1991 US-backed coup. Aristide had been forced to travel to Washington and, despite popular calls for his return, there was no way he could remove the para-military junta without military back-up.

Recognising the manifest hypocrisy of supporting a brutal military dictatorship against an elected President "the Clinton administration offered Aristide a deal: US troops would take him back to Haiti – but only after he agreed to a sweeping economic programme with the stated goal to "substantially transform the nature of the Haitian state"." (Klein Guardian 17 July 2005)

There may be a feeling of deja vu when you hear that Aristide was forced to agree to pay the debts accumulated under the larcenous

Duvalier dictatorships, – just as Haiti had to pay the French the 'debt' built up during the enslavement period – decimate the civil service, open up Haiti to "free trade" and cut import tariffs on rice and corn. It was a heads US wins tails Haiti loses deal but, Aristide conceded that, he had little choice but to acquiesce. "I was out of my country and my country was the poorest in the western hemisphere, so what kind of power did I have at that time?" (Klien 2005)

There was only one sticking point, but this proved to be a deal-breaker. Washington's negotiators demanded the immediate sell-off of Haiti's state-owned enterprises, including phones and electricity. Aristide recognised that unregulated privatisation would transform state monopolies into private oligarchies, and that this move, in accord with classic US domestic and foreign economic policy, would increase the riches of Haiti's elite and strip the poor of their national assets. Aristide was clear; he told Klein that the proposal simply didn't add up: "Being honest means saying two plus two equals four. They wanted us to sing two plus two equals five."

In an attempt to hold on to power whilst retaining some degree of integrity "Aristide proposed a compromise: Rather than sell off the firms outright, he would "democratise" them. He defined this as writing anti-trust legislation, ensuring that proceeds from the sales were redistributed to the poor and allowing workers to become shareholders. Washington backed down, and the final text of the agreement called for the "democratisation" of state companies." (Klein Guardian 17 July 2005).

However the deal broke down when Aristide announced that the proposed new laws would have to be ratified by parliament before any sales could take place. This was like a red rag to an American imperialist bull. How dare the President seek to consult with his parliament. What was this, Democracy? Aristide described the Washington tactics as akin to attempting an "economic coup". "The hidden agenda was to tie my hands once I was back and make me give for nothing all the state public enterprises." (Klein Guardian 17 July 2005).

The US accused him of reneging on the deal because of his desire to prevent a fire sale of Haitian national assets.

In time honoured tradition the US applied the financial squeeze cutting off more than $500m in promised loans and aid and directing millions into the coffers of opposition groups. The final blow was the US backed armed coup of February 2004.

This was by no means the end of the attack on poor Haitians. "On June 23 Roger Noriega, US assistant secretary of state for western hemisphere affairs, called on UN troops to take a more "proactive role" in going after armed pro-Aristide gangs. In practice, this has meant a wave of collective punishment inflicted on neighbourhoods known for supporting Aristide, most recently in Cité Soleil on July 6." (Klein Guardian 17 July 2005)

However the warmongers of Washington obviously do not read their history books and do not know who they are dealing with. Despite the US sponsored wave of terror that has been directed at Aristide's supporters Haitians are still on the streets protesting. They have rejecting the planned sham elections, are still opposing privatisation and continue to demonstrate their support for Aristide by holding his photograph aloft. The arrogance and condescension of Washington's 'experts' is demonstrated by their inability to anticipate the possibility, let alone the likelihood, that Aristide would have rejected their advice a decade ago, and that today his poor supporters could be acting of their own volition. "We believe that his people are receiving instructions directly from his voice and indirectly through his acolytes that communicate with him personally in South Africa," Noriega said. (Klein Guardian 17 July 2005)

Aristide claims no such powers. "The people are bright, the people are intelligent, the people are courageous," he says. They know that two plus two does not equal five. (Klein Guardian 17 July 2005)

Check out the significance of Klein's article. Firstly, over the past ten years I have never heard any of the key issues covered in this article even alluded to; let alone directly covered by any television programme in the UK and we always need to remember that television is where the majority of people get most of their news, especially in relation to foreign affairs. Secondly, look at the role of the supposedly 'liberal' Clinton regime. Supporting big time criminals so that US transnational corporations and their Haitian friends could economically rape the land.

As I mentioned in my previous book (Grant 2003) when reviewing Clinton's leadership, if his Afrikan-American supporters would take the time to remove their heads from his anus they would see more clearly that he does not give a shit for Afrikan people, although he is more than willing to defecate on us. Remember, this is the President who placed an illegal blockade around Haiti to stop refugees fleeing, from the worst excesses of the despots Clinton's government installed in power, reaching sanctuary in the USA, whilst laying out the red carpet for the steady flow of mainly Caucasian Cuban refugees arriving in the US from Cuba. Could anyone but the most rabid right-wing ideologue claim that the Castro government of the time was worse than the rulers of Haiti?

Thirdly, the support of successive US governments, Democratic and Republican, for the murderers ruling Haiti once again highlights the hypocrisy and mendacity of their claims that spreading democracy is a high priority of US foreign policy. As a former US President said many years ago *'America's business is business'*. Ya get me!

May the Creator bless Haiti.

The 1791 slave revolt in St Dominique
brought independence to Haiti

Vampires Running Bloodbanks

Nearly half of the world's population live on less than £1.40 a day and over 30,000 children die from poverty every day. The richest 1% of people earn as much as the poorest 57%. Almost a third of the largest economies in the world are not countries, but transnational corporations.

Source: *World Development Movement*

"In a quarter of the roughly 50 wars and armed conflicts active in 2001, resource exploitation has played a key role. These are known as resource wars....A poor country with weak infrastructure, few options for making money and possessing significant 'lootable' resources is four times more likely to experience war than a similar country without them." (New internationalist 2004:10-11).

So what is the connection between gross income inequality and poverty, mineral wealth and wars? Well a large part of the answer lies in the last two words of the first paragraph of this chapter...transnational corporations. This is the accurate description for what are normally referred to as multinational companies. However multinational company is a gross misnomer suggesting that these are organisations with ownership spread across the world when in reality these are economic organisms without national allegiance operating across the globe. Their function is to make the very rich even richer and the by product of this process is that the very poor become even poorer.

Their partners in crime are governments, of the richest countries in the world in particular, who set the legislative and economic framework to ensure that their corporate friends and funders are free to 'compete' whilst playing downhill, with the wind at their backs and the sun and rain obscuring their shoeless opponents' vision. This is heads I win tails you lose economics in which nearly all the stock phrases and mantras such as 'free market' have exactly the opposite meaning. As Susan George pointed out in examining the use of public funds to subsidise collapsing banks in the USA and Europe, Japan " appears to be the only genuinely capitalist country in the OECD group," (George cited in Chomsky 1996: 107).

The OECD (Organisation for Economic Co-operation and Development) is a club run by and for the rich countries of the world (with Japan playing their usual role of honorary Caucasians) to ensure they remain just that. George was referring to the fact that Japan was the only OECD country that stuck to the stated capitalist principle that the taxpayer or state should not pay for the commercial failings of banking or any other commercial sector. By contrast that proponent of laissez faire capitalism Ronald Reagan performed the "biggest nationalization in U.S. history (the Continental Illinois Bank bailout)....leaving the taxpayer with costs running to hundreds of billions of dollars." (Chomsky 1996: 107).

It is important to note at this point that countries generally only believe in free trade when it will yield them an economic advantage and that all the most economically powerfully countries in the world have, and in most cases still do, used protectionist measures to shield particular industries from competition. Britain was the first global superpower to demand the lifting of trade barriers, knowing that as the first country in the world to industrialise it had a massive economic advantage and could decimate fledging industries in foreign countries.

Later on we had the new bully in the economic playground, the USA, demanding that foreign governments give it unfettered access to their markets. But what was the US doing on the home front? The free market loving Reagan administration had not only massively increased state expenditure as a share of GNP (Gross National Product) to over 35% – mostly as a result of massive increases in military expenditure – by 1983, which was more than a third higher than a decade earlier, they also nearly doubled import restrictions to 23% which was more than all post-war US administrations combined (Chomsky 1996).

These are the same people who then instruct – via the IMF and

World Bank – Afrikan governments to privatise their industries and throw open their domestic markets to (heavily subsidised) US goods which then undercut local producers leading to the closure of indigenous businesses, resulting in reduced local production and massive unemployment.

Zambia is a classic example. In 1993 they were prescribed the IMF medicine of economic austerity combining an end to food and other key goods subsidies (after all why would you want to prevent your people from going hungry) and immediate large scale privatisation of key industries. Eleven years on with the privatised companies collapsed due to cheap imports, 80% unemployment and large-scale malnutrition, the IMF's Afrikan lackey in Zambia happily told the BBC of the positive impact they had made in Zambia and that whilst no one likes to see people lose their jobs this pain is a necessary part of the reconstruction of the Zambian economy.

The IMF is like a doctor who does not recognise that if the patient dies the treatment cannot be deemed an unqualified success! But the reality is that the IMF is there to serve the interests of rich countries and rich companies and most particularly the US. Afrika is like one giant warehouse full of fabulous minerals and gems, and keeping its constituent countries poor is the best way of ensuring that the price of these raw materials remains incredibly cheap. If Afrikan governments gained some economic strength they would exercise control over the supply of their raw materials and hence prices would increase dramatically. The 'West' does not want this to happen since this would impact negatively on domestic inflation and begin to transform the flow of resources between North and South in a more equitable manner.

The massive subsidies paid out by the US government to its domestic cotton producers are one of the best examples of Caucasian economic hypocrisy. In a landmark case brought by Brazil, the World Trade Organisation (WTO) ruled that most of the $1.5bn in annual subsidies that the U.S. government pays to its 25,000 cotton farmers is illegal. This $1.5bn is just a fraction of the estimated $300bn of subsidies that governments in the rich world dole out to their farmers. This is the nature of 'free trade'. One of the economic centrepieces of

'The New World Order' is to ensure that their system of *Welfare For The Rich* remains unchallenged.

And what is the price of such largesse for those in the poor world. The Guardian Newspaper quoted Oxfam spokeswoman Celine Charveriat who noted that the WTO ruling "....would be a huge victory, not just for Brazil but particularly for 10million poor African farmers whose livelihoods have been crippled by unfair competition." (Guardian 28 April 2004: 17). This is the same type of calculation the U.S. uses in balancing civilian vs. US military casualties during any of its numerous massacres of non-Caucasians. In military and media terms 1 Caucasian life is worth between 1,000-10,000 Afrikan lives. The ratio falls a bit for other non-Caucasians, for e.g. I reckon it takes about 100 Arab lives to equal 1 Caucasian life. Anyway based upon this type of reasoning the absolute impoverishment of 10 million Afrikan farmers (and with their families maybe 40-60 million Afrikans in total) counts as nothing against the need to keep 25,000 overwhelmingly Caucasian U.S. farmers living high on the hog.

The Minneapolis based think-tank the Institute for Agriculture and Trade Policy calculates that the US has increased its share of world cotton exports from 24% in 1996 to more than 40% in 2004. The aforementioned Guardian article notes that the effect of these US subsidies and market share domination "has been to depress cotton export prices by two-thirds over the same period to 37 cents a pound, 61% below the cost of production." (Guardian 28 April 2004: 17). Naturally the effect of this artificial lowering of prices is to destroy the income and livelihood of farmers in the poor world who do not benefit from huge subsidies. And let's be clear; that is exactly the aim of these subsidies, to destroy competition by decimating indigenous production. The second aim of this policy is to create artificially low prices for the consumption addicted domestic populations of the US and Europe. If you ever wondered why the cost of so many goods in your supermarket seems to keep on falling, you now know. You also now know the real price of these cheap goods... poverty, malnutrition and death for millions of people around the globe.

As an example of who is living large in the world. According to the Food and Agriculture Organization's measure of Body Mass Index

55.3% of U.S. citizens are overweight or obese whilst 3.5% are malnourished whereas 50% of Indian citizens are malnourished whilst 5% are overweight or obese. The most amazing of these statistics is that not far short of 10million people are malnourished in the supposed greatest nation on Earth.

However beneath these generalised statistics concerning the disparity between rich and poor nations are some equally shocking facts revealing the economic and social disparities within nations. Take the USA as an example.

In an article published in '*The Independent*' newspaper in the UK (09 September 2005) journalist Paul Vallely highlighted some shocking statistics contained within a United Nations report on global inequality. The report highlighted the fact that parts of the United States are as poor as the Poor (referred to as Third) World, and that the US is the only wealthy country with no universal health insurance system. It is worth noting that just 13 per cent of European-Americans are uninsured, compared with 21 per cent of Afrikan-Americans and 34 per cent of Hispanic-Americans. Being born into an uninsured household increases the probability of death before the age of one by about 50 per cent.

The document produced prior to the UN's 60th anniversary conference in mid September 2005 – which was the biggest gathering of world leaders in history – provides a stinging indictment of US domestic policy and its love affair with 'trickle down economics'.

The annual Human Development Report normally focuses upon the Poor World, but the 2005 edition scrutinized inequalities in health provision inside the USA as part of an examination of how inequality worldwide is retarding the eradication of poverty.

Some of the headlines from the report include:

- The infant mortality rate has been rising in the US for the past five years – and is now the same as in Malaysia which has a quarter of the US' per capita income. America's Afrikan children are twice as likely as Caucasians to die before their first birthday,
- The report accuses the US of having "an overdeveloped military strategy and an under-developed strategy for human security".

- The report emphasizes that the US policy of promoting growth and trade liberalization on the assumption that this will trickle down to the poor will not stop children dying. Growth alone will not reduce poverty so long as the poor are denied full access to health, education and other social provision. Among the world's poor, infant mortality is falling at less than half of the world average.

- The report highlights India and China as examples of the severe limitations of this growth alone model of tackling poverty. Both countries the UN says have been very successful in wealth creation but have not enabled the poor to share in the process. A rapid decline in child mortality has therefore not materialized. Indeed, when it comes to reducing infant deaths, India has now been overtaken by Bangladesh, which is only growing a third as fast.

- Poverty could be halved in just 17 years in Kenya if the poorest people were enabled to double the amount of economic growth they can achieve at present.

- Inequality within countries is as stark as the gaps between countries, the UN says. Poverty is compounded by social ills such as patriarchy and misogyny (see later chapter on these subjects). The death rate for girls in India is now 50 per cent higher than for boys. Misogyny means girls are not given the same food as boys and are not taken to clinics as often when they are ill. Fetal scanning has also reduced the number of girls born as female fetuses are disproportionately aborted.

- The only way to eradicate poverty, it says, is to target inequalities. Unless that is done the Millennium Development Goals will never be met and 41 million children will die unnecessarily over the next 10 years.

- Child mortality is on the rise in the United States. For half a century the US has seen a sustained decline in the number of children who die before their fifth birthday. But since 2000 this trend has been reversed. A baby boy from one of the top 5 per cent richest families in America will live 25 per cent longer than a boy born in the bottom 5 per cent

- Afrikan-Americans in Washington DC have a higher infant death rate than people in the Indian state of Kerala
- If the gap in health care between Afrikan and Caucasian Americans was eliminated it would save nearly 85,000 lives a year. Technological improvements in medicine save about 20,000 lives a year.
- Child poverty rates in the United States are now more than 20 per cent. Child poverty is viewed as a particularly sensitive indicator for income poverty in rich countries. It is defined as living in a family with an income below 50 per cent of the national average. The US – with Mexico – has the dubious distinction of seeing its child poverty rates increase to more than 20 per cent which leads one to question the benefits of NAFTA (North American Free Trade Agreement), to Mexico in particular. By comparison in the UK – which at the end of the 1990s had one of the highest child poverty rates in Europe – the rise in child poverty, by contrast, has been reversed through increases in tax credits and other forms of benefits targeting households with children.

These are the statistics which the hurricane Katrina could not blow away on the US Gulf coast as it lifted the lid on the USA's not so secret ugly secret of systemic poverty and racism.

Of course in accord with the adage that you don't get something for nothing (unless you are rich) we consumers pay some of the real price for the aforementioned cheap goods because the subsidies paid to these farmers (the bigger they are the more they get) is paid for out of our taxes.

Afrikan will never get out of poverty following the advice and ministrations of U.S. run pseudo global institutions such as the IMF and World Bank. Their prescriptions do not even work for the poor in the rich world, let alone for the poor in the poor world.

This chapter will provide you with a relatively brief summary of the processes and mechanisms used by Caucasian governments, and the US in particular, to ensure their continued economic domination of the world under the guise of free trade and globalisation. In particular I will examine the role of the IMF (International Monetary Fund) World Bank, WTO (World Trade Organisation) – which was born out of GATT (General Agreement on Tariffs and Trade) – and NAFTA (North American Free Trade Area) in keeping Caucasian hands firmly gripped around non-Caucasian throats.

When people talk about the 'New World Order' one often hears a lot of farfetched talk from fundamentalist Christians about Devil Worshipers in Government planning to take over the world, whilst on the other hand New Age mystics such as David Icke warn us about shape shifting Lizard looking aliens. The reality is that several thousand, mainly very rich; mostly Caucasian men; who occupy the higher reaches of the largest corporations, and a handful of Caucasian governments plan to exercise absolute political and economic control over the world. They are not devils, except in the sense that they exhibit a complete absence of concern for the human suffering engendered by their actions, and they are not aliens except in the sense that their anti-human mentality is alien to anyone with a spark of humanity. They crave wealth, but above all power and control.

The BBC's economics correspondent James Morgan writing in the Financial Times described the "de facto world government" that is emerging in the shape of the IMF, World Bank, G7, GATT and other US controlled 'international' economic institutions. He also made reference to the "new imperial age" that has dawned, with the only correction required to this statement being the removal of the word 'new'.

Chomsky cites the former Chairman of the Group of 77 (which advocates on behalf of poorer countries) Luis Fernando who suggested that The New World Trade Organization established by the latest GATT agreements will align itself with the World Bank and IMF in "a New Institutional Trinity which would have as its specific function to control and dominate the economic relations that commit the developing world" (Chomsky 1996: 179) whilst the rich countries continue to play by their own rules as formed at G7 meetings and other select gatherings.

Echoing this religious wordplay Richard Peet named his book on the IMF, WTO and World Bank 'Unholy Trinity' and like Chomsky, but in more detail, explores the role of these institutions in cementing 'Western' economic hegemony.

1945 onwards – The warmongers share the spoils

When examining the post 2nd European tribal World War economic order one must be clear that it was planned and developed not only during the early stages of that war, but in terms of US economic policy had its earliest antecedents in the U.S. response to the Great Depression of the 1930's. The U.S elite had successfully defeated "the newly realized political power of the masses" as the National Association of Manufacturers described the granting of meagre rights to workers in the 1930's that had been established in Britain for 50 years (Chomsky 1996: 84) through the use of "scientific methods of strike breaking and human relations" (Chomsky 1996: 85). With the disquiet on the domestic front now quelled US policy makers turned their attention to the economic conquest of the world and identified the most probable scenarios for carving up the world following the end of the war.

It should be remembered that at the end of the European tribal WWII the U.S. held approximately half the world's wealth and US production had quadrupled during the war whilst production in all other rich countries had fallen dramatically (Chomsky 1996).

The Council of Foreign Relations which brings together the corporate and governmental worlds was the arena for this planning and strategising and came up with the idea of the 'Grand Area' which encompassed all those parts of the world which were to operate under U.S. economic hegemony. This economic empire would provide the US with all it required by way of cheap goods and raw materials and allow the existing economic order within the U.S. to remain unchallenged and indeed be strengthened. The initial plans assumed that Germany would emerge from the war intact as a major power and that the Grand Area would encompass the Western Hemisphere, The Far East and the British Empire. As you can see no one can accuse the U.S. of being greedy! The US also wanted to exclude other traditional colonial powers that operated in its 'back yard' of South America and the Pacific.

With the demise of Germany, well the world was the U.S.' oyster and there was only the Soviet Union and China blocking total world domination. With the economic and political collapse of the Soviet Union only China remains and they have been reincorporated into the capitalist fold.

From 1-22 July 1944 44 nations led by the U.S.A., with the ever faithful UK at their side, met at The United Nations Monetary and Financial Conference held at Bretton Woods in New Hampshire to discuss how the post-war world economy was to be managed. Now of course in reality the type of discussions most countries have with the U.S. is the same type of discussion an eight year old has with the local fifteen year old thug who says can I have a bite of your hot dog. There is a pretext of choice but both sides are well aware of the consequence of refusal.

If you want a flavour of how the show was run, ponder these following facts. Firstly, many of the delegates had not seen the many complex papers tabled at the conference prior to their arrival. Secondly, the conference proceedings were held in English which many of the delegates did not speak, and with no organised system for interpreting in place. The following quotes provide sufficient explanation of the real context of this supposed meeting of equals:

"At Bretton Woods representatives of forty-four delegations signed the agreements without having the time or opportunity to read them." (Van Dormel cited in Peet 2004: 40)

"twenty-one countries have been invited [to Bretton Woods] which clearly have nothing to contribute and will merely encumber the ground...The most monstrous monkey-house assembled for years" (Sanderson cited in Peet 2004: 40).

"Bretton Woods was a drafting meeting, with the substance having largely been settled previously by the U.S. and U.K. delegations supported by the Canadians" (Mekesell cited in Peet: 2004: 40).

The foregoing quotes pretty much sum up the true nature of how international accords, United Nations resolutions and the like are put in place. A few powerful countries meet beforehand to decide what should happen and then they 'persuade' the rest that it would be in their best interests to give them a bite of their hotdog!

Notwithstanding the enormous disparity in power and influence at these discussions, most countries did share a common goal which was to ensure future economic stability following the trauma of the Great Depression during the 1930's which dealt a tremendous blow to capitalism and to some extent precipitated the Second European tribal World War. In line with this agenda of minimising the unpredictable nature of free market economics the need to create regulatory institutions was acknowledged.

The participants at Bretton Woods did still cling to much of 'classical' neo-liberal economic theory – despite an emerging recognition of the imperfections of the free market – and this included the idea, as espoused by people such as the British economist J.S. Mill, that commerce rendered war obsolete, and this notion, which seems so ridiculous as one surveys the war torn ruins of the 20th century, lay at the heart of the Bretton Woods strategy. What also lay underneath, but was never articulated publicly was the desire of the Caucasian capitalists to further expand their industrial boundaries and fully exploit the resources of the poor non-industrialised world.

What emerged from this three week summit were the formalisation of the IMF and the International Bank for Reconstruction and Development (IBRD, later to be known as the World Bank), with a proposal for an International Trade Organisation (ITO) – which came to life as the General Agreement on Trade and Tariffs (GATT), and only much later evolved into the WTO – which was formalised as part of the Havana Charter of 1947 (Peet 2004).

The Marshall Plan developed by the US to fund the reconstruction of post war Europe (including Germany, for Caucasians will forgive the sins of their brothers unlike the U.S. response to Vietnam) was used as a bargaining chip to force colonial powers such as Britain to agree to give up their colonies over a period of years. Churchill wanted Britain to hang on to its empire, however the U.S. was determined to be the new neo-colonial power in town and thus kept a keen eye on proceedings in the colonies and ensured that U.S.

corporations were given access to their booty. As discussed above both during and following European tribal WWII the U.S. put in place the institutional infrastructure to ensure it would maintain a vice like grip on world trade and global economic development. As usual as soon as you see the word 'World' or 'International' in the title of an institution you know two things. Firstly, that it has been set up by Caucasians, secondly that its values will stem from, promote and mirror Caucasian values and thirdly, that any benefits accruing from its operation will invariably flow almost exclusively to Caucasians.

Therefore it was in this spirit that these global economic regulatory institutions were set up.

Let's now look at these 'global' institutions, their stated aims and their real purpose.

The International Monetary Fund

The Bretton Woods Agreement established the International Monetary Fund "to promote international monetary co-operation and provide the machinery through which countries consult and collaborate" (Peet 2004:49). The purpose of the IMF was "to facilitate the expansion and balanced growth of international trade and to contribute thereby to the promotion and maintenance of high levels of employment and real income and to the development of the productive resources of all members as primary objectives of economic policy" (Scammell cited in Peet 2004 :49).

Be clear, the Bretton Woods agreement and the institutions it spawned were part of the planned process of cementing US economic and political hegemony over the 'free world'. As Peet (2004) highlights many of the delegates to the conference were not clear as to what they had signed up to and neither were their respective governments. He cites Van Dormel to illustrate this point:

"....Parliaments had hardly, or not at all, been involved in the negotiations, and did not know what they were all about. In most cases, it was a simple formality" (Peet 2004:51). Peet makes it clear that in his opinion the IMF was created as part of an effort to formalize US and UK economic dominance into an international monetary agreement and was one of the enforcing institutions created out of Bretton Woods. He suggests that it was not until 1959 and the birth of widespread currency convertibility that the IMF was really able to begin to flex its monetary muscles and this role developed to include "surveillance of national economic policies and disciplinary controls over them...The voting system was deliberately designed to enable the US will to prevail, and to prevent policies not in the US national interest from being adopted, or perhaps even discussed (Peet 2004:53). Peet highlights a point I made earlier about international institutions when saying that "US domination could be clothed in the raiments of 'international consultation and collaboration' because of the apparently international nature of the conference (Peet 2004:53).

There were two parts of the IMF's role as conceived at Bretton Woods. The first related to the control of currency exchange whilst the second revolved around the granting of loans to member countries experiencing economic hardship. It is the second of these two roles that has gained in prominence and caused increasing controversy over the past thirty years as the independence and helpfulness of the IMF's policies have come under increasing scrutiny.

The IMF has become increasingly directive in its approach to granting loans. Whereas its original loans conditions required "an effective program for establishing or keeping the stability of the currency of the member country at a realistic exchange rate" (IMF 1958: 404). However, this limited restriction on the economic policies of loan recipients has changed considerably over the years and the IMF now takes every opportunity to direct almost all aspects of the economic life of its client countries.

The IMF's role in the economic development of Eastern European countries following the fall of the Berlin Wall and collapse of communism is instructive and typical.

Taking a look at the 'big prize' in Eastern Europe, Russia, Noam Chomsky in his excellent book 'World Orders Old and New' cites Canadian economist Michel Chossudovsky who notes how "The IMF-Yeltsin reforms constitute an instrument of 'Thirdworldisation'" (Chossudovsky cited in Chomsky 1996: 152) and the same economist notes how the IMF's ministrations led to a hundred fold increase in consumer prices in one year, an 80% reduction in real earnings and the decimation of ordinary Russians' lifetime savings. Of course the new Russian capitalist oligarchy achieved enormous gains as Yeltsin and his cronies managed the 'opening up' of the Russian economy, which centred around the virtual give away of formerly state owned industries at bargain basement prices. Russia now has more billionaires (in sterling and dollar terms) than any other country in the world whilst the majority of its population has never been poorer and continues to suffer under IMF guided economic 'shock therapy'.

People such as Roman Abramovich the Russian billionaire owner of Chelsea football club are beneficiaries of this "…pillage of Russia's primary resources" (Chomsky 1996: 152). Russia is now experiencing what Afrika and large parts of Asia have experienced; with a small elite supporting 'economic reform' whilst poverty and hunger visit the masses.

The World Bank

The World Bank is the second of the four horsemen of the economic apocalypse. Its mission statement says that 'our dream is a world without poverty' however poverty was the last thing on the minds of the leaders of the USA and Europe when this development agency was conceived. Although formed – as the International Bank for Reconstruction and Development (IBRD) – at Bretton Woods to play a part in the post-war reconstruction of Europe, the World Bank was very much an afterthought in comparison to the attention focused upon the development of the IMF.

The World Bank has come a long way. It now lends over $17 billion a year to client countries and exercises tremendous influence over the economic and social development policies of these countries via its two modes of intervention, (i) the provision of direct loans to client countries, and (ii) setting the policy conditions under which future loan capital will be made available to countries in the Poor World. As Peet (2003) notes one commentator suggested that the World Bank 'is to economic development theology what the papacy is to Catholicism, complete with yearly encyclicals' (Peet citing Holland 2003: 111).

As should be obvious by now; the World Bank, like the IMF and all the other 'Worldwide' institutions created by the Caucasian elites has the singular, overriding and unstated purpose of cementing the economic and political hegemony of the rich Caucasian countries, and the USA in particular, over the rest of the world by 'rewarding' countries that tow the neo-liberal economic development line and punishing those countries that seek alternative, independent methods of economic, social and political development. All other stated aims and ambitions are secondary and must be viewed and understood as such.

There are five integral component parts of the World Bank Group which is the preferred name of the institution. The five parts of the Group are:

1. The International Bank for Reconstruction and Development (IBRD) which makes and guarantees loans to 'creditworthy countries', as well as providing economic advisory services. It currently has around 36 client countries.
2. The International Development Association (IDA) provides loans to countries that are 'not usually creditworthy' in the global financial markets.
3. The International Finance Corporation (IFC) provides the largest multilateral source of loan and equity financing for private sector projects in the poor world.
4. The Multilateral Investment Guarantee Agency (MIGA) provides investment insurance.
5. The International Centre for Settlement of Investment Disputes (ICSID) facilitates the settlement of investment disputes between governments and foreign investors (World Bank website).

Peet (2003)

The first two parts of this powerful financial institution, the IBRD and IDA, really form what we refer to as the World Bank.

With its headquarters in Washington, and 8,000 of its 10,000 staff based in Washington, like its apocalyptic sibling institutions, this is US economic muscle garbed in international clothing. The World Bank was a child of the U.S. right from the get go. Most of its leadership, general staffing and a large portion of its capital, all being supplied by the land of the brave and home of the free.

The World Bank emphasised monetary and fiscal discipline in the economic policies of client countries and was invariably more economically 'conservative' and market oriented than its clients. It generally emphasised large economic infrastructure projects and only began to take an interest in lending to poorer nations as the Cold War standoff between the US and USSR gained momentum. Peet cites US Secretary of State John Foster Dulles who said, in seeking to overcome conservative Congressional objections to soft loans to poor countries, "It might be good banking to put South America through the wringer, but it will come out red" (La Faber cited in Peet 2004: 115).

The World Bank like its ugly institutional siblings was and remains a very political creation. Under the leadership of first George Woods (1963-1968) and then Robert McNamara (1968–1981) the Bank slowly transformed from a bank lending to economically middle ranking countries to more of a development agency with a predominantly poor clientele. However even at the peak of the poverty alleviation thrust in the Bank, during McNamara's tenure, no more than a third of its lending was directed to this issue, with the rest going to traditional infrastructure projects.

By 1979 McNamara was suggesting that the Bank should use its programme loans to induce 'reforms' and before long the IMF was linking its lending to short-term 'stabilization programmes' whilst the Bank was requiring clients to implement 'structural adjustment programmes' to tackle more deepseated long-term structural economic problems. Since this time the World Bank has focused ever more on a 'policy interventionist stance' (Peet 2004: 122) i.e. telling the governments of poor countries not how they should run their economies but rather how they **will** run them and with precious little attention on trying to alleviate poverty. All the time within an increasingly neo-conservative laissez faire economic paradigm that abhors 'big government' except when it is subsidising the activities of transnational corporations. The rest as they say is economic history as the Bank and IMF continue to urge and coerce poor countries with malnourished populations to adopt an export oriented agricultural policy and development strategy leaving the most fertile land reserved for 'cash crops' whilst children die of the diseases of malnutrition.

If one wants concrete illustrations of the insanity and stupidity that passes for policy making and strategy in the World Bank there are few better reads than Peter Griffith's book '*The Economist's Tale*' (2003) in which he describes his time working as an economic advisor for the World Bank in Sierra Leone in the 1980's. During the book he describes a meeting in Freetown in September 1986 where a Danish consultant was presenting his final report on a World Bank credit scheme to the Ministry of Agriculture which involved the supply of credit to farmers as a means of increasing production. The scheme involved the World Bank lending one million dollars to Sierra Leone for the credit scheme. The consultant described during his presentation how the administration of the scheme – by a World Bank staff member – cost seven leones for every leone lent out i.e. 87.5%, and of the 12.5% actually loaned out only 10% i.e. 1.25% or $12500 of the original $1,000,000 dollars could be recovered when the time for the money to be repaid arrived. As Griffith points out in his book this repayment scenario – if not the huge administration costs – could have been predicted given that food prices were so low that it was uneconomic to buy fertilizers and sprays.

The Danish consultant concluded his presentation, and no doubt his career as a consultant to the World Bank, by suggesting that it would have been far cheaper not to have lent the money to the farmers at all and a more economic course of action would have been to drive through the villages throwing the money through the window. In response to this the World Bank official Mukkerjee insisted furiously that "Mr Larsen is quite wrong in his calculation. It would not be cheaper to throw the money out of the window. He has not costed the petrol."

Just about says it all. Stupid vampires running bloodbanks!

The World Trade Organisation

The General Agreement on Tariffs and Trade (GATT) and the World Trade Organisation (WTO) are the third and fourth horsemen of the economic apocalypse. This is a bit of a cheat really since the WTO is the institutionalised version of the GATT which was signed in 1947 by 23 countries.

These apocalyptic twins are designed to 'regulate' or more accurately control international trade in goods and services using a system of rules laid out in articles of agreement among member governments. The WTO is a powerful advocate of 'free trade' or 'trade liberalisation' which are the euphemisms for the unfettered opening up of the economies of poor and middle income countries to the transnational corporations of the rich countries. However, despite the rhetoric there is no illusion of trade reciprocity and the poor find their goods blocked by a myriad of tariffs and regulation designed to protect the indigenous markets and producers in rich countries. The recent (2005) move by the European Union to limit the flow of imported Chinese clothes is a classic example of the reality of *'the free movement of goods and services'* that these hypocrites are forever spouting on about.

The WTO more than any other economic institution has come to symbolise the fierce debate over globalisation and the economic New World Order.

Let us be clear, for the majority of the 400 odd year history of developed capitalism, in its varying forms, very few people and certainly very few of the economic and social elite in the richer countries of the world have believed that trade between countries should take place in an environment free of government intervention, i.e. so called 'free trade'. Vigorous state intervention was the norm – as it still is today in the rich countries.

Chomsky (1996) highlights how John Maynard Keynes, one of the giants of centre-left capitalist economics commented on the fact that the foundation and origin of British foreign investments', international networks and wealth was based upon Elizabethan piracy and plunder, as Chomsky rightly points out "terrorists, in contemporary lingo" (Chomsky 1996: 113). It was military might,

46

state monopolies and government intervention that laid the foundation for Britain's 'golden years' of empire which were initially based upon gaining mercantile supremacy in the Mediterranean during the seventeenth century.

Once Britain's economic supremacy was secured and its industrial revolution led to a shift in the balance of class power from mercantilists to industrialists the need for cheap food for factory workers led to calls for trade liberalisation to allow for the import of cheap food from abroad. Hence the British Corn Laws introduced in 1815 and which maintained artificially high food prices by restricting the import of grains, thus benefiting the landowning aristocracy, were scrapped in 1846. It is important to note that this key moment in British capitalist history was based upon the self interest of the new dominant social class not any rigid or principled adherence to neo-liberal capitalist economic theory. And this has been the way of the world until the present day. The British pushed for liberalisation in all areas where they held the economic advantage e.g. in the production of textiles – N.B. only after they had destroyed the highly efficient Bengali textile industry which had the capability to decimate the British textile industry and lead India to an industrial revolution over 100 years before it actually took place in the sub-continent.

Similarly, the US introduced trade tariffs on the import of British textiles in the 1860's to save the New England textile industry, more than half of which would have been destroyed – seriously undermining the US Industrial revolution – if left to compete in open competition with British manufacturers. Free trade is for the economically weak to practice, the rich are not interested in it except when they can pick and choose the arena of competition and the referee.

Many of the poorer countries of the world, led by Brazil and India, have been fighting back against this 'heads I win tails you lose' brand of economics and trade relationships and this has led to serious deadlock in trade and treaty negotiations at the WTO. As usual the USA wants everyone's cake and to eat it. They are at the forefront of blocking access to their markets by poor countries whilst seeking agreements that will allow US corporations to sue foreign governments that enact any legislation that has an adverse effect upon their access to markets.

This is the economic face of global white supremacy. Carving up the world in ways that will further enhance their global hegemony whilst further deepening the dependency and impoverishment of the poor.

The IMF/World Bank Some Facts

The following information was taken from the March 2004 (Issue 365) edition of the New Internationalist magazine pages 18-19.

- The 30 countries of the OECD (Organization for Economic Development and Co-operation control over 60% of the votes in the IMF (63.55%) and World Bank (61.58%). The G8 countries by themselves control almost half the votes in the IMF (48.18%) and the Bank (45.71%).
- Day to Day power in the IMF and World Bank rest with its Board of Directors. The US Director controls 17.14% of the vote in the IMF and 16.39% in the Bank. The US has stated that it will not allow its voting power in the IMF to drop below 15%, which gives it a veto over all key decisions.
- In 1999 the HIPC (Highly Indebted Poor Countries) repaid $1,680 million more than they received in the form of new loans. For every dollar in grant aid to developing countries, more than 13 come back in debt repayments.
- According to the US Government's International Financial Institution Advisory Commission, the IMF World Bank and regional development banks can easily garner the resources for total debt cancellation for the HIPC countries as it represents just 5% of their effective capital.

So as you can see THERE IS NO ECONOMIC JUSTICE, JUST US.

Waging War on the World

"In a bullfight after being brutalized while making innumerable charges at the movement of a cape, there comes a time when the bull finally turns and faces his adversary with the only movement being his heaving bloody sides. It is believed that for the first time he really sees the matador. The final confrontation is known as "the moment of truth." For the bull, this moment comes too late.............it is Blacks' moment of truth; it is time for Blacks to look at the matador."

Bobby E. Wright (1984: 1-2)

The above quote is taken from a wonderful little book written by Clinical Psychologist Dr Bobby E. Wright entitled 'The Psychopathic Racial Personality'. This book is essential reading for any Afrikan who wants to get an insight into what we are truly up against. It is short, concise and straight to the point. Instead of buying your teenagers CDs by morons for their birthday or Christmas, why not buy them this book. The understanding gained will stay with them for a lifetime and serve them well.

In his book, the sadly departed Dr Wright highlights how the Afrikan bull has been charging at a host of banners held in front of us by Caucasian matadors. He says that "Those banners have been represented by concepts such as democracy, capitalism, Marxism, religion, education." (Wright 1984: 1)

The United States is the latest in a line of European empires and needs to be viewed and analysed in this context. One of the hallmarks of imperialistic regimes is their need to invent enemies as a pretext for launching some new act of war or aggression in order to garner more territory and resources. You can go through the history of the world and see this tendency and Caucasians being the most aggressive branch of the most aggressive species (human beings) to walk or crawl on Earth demonstrate this trait more than any other people.

One of the most aggressive of all Caucasian empires was Rome which is one of Europe's two – along with Greece – 'classical civilisations'. Although the Greeks did more for Caucasians in terms of cementing the Caucasian worldview and cognitive mode (the way they think), Caucasians love the Romans for their aggression and conquest. The Romans were bloodthirsty savages. Yes, they had a high degree of technological development and possessed a literate elite, however morally they were as savage as the Greeks and almost as hedonistic and sexually debased (see later section on Relationships).

In order for a Roman military office to be granted the honour of parading through Rome itself they had to provide evidence of having killed at least 5,000 of the enemy in battle. Now of course no one was going to question if this figure included a significant number of children and other non-combatants or what the U.S. now refers to as 'collateral damage'. All people who were not Roman citizens were regarded as barbarians and were therefore dispensable. This is the same view the United States government has of those people who are not their loyal, forelock tugging allies.

Let's look at what a couple of Caucasian historians tell us about the Roman Empire and see whether you see the parallels with the New World Order.

"There was no corner of the known world where some interest was not alleged to be in danger or under actual attack. If the interests were not Roman, they were those of Rome's allies (**Pinochet in Chile**); and if Rome had no allies, the allies would be invented. When it was utterly impossible to contrive such an interest – why, then it was national honour that had been insulted (**Noriega in Panama**). The fight was always invested with an aura of legality (**Coerced UN resolutions**). Rome was always being attacked by evil-minded neighbours (**axis of evil**)....The whole world was pervaded by a host of enemies (**communists, Muslims, uncivilised savages**), it was manifestly Rome's duty to guard against their indubitably aggressive designs (**world's policeman and defender of democracy**)....Even less than in the cases that have already been discussed, can an attempt be made here to comprehend these wars of conquest from the point of view of concrete objectives. Here there was neither a warrior nation in our sense, nor in the beginning, a military despotism or an aristocracy of specifically military orientation (**Grenadan invasion, assault on Nicaragua**). Thus there is but one way to an understanding: scrutiny of domestic class interests, the question of who stood to gain (**U.S. transnational corporations**)." (Schumpeter 1955 cited in Blum 2003 125-126) My additions in bold in brackets.

In the above quote Schumpeter correctly identifies the many spurious reasons offered by the Romans to excuse their unrelenting aggression and warring against foreign states. I have added into his quote contemporary examples of where the U.S. has used these many excuses and pretexts. Schumpeter correctly identifies the economic drive behind this aggression, but what he does not address are the psychological drives, namely the Caucasian's obsessive desire for Power and Control (Ani 1996).

The next quote on Rome offers us further insight by explicitly drawing parallels between the two empires.

"America is today the leader of a world-wide anti-revolutionary movement in the defense of vested interests. She now stands for what Rome stood for. Rome consistently supported the rich against the poor in all foreign communities that fell under her sway; and since the poor, so far, have always and everywhere been far more numerous than the rich, Rome's policy made for inequality, for injustice, and for the least happiness of the greatest number." (Toynbee 1961 cited in Blum 2003:126)

So we see that some Caucasians can identify the deceit, lies and insatiable appetite for expansion of their greatest empires, and subject them to honest if limited analysis. However what they cannot do is to provide a satisfactory explanation of the millennia old history of relentless violence and aggression, particularly as directed against non-Caucasians. Why not? Because the answer is too damning, horrific and distasteful for almost all Caucasian intellectual palates.

Bobby E Wright was not hampered by such restrictions and

provides an explanation that would be considered ludicrous by virtually all Caucasians and most Afrikans, but which I think provides the best fit with Caucasians overt and recorded behaviour, as opposed to their rhetoric, and most Afrikan's desire to believe in the (Caucasian) myth of the brotherhood of man. In his work 'The Psychopathic Racial Personality' Wright states his case clearly, "..in their relationship with the Black race, Europeans (Whites) are psychopaths...The psychopath is an individual who is constantly in conflict with other persons or groups. He is unable to experience guilt, is completely selfish and callous, and has a total disregard for the rights of others." (Wright 1984: 2). Wright goes on to clarify a common misunderstanding about psychopaths, namely that it is not that they do not understand the difference between right and wrong, it is that they choose to ignore the concept of right and wrong.

He further states "By ignoring this trait in the White race (the lack of ethical and moral development) Blacks have made and are still making a tragic mistake in basing the worldwide Black liberation movement on moral suasion. It is pathological for Blacks to keep attempting to use moral suasion on a people who have no morality where race is the variable." (Wright 1984: 5). See it deh!

Now that we have put Caucasians' behaviour – as a group – toward non-Caucasians into the proper psychological context, let us move on and take a look at the many examples of U.S. warmongering and military interventions in the post tribal European WWII period leading up to their current military escapade in Iraq. This will help you to understand why the U.S. spends more on their military than the next twenty top military spending countries put together. Unbelievable, but very true.

The following list is taken from chapter 17 of 'Rogue State' (2002) by William Blum which in my opinion is the best book currently available on the subject of US foreign interventions.

China 1945 – 1951
France 1947
Marshall Islands 1946-58
Italy 1947-1970s

Greece 1947-1949
Philippines 1945-53, 1970s-1990s
Korea 1945-53
Albania 1949-53
Eastern Europe 1948-56
Germany 1950s
Iran 1953
Guatemala 1953-1990s
Costa Rica mid 1950s, 1970-71
Middle East 1956-58
Indonesia 1957-58
Haiti 1959
Western Europe 1950s-1960s
British Guiana/Guyana 1953-64
Iraq 1958-1963
Soviet Union 1940s-1960s
Vietnam 1945-1973
Cambodia 1955-73
Laos 1957-73
Thailand 1965-73
Ecuador 1960-63
The Congo/Zaire 1960-65, 1977-78
France/Algeria 1960s
Brazil 1961-1964
Peru 1965
Dominican Republic 1963-65
Cuba 1959 to present
Indonesia 1965
Ghana 1966
Uruguay 1969-72
Chile 1964-73
Greece 1967-74
South Africa 1960s – 1980s
Bolivia 1964-75
Australia 1972-75
Iraq 1972-75

Portugal 1974-76
East Timor 1975-99
Angola 1975-1980s
Jamaica 1976
Honduras 1980s
Nicaragua 1979-90
Seychelles 1979-81
South Yemen 1979-84
South Korea 1980
Chad 1981-82
Grenada 1979-83
Suriname 1982-84
Libya 1981-89
Fiji 1987
Panama 1989
Afghanistan 1979-92 and 2002 – present
El Salvador 1980-92
Haiti 1987-94
Bulgaria 1990-91
Albania 1991-92
Somalia 1993
Iraq 1990s, 2003 – present
Peru 1990s – present
Mexico 1990s – present
Columbia 1990s – present
Yugoslavia 1995-99
Venezuela 2002 – present

As you can see the USers have been extremely busy. What is most interesting is that the above list shatters the myth surrounding the US love for democracy. If you read Rogue State (2002) you will see described the US attempts – many of which were successful – to destabilise and overthrow 'democracies' all over the world as well as its support for some of the most brutally repressive regimes in the world.

Iraq needs to be viewed in the context of Caucasians' need for

Power and Control and the US 'national interest' which is code for the desire of the rich elite who run the US to get even richer. The US wants another Israel in the 'Middle East' to protect its economic interests and 9/11 provided the perfect cover to invade the region and install a regime more to their liking. The 150,000 Iraqis who died in the first Gulf War massacre, the 500,000 to 1,000,000 Iraqis (mainly children) who died as a result of the sanctions between the first and second massacres and the 50,000-100,000 Iraqis who have died during the second Iraqi massacre are simply 'collateral damage'.

Gideon Polya, an Australian writing on the countercurrents website suggests that... "the current resurgent racism in White Australia is part of a bigger picture. White Australia participated in 2 centuries of racist, violent and brutal British imperialism on all continents except for the Americas. In the post-1950 era the under-5 infant mortality in countries in which Australia has been involved militarily as a UK and/or US ally (most notably Korea, Indo-China, Iraq and Afghanistan) has totalled about 35 million. The latest UN and UNICEF reports (2005) indicate that the total post-invasion avoidable mortality (excess mortality) in the Occupied Iraqi and Afghanistan Territories has been 1.9 million – and the post-invasion under-5 infant mortality has totalled 1.5 million (for detailed articles see: http://members.optusnet.com.au/~gpolya/links.html).

All Western civilian deaths from jihadist or Arab insurgency violence (currently totalling about 5,000 for the last 20 years) are assiduously reported in Australia. However the mainstream media of White Australia steadfastly refuse to report the horrendous civilian death toll from Anglo-American imperialism (democratic Nazism) in the Occupied Iraqi and Afghan Territories." **By Gideon Polya** 01 June, 2005 Countercurrents.org

The foregoing puts all of Bush and Blair's talk of terrorists into context.

The U.S. Senate report (July 2004) into 'intelligence failings' highlighted the numerous falsehoods upon which the Iraqi massacre was based, however as expected kept the spotlight on the CIA and off the White House. This was the price demanded by the Republicans on the committee to get a final report with unanimous bipartisan agreement. Jay Rockerfeller the Democrat Chair of the committee made it quite clear that he was of the opinion that Little Bush and his cronies had made up their minds to invade Iraq shortly after 9/11 and that the 'intelligence reports' were commissioned to substantiate the case not investigate it.

What makes the case to go to war purely on the basis of 'intellligence' so ridiculous is the record of consistent and spectacular intelligence failings by the CIA, NSA (National Security Agency), FBI and other more covert security agencies. As the former US President Lyndon Baines Johnson remarked so memorably in summing up the capabilities of the CIA,

"Those guys couldn't pour piss out of a boot – not even if the instructions were written on the heel."

It also has to be remembered that along with the incompetence and mistakes is the reality that part of these agencies' role is to create and manufacture fraudulent 'evidence' to justify US bellicosity and aggression against foreign governments.

Check out the following article that highlights how the second Iraqi massacre had long been predicted and is part of a more than 100 year old struggle between the most powerful Caucasian nations for control of other people's resources.

"To the Western peoples it still appears that they believe this American War upon the World is based on 'terrorism', but to the rest of the World it has long been known what the Military Leaders of the United States were planning, and even to as far back as 1998 were the warnings of these wars being reported, and as exampled by one such warning issued by the World Socialist Web Site News Service in their article titled

New Caspian Oil Interests Fuel US War Drive Against Iraq
http://www.wsws.org/news/1998/nov1998/casp-n16.shtml

and which had said

"Powerful geo-political interests are fuelling the American war drive. In many respects US policy in the Persian Gulf is driven today by the same considerations that led it to invade Iraq nearly eight years

ago. As a "senior American official"—most likely Secretary of State
James Baker—told the New York Times within days of the Iraqi
occupation of Kuwait in August of 1990: "We are talking about oil.
Got it? Oil, vital American interests."

http://www.wsws.org/news/1998/nov1998/casp-n16.shtml

This struggle recalls the protracted conflict between Britain and
Russia at the end of the nineteenth century for hegemony in the
Middle East and Central Asia that became known as the Great Game.
Germany made its own thrust into the region with its decision to
build the Berlin to Baghdad railroad. The resulting tensions played a
major role in the growth of European militarism that erupted in
World War I. This time American imperialism is the major
protagonist. Over the past several years, the battle for dominance in
the region has come to center on one question: where to build a
pipeline to move oil from the Azeri capital of Baku to the West.
http://www.wsws.org/news/1998/nov1998/casp-n16.shtml

"The Caspian region has emerged as the world's newest stage for
big power politics. It not only offers oil companies the prospect of
great wealth, but provides a stage for high-stakes competition among
world powers.... Much depends on the outcome, because these
pipelines will not simply carry oil but will also define new corridors
of trade and power. The nation or alliance that controls pipeline
routes could hold sway over the Caspian region for decades to come."

What is perhaps most insane about these Western peoples
reactions to these true things is their not caring to know that both
Russia and China are not going to lose Central Asia, or the Middle
East, by anything other than Military defeat. The suddenness of this
Wars escalation will surprise these Westerners, even as their Military
Forces had been the ones who started it, and as we can read as
reported by the Washington Post News Service in their article titled

Undeclared Oil War
http://www.washingtonpost.com/wp-dyn/articles/A10714-
2004Jun27.html

In other words, we are on the cusp of a new kind of war — between those who have enough energy and those who do not but are increasingly willing to go out and get it. While nations have always competed for oil, it seems more and more likely that the race for a piece of the last big reserves of oil and natural gas will be the dominant geopolitical theme of the 21st century."

http://www.npr.org/templates/story/story.php?storyId=4284299
By Sorcha Faal www.rense.com
13 July 2005

The foregoing has hopefully reinforced your understanding that the USA is the largest sponsor of terrorism in the world today and that this is as it has been for the past 50 years.

It's always about money

As a 19th century US president baldly stated "America's business is business" and war is big, big business. There may be many losers in war; however there are always a relatively small number of bigtime winners. During the Iraq invasion President Bush has ensured that the group he refers to as "his base", who are commonly referred to as the super-rich, have been well looked after. There have been many lucrative contracts awarded to Bush's cronies during the onslaught on Iraq but nothing as blatant and criminal as the contract described below.

For over 20 years now, Bunnatine "Bunny" Greenhouse has overseen contracts at the Army Corps of Engineers and up until August 2005, Greenhouse was the highest-ranking civilian member of the Army Corps of Engineers. She has been demoted for "poor job performance," despite an untarnished career as one of the country's highest-ranking procurement officers.

So what did she do wrong? What was her misdemeanour? Well, she did not keep her head down and tried to blow the whistle. She raised the flag for honesty and probity over the Pentagon's no-bid contracts to Kellogg Brown & Root (KBR), the fully owned subsidiary of US Vice-President Dick Cheney's old company

Halliburton. The Greenhouse/KBR story commenced way back in the early months of 2003, when KBR was awarded a handful of government contracts in anticipation of the invasion of Iraq. One of KBR's major prewar contracts, the one that got Greenhouse in hot water with the Bushites was designed to rebuild Iraqi oil fields.

Joshua Frank notes on the www.countercurrents.org website (31 August 2005) that,

"American military strategists were anticipating that Saddam's oil fields would be set afire as the U.S. invaded. It never happened. The Pentagon dubbed the program Restore Iraqi Oil (RIO). They wanted the pipelines to keep on flowing. Indeed, the lucrative contracts to rebuild the oil fields came easy for KBR. They didn't even have to bid for it. KBR was handed $7 billion for the RIO contract without a question asked.

Describing the RIO fiasco in his forthcoming book Grand Theft Pentagon, Jeffrey St. Clair writes:

"On February 26, 2003, less than a month before the invasion of Iraq, a meeting was convened in the inner sanctum of the Pentagon. The purpose of this conclave was to devise a project that would come to be known as RIO or Restore Iraq Oil. The top priority on that February morning was to decide which U.S. company would receive the juicy contract to put out the expected oil field fires and to rebuild and manage Iraq's oil infrastructure, from the wellheads to the pipelines to the big oil terminals off the coast near Basra.

"In a way, this meeting in the bowels of the Pentagon was all for show, a kind of mating ritual between the government and its favorite contractor. There was little doubt about who was going to land the deal. So little doubt, in fact, that a Halliburton executive had been invited to attend the secret conclave. There were several other companies that could have done the job that was given to Halliburton. Fluor-Daniel, Parsons, and GSM Services were all were just as qualified for the task. Yet, none of these firms were invited to submit a bid or a plan of action.."

So everything seemed set for a smooth $7bn backhander to KBR when Bunny Greenhouse, argued that the negotiation and preparation of the RIO contract was unheard of, and not in a good way. The first point to note is that procurements of this type are never processed through the offices of the Army Corps. Secondly, despite the assignment to the Corps, the negotiating process remained in the hands of Secretary of Defense Donald Rumsfeld. Thirdly, Greenhouse was rightly critical of KBR's integral role in developing the contract, something that goes against all the normal rules and procedures on procurement. Finally, Greenhouse questioned why the RIO contract was written so that any future contractor that wanted to bid on the Iraq reconstruction had to submit their bid for work in correspondence with KBR's agreement. Greenhouse recognised that this requirement was completely unrealistic, for nobody had access to the contract but KBR and the appropriate government offices.

Greenhouse also objected to the length of the initial contract, which was for a five year period. In order to ensure her disapproval was duly noted Greenhouse wrote "I caution that extending this sole source contract beyond a one-year period could convey an invalid perception that there is not strong intent for alimited competition" right next to her signature on the original RIO contract.

Inevitably the screws were immediately turned and shortly after she penned her objection, she received her first ever negative performance evaluation, in which her reviewer commented, "nobody like[s] her." She was soon demoted and stripped of budget authority and staff management responsibility. Seemingly it was only her decision to hire a lawyer that kept the neo-con stooges at bay.

On June 27, 2005, as part of the ongoing investigation into KBR's no-bid contracts, Greenhouse agreed to testify before the Democratic Policy Committee that was looking into the Halliburton/KBR contract debacle. She had been warned only three days prior that testifying "would not be in her best interest..", however she didn't listen and spoke openly and honestly to the committee.

"I have been involved with government contracting for over 20 years," she said. "[And] I can unequivocally state that the abuse related to contracts awarded to KBR represents the most blatant and improper contract abuse I have witnessed during the course of my professional career."

The axe soon fell and shortly after Greenhouse's brave testimony, she was placed on a 90-day performance review. This is how the Bushites reward honest and brave public servants prepared to risk their careers to expose the fraud and corruption of Pentagon no-bid contracts. On Aug. 27, the guillotine came down. Greenhouse was demoted.

These are the stories NBC, ABC, BBC and other so-called 'respected news outlets' don't cover. You have to ask yourself why?

What Goes Around

Take a look at the following photographs. The first two were taken in Fallujah in Iraq on 31 March 2004 whilst the second two date back to 1919 in the USA. As soon as I saw the Iraqi images, as moving images on television and still photographs on the web, my mind immediately went to the www.maafa.org website which archives images of lynchings of Afrikan-Americans in the 20th century.

What struck me about these images were the similarities and differences in both the social and emotional context. The similarities related to the use of burning and lynching and the obvious pleasure derived from killing 'the enemy'. The differences are perhaps even more interesting and revealing. The US civilians were killed brutally but were not tortured for any length of time. Their murders were opportunistic, frenzied and random. One can observe the heightened emotional atmosphere by observing the expressions on the faces of the Iraqis in both pictures. In other pictures from these murders there is almost a joyous frenzy. The latter two images of the US lynchings tell a different tale. The unseen context is that many lynchings were not random, unplanned or frenzied. Many lynchings were advertised in local newspapers in the days leading up to the 'entertainment' and special trains were sometimes put on to transport spectators. On the aforementioned website there is a photographic image of a huge crowd waiting for a lynching to commence. The words 'waiting for the show to begin' which are written on the photograph are an apt description of the scene.

You will see how calm and matter of fact the murderers appear. There is pleasure; however it is a cool almost dispassionate pleasure. This is not surprising since it is unlikely to have been the first time that most of them had participated in such an act.

Given the organised nature of lynchings it was important that the victim was not killed too quickly to ensure that the crowd got full value for their time and effort in travelling to witness the event. The prolonged torture also served to bolster Caucasian self-confidence in their power and mastery over the Afrikan. Such torture would include: severe beating, partial hanging then reviving, non fatal stabbing, more partial hanging then reviving, sometimes burning of the skin with hot irons (sometimes red hot pokers were pushed into the victim's mouth and throat), eventually followed by fatal hanging. The victim's penis and testicles were often cut off and kept as trophies – no doubt in a psychological attempt to capture and tame the reputed power of the Black phallus and genetic material (see Welsing 1991) – and then the body was cut down and burned, as depicted in the first of the two lynching photographs. All this 'entertainment' could last for up to two hours.

You tell me, which of the people depicted is more sick, barbaric and uncivilised?

African American Holocaust
http://www.maafa.org

African American Holocaust
http://www.maafa.org

John Hartfield
Ellisville, Miss.
June 26, 1919. 5 pm

Now you may well be thinking there is a hell of a lot of a difference between 2004 and 1919 and Caucasians in the US have become a lot more humane and learnt from their bad old racist ways since then. Even whilst noting that the last 'officially recorded' lynching in the US took place in the early 1980's my response would be, let's compare the contemporary with the contemporary. We are told by 'Bush the Little' that the murders in Fallujah, the decapitation of hostage victims and the like are proof of the barbarity of the Iraqi terrorists. So how do we weigh the ghastly murder of a few dozen people in this way with the killing of 150,000 Iraqi soldiers in the first Gulf massacre, at least 500,000 children as a result of the US directed sanctions between the two massacres and the more than 50,000 Iraqis killed in the second massacre?

Would Bush have the nerve to strangle, suffocate or decapitate those half a million children personally? Is it more barbaric to have your head chopped off, or to die in agony from malnutrition, radiation poisoning induced cancers over a period of many months? Caucasians have developed the technology to kill people at a distance in more and more impersonal ways. They seem to feel that if you do not know the victim's name and do not see their face then killing them leaves no moral stain.

The process of long distance killing is in perfect keeping with Caucasians' cultural psychology and cognitive mode. It was Plato in his work 'The Republic' who first, and perhaps best, encapsulated what was to become the European epistemological (nature of truth) and ontological (nature of existence) paradigm. Plato set out a world full of objects (inanimate things, animals, Greek women and Barbarians [non-Greeks]) that were to be acted upon and manipulated by the subject (Greek man) who would put these objects into an order and place that was pleasing to his civilised mind. There was nothing but dead space between the subject and object, no interrelationship or connection. This cognitive mode provided the basis for the development of European science whose machines reflect the coldness and despiritualised nature of the European psyche. Of course these machines have also allowed Europeans to develop important and useful technologies as well as conquer the world, and to develop the ability to kill ever greater numbers of people in a more and more detached and emotionless way. Europeans have turned war into a video game – for the television viewers back home at least – and this along with the racism of Caucasians – is why their domestic audiences so readily accept the slaughter of tens of thousands of innocent non-Caucasian people as a price well worth paying to set the dead free!

You be the judge? More than 650,000 Iraqis killed with bombs, disease and hunger versus a few dozen hostages killed with swords. Maybe both are barbarians, but one set of barbarians has perfected the art of killing on a grand scale.

Be clear. Caucasians do not, never have and never will equate non-Caucasian lives with Caucasian lives. Bush would never have done what he has done in Iraq to Caucasians, especially if they were pseudo-Christians like him. As a rough rule of thumb the following sets out the relative value of various racial/ethnic groups from a White Supremacist viewpoint:

10000 Afrikans = 1 Caucasian
1000 Far East Asians (excluding Japanese and Chinese) = 1 Caucasian
100 Indians = 1 Caucasian
100 Arabs = 1 Caucasian
50 Chinese = 1 Caucasian
20 Japanese = 1 Caucasian

Watch the news, read the newspapers and see if I am wrong.

Working for 'The Man'

How do Afrikans get by working within Caucasian organisations? Most people I meet seem to be dissatisfied with their lot at work and this tendency increases sharply for Afrikans. However, most people have no intention of leaving their job, or at least giving up doing the type of work they say they dislike. Again, this tendency increases for Afrikans. Many Afrikans moan and complain about their jobs and racist Caucasian managers, however due to a combination of economic and psychological dependency cannot get off the White financial breast.

In my previous book I compared the psychology of Afrikan men with the field slave, house slave, runaway and Maroon. That great ancestor Professor Jacob Carruthers suggested that 10% of Afrikans suffered from mild cultural dislocation, 80% from moderate cultural dislocation and 10% severe cultural dislocation. The latter 90% if put in the position of a runaway would not know where to run and this is the position of most Afrikans in employment. Most Afrikans I know dislike/hate their jobs but are even more afraid of the forbidding land outside of the bureaucratic plantation. With signposts marked 'Self-Sufficiency' and 'Economic Independence' it is indeed a strange and frightening prospect for most Afrikans. We were born on the White financial breast and that is where most of us will die.

So how do Afrikan employees cope psychologically in Caucasian Institutions? Apart from individual personality traits and coping mechanisms, which are of course extremely important, I believe the most important determinant of how we behave, cope and 'get on' in white organisations is our worldview, which determines whether we will believe in the capacity of our employing organisation, and Caucasian Institutions in general, to bring about fundamental change in their area or field of operation.

I have set out below a generalist model illustrating four psychological positions from which I believe most people – irrespective of ethnicity – operate within Institutions. As suggested earlier, personality characteristics will have a strong bearing on an individual's 'institutional modus operandi', for example some people are innately sceptical and suspicious of authority, however worldview will be perhaps even more important, especially when the factor of race is added to the employment equation.

Diagram (i) – Psychological Positions within Institutions

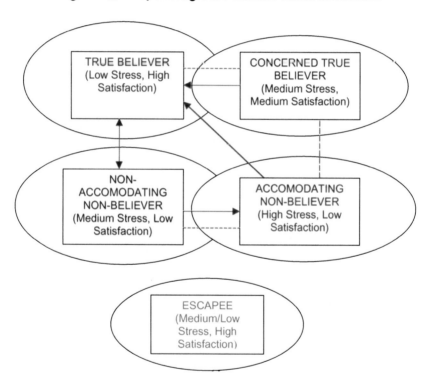

Key: Arrows between ovals represent potential lines of conflict
(arrowhead indicates direction of emotional energy)
Dashed lines between ovals represent potential lines of alliance

In relation to the above diagram I would suggest that as a generalisation the 'True Believer' and 'Concerned True Believer' psychological positions most comfortably fit with a Negro assimilationist/integrationist worldview (as described in my previous book). A classic example of a 'True Believer' is Trevor Phillips the Head of the Commission for Racial Equality (CRE) and a man aptly described by Diane Abbott MP (Member of Parliament) as the 'most important Negro in Britain'. Mr Phillips delights in attacking Afrikan people – particularly men – and adopting political positions that are so anti-Afrikan that they win him plaudits from Richard Littlejohn (a notorious rightwing journalist) and the British National Party (a neo-nazi political party) amongst others.

The 'Accommodating Non-Believer' and 'Non-Accommodating Non-Believer' positions fit with a 'Black/Runaway' worldview and where someone sits in relation to these two boxes will largely be determined by personality type.

All things being equal, in general terms The True Believer will be the happiest and least stressed of our four employee types. The Accommodating Non-Believer will be the least satisfied and most stressed given their lack of belief in the organisation's purpose and constant battle to 'stay in the loop' whilst maintaining their principles. They will constantly wrestle with their conscience and dream desperately of 'escaping', however it should be noted that this group can still be quite effective in levering change for Afrikan people within the confines of what is possible within a Caucasian Institution.

The Non-Accommodating Non-Believer will gain little satisfaction from their work and may experience a significant degree of stress due to being isolated and labelled as a troublemaker by many of their colleagues. They will however feel more at ease than the Accommodating Non-Believer and experience lower levels of stress. The Non-Accommodating Non-Believer runs the risk of tilting at lots of windmills and fighting lots of battles but never winning a war. There is a danger that this type of person comes to view the battle as the end rather than the means, however they are just the type of person you want with you when your back is against the organisational wall.

The Concerned True Believer may have concerns in relation to specific aspects of their work, however they do not aspire to escape and believe in the capacity of Caucasian organisations collectively to bring about transformational societal change, which they are much more likely to think about in class rather than race terms in any case.

The fifth and final position is beyond the institutional walls. The escapee is the Afrikan/Maroon in worldview. The escapee has not just escaped from employee status economically, for there are many successful Negro businesspeople. The escapee has escaped spiritually, culturally and psychologically. They have spat out the White breast and found the means for physical and metaphysical sustenance. The Believers cannot even comprehend what it is to be an escapee, whilst most Non-Believers only dream of it. It is the Non-Believers who tie their dreams to plans and have courage who will escape the plantation boundaries.

As said earlier it is your worldview that determines your behaviour. Whilst it is possible to keep your thoughts to yourself when the organisation demands action contradictions can come to the fore.

Diagram (ii) – The interface between culture, thought and behaviour

Culture	Attitudes	Behaviour
Values, cognitive mode, language, food, dress, clothes, music etc.	Thoughts, ideas, opinions	Speech, Body Language, Written Documents

Point of Psychological Disjuncture for Non-Believers

It is when forced to act on certain crucial value laden issues that one has to reveal one's cultural/psychological hand – or act against one's beliefs – and this is when institutional life can become difficult for non-believers.

Let us now move on to look at how institutions deal with dissent and examine how this alters depending upon a person's position within the organisational hierarchy.

Table 1: Common Institutional Behavioural Expectations of Employees

Position in Contemporary Hierarchy	Plantation Hierarchical Equivalent	Organisational Expectation	Allowable contemporary limits of Non-compliance	Contemporary Organisational response to unacceptable non-compliance
Junior	Field Slave/House Slave	Passive	Grumbling	Paternalistic indulgence or the Sack
Junior Middle Manager	Trustee Slave	Representational	Querying	Censure
Senior Middle Manager	Overseer	Advocate/Cheerleader	Questioning	Marginalisation, Career Blockage
Senior Executive	Senior Overseer	Proselytiser	Challenging	Walk The Plank, Jump or get Pushed

Now you may be wondering why I have correlated positions in an institutional hierarchy with those on a plantation. You may even be feeling particularly aggrieved depending upon where you are in your organisational hierarchy. You may be thinking this is another example of the Afrocentric obsession with slavery and a victim psychology. Well, we always have to go back to the essential nature of things then examine the context in which events or activities take place. Chattel slavery was an institution, a cultural institution. As I noted in my previous book (Grant 2003) the fundamental essence and defining qualities of an Institution are not the buildings or objects associated with its operation, but rather its ability to create and maintain thoughts, ideas, practices and processes and to function over a prolonged period of time irrespective of leadership/personnel changes. By this definition European chattel slavery was an institution.

Chattel slavery was a product of European cultural thought and practice. The European organisations/institutions in which most Afrikans work are also the products of European cultural thought and practice. The same mindset created both. They operate differently on a surface level because of the changed context – social, political, economic, technological and environmental – in which we operate. This means for example that the type of penalties enforced for non-compliance on a plantation are of a completely different order to those used by contemporary organisations. However, one thing that is shared by both is the use of psychological techniques to create compliance and this is how Caucasian behaviour towards Afrikans in 'the West' has changed over the years. Overt violence is used more sparingly whilst there is an ever increasing focus on the use of psychological techniques (and medical warfare) to pacify and conquer Afrikans.

In working for Caucasian institutions there are some simple tips I would offer for Non-Believers (True Believers will probably have put this book down by now):

- Think explicitly about how you operate psychologically and politically within your organisation
- Know the things you can change, those you can't, and how to tell the difference
- Hatch an Escape Plan as soon as you start a new job. Be clear with yourself about how long you want to stay with that employer and what you want to get out of your time in post
- Be on your guard. Seek allies but vet them carefully. Do not engage in 'free talk', especially with non-Afrikans or Negroes
- To know what you are for is even more important than knowing what you are against
- Save for a hurricane and not just a rainy day
- Do not believe that you can get away with what Caucasians get away with without possible adverse consequences (Do as the policies say not as they do)
- Do not be naïve enough to believe that you are going to transform institutional practice. Try to make sure the

institution does not transform you.

- Always strive for excellence and do not collude with or support Afrikan incompetence. Work in line with Afrikan principles (e.g. Ma'at, The Ten Afrikan Virtues [see Part IV for latter]) and you will not go far wrong.
- Be ready for the test. At some point Caucasians will seek to test your loyalties and allegiance. If you are economically vulnerable or culturally weak you will find it hard to resist.
- Keep written records of supervision notes, important decisions, your key achievements etc. You never know when you will be asked to justify your role
- Remember that stress is a function of feeling powerless allied to attaching great importance to your work (either economically, psychologically or both). Do not be afraid to say that you have too much work (and justify it in writing). Do not be afraid to take your holidays. Do not invest too much of your self image in your work for Caucasian Institutions.
- IF YOU ARE UNHAPPY GET OUT AS SOON AS YOU CAN! (I need to take my own advice).

As usual Marcus Mosiah Garvey gets to the heart of our dependency.

"Oh, how disgusting life becomes when on every hand you hear people (who bear your image, who bear your resemblance) telling you that they cannot make it, that Fate is against them, that they cannot get a chance. If 400,000,000 Negroes can only get to know themselves, to know that in them is a sovereign power, is an authority that is absolute then in the next twenty four hours we would have a new race, we would have a nation, an empire, – resurrected, not from the will of others to see us rise, – but from our own determination to rise, irrespective of what the world thinks." (Garvey 1986: 39)

Marcus Garvey is speaking here of the psychological component of Kujichagulia (Self-Determination), without which no kind of freedom – be it economic, social, cultural or political – is possible. If we learn nothing else we must learn this.

Patriarchy – Father of Misogyny

'The world is full of women and their children'

In my previous work 'Niggers, Negroes, Black People and Afrikans' (2003) I set out what I believe to be some of the critical challenges facing Afrikan people at this time. I described a connecting causal chain linking despiritualisation, patriarchy and survivalism in the Afrikan psyche and manifesting itself in some very disturbing behaviour patterns amongst a large minority of Afrikan males.

This chapter will explore the transformation of Afrikan cultural practice – as opposed to some of the cultural theory, be it Afrocentric or otherwise – from generally the most gender balanced – though by no means ideal – and feminine embracing of any group of people, to the contemporary patriarchal, male dominated reality which has bred an oppositional male/female schism in Afrikan gender relations that has traditionally been the hallmark of Caucasian culture with its 'war of the sexes' psychology, which is a euphemism for the 'War On the Female Sex' reality of European history.

In examining how Afrikan men can take steps to right this wrong, for it is the responsibility of Afrikan men to take the first step forward in seeking reconciliation and restitution of the Ma'atian principles of Harmony and Balance, I will initially have to provide a relatively brief historical overview of the fundamental philosophical beliefs underpinning European and Afrikan culture. The overview may seem long to the reader but believe me it really is brief in the context of the subject matter we are dealing with.

This process is necessary in order to reinforce one of the central arguments within this chapter, namely that the historical and contemporary Caucasian approach to gender relations and politics offers little of value to Afrikans in our search for a better; more just, relationship between the sexes. 'Feminism' is 'Caucasian Feminism' and is the product of European female thought and cultural practice.

--

Just as we require our own paradigms in other areas of life so we require an Afrikan paradigm to guide gender relations.

Part III of this book is about relationships, including a chapter on female/male sexual relationships, so some of the work in this chapter will act as a preface to the ideas explored in Part III; however since male/female relationships are so much broader than sexual relations the overlap will be much less than one might have initially imagined. What this chapter will hopefully do is to provide the philosophical framework underpinning the practical ideas for improving Afrikan female/male sexual relationships in that later chapter.

In my previous book (Grant 2003) I voiced my scepticism over the widespread occurrence of matriarchal societies in pre-enslavement/pre-colonial Afrika. This was not in any way to suggest that I know more or have access to new material that has not been uncovered by some of our greatest historians who have concluded that matriarchy was the predominant Afrikan social system, but rather an indication of the fact that I felt that matrifocal or mother-centred was a better description of those societies. I express this opinion with some caution, but express it nonetheless as an honestly held view.

Notwithstanding the foregoing semantic argument, I believe that the historical evidence clearly attests to the fact that in general the role of women and status of womanhood/motherhood was held in much higher esteem and afforded women much greater rights and privileges in Afrika than in comparison to their European counterparts (Carruthers & Karenga 1986).

The following section describes some of the core differential aspects of Afrikan and European culture in relation to women's status and role. I use the words European, Caucasian and Indo-European interchangeably in this chapter since when one speaks historically one is essentially referring to the same people.

The Afrikan Cultural Model
In exploring the Afrikan cultural model I will start with a very old passage taken from the book THE HUSIA – SACRED WISDOM OF ANCIENT EGYPT by Professor Maulana Karenga which is a

compilation of works from the sacred texts of Kemet. In many cases these works date back to over 4,000 years ago. It is worth remembering that Homer was the first European to write anything of significance around 2500 years ago. The following quote is taken from the Book of Ani which is contained within the Books of Wise Instruction. When analysing this text remember how long ago it was written and skip forward in this chapter and compare it to the writings of Manu highlighted under the Caucasian Cultural Model section under the heading 'The Law Code of Manu'.

"Do not order your wife around in her house when you know she keeps it in excellent order. Do not ask her "where it is" or say to her "bring it to us" when she has put it in the proper place. Watch her carefully and keep silent and you will see how well she manages. How happy is your house when you support her. There are many men who do not know this. But if a man refrains from provoking strife at home he will not see its inception. Thus every man who *wishes* to master his house, must *first* master his emotions." (Karenga 1989: 57)

I reckon there are plenty of brothers in 2005 who could learn a lot from the above passage!

Let us now look at what the ancient Kemites tell us about the proper relationship between a man and his mother:

"Double the gifts your mother gave you and care for her as she cared for you. She bore a heavy burden in you and did not abandon you. When she brought you forth after your months, she was still bound closely to you. For her breasts were still in your mouth for three years. While you grew, she cleaned your filth without disgust in her heart and without saying "O what can I do?" She placed you in school to be educated and came there daily on your behalf with bread and beer for your teacher. Thus when you become a young man and marry a wife and establish your house, lose not sight of your own childhood. Raise your children as your mother did you. Do not let her find fault

--

with you, lest she raise her hands to God against you and God hears her complaints and punishes you." (Karenga 1989: 56)

Again, skip forward to the Caucasian cultural model section and compare with the writings of Manu. The contrast will be obvious.

In terms of the role and status of women in Ancient Afrika Ife Jogunosimi tells us that "Unlike her counterpart in the Ancient Near East and Classical Greece and Rome, the woman in Africa occupied a position of equality and respect. She inherited as well as sold property; signed legal documents and played a very important part in the daily life of the state. In addition to these powers the natural line of inheritance was through the woman." (Jogunosimi in Carruthers & Karenga 1986: 31). It should be noted that many women did not attain these rights in 'modern Europe' until the 20th Century.

Ifi Amadiume in her excellent book 'Reinventing Africa – Matriarchy, Religion and Culture' provides a detailed critique of how European social scientists have consistently downplayed and degraded the role of the female and feminine in African societies. She also provides an overview and critique of the theories and ideas of Cheikh Anta Diop regarding the role of Matriarchy in the African social system.

In reviewing his work she says "Under this African state model the queen mother was important in Nubia, Egypt and the rest of Black Africa. Holding Egypt as the authentic model of this system, Diop shows the economic, political and religious importance of matriarchy. The queen was the true sovereign, landowner, keeper of the royalty, and guardian of the purity of the lineage. When through marriage, she transmitted the crown to her husband, he acted only as her executive agent." (Amadiume 2001: 56).

Amadiume goes to say that "Diop's theory of matriarchy is largely based on rules of succession and inheritance through the female line, and the reigns of queens in African kingdoms. I, on the contrary, have preferred to define matriarchy in terms of deeper ideological structures which have wider socio-political expressions in a well recognized viable women's system. However, I have no quarrel with Diop on the central importance of the concept of motherhood."

(Amadiume 2001: 112)

Amadiume touches upon a point I made in my previous work (Grant 2003) and later in this chapter – although she does not reach the same conclusion – when I suggested that there was a need for greater clarity and distinction in the use of the terms matrilineal, matrilocal, matrifocal and matriarchal. Diop's focus in his work was often on matrilineal structures of succession and inheritance as proof of matriarchy, whereas I would say that whilst matrilineal structures may be a part of matriarchy they are not in and of themselves proof of matriarchy or necessarily sufficient to classify a society as matriarchal.

Amadiume provides a broader definition for Afrikan matriarchy. She says "The traditional power of African women had an economic and ideological basis, which derived from the importance accorded motherhood. I have argued that this issue of the structural status of motherhood is the main difference between the historical experiences of African women and those of European women. This is directly linked to the histories of the family in these different systems. Frederick Engels (1972) argued that the European patriarchal family has been the root and seat of women's oppression. I believe that it also explains why European women never achieved women's organizations and self government as African women did." (Amadiume 2001 112)

The Caucasian/Indo-European Cultural Model

Marimba Ani in her book Yurugu states that "Indo-European culture did however contribute characteristics to European Judeo-Christian ideology. Although it is possible to identify practices of male dominance in most societies of the world, patriarchy as an institutionalised value, as an intrinsic characteristic of *utamaroho* (see glossary) can be associated with the Indo-European origins of Western civilisation. One of the aspects of cultural development that demonstrates this most clearly is religion." (Ani 1996: 171)

In my previous book (Grant 2003) I described the earliest known ordering of a racist philosophy as developed within the Vedas of the

Hindu religion and manifesting itself as the racist caste system as developed in India. As I had noted the Vedas had been initiated by the Black Dravidian (Harappan) civilisation about 2000 BCE but were substantially enlarged and changed following the Aryan/Indo-European invasion of India around 1300BCE. Aryan originally denoted an archaic Indo-European language from which developed contemporary European and Indian languages but came to denote the ancestors of contemporary Europeans, particularly those of Germanic and Scandinavian origin. Aryan people are said to originate from the region between the Carpathian and Caucasus mountain regions north of the Black Sea.

Now since we saw the structured flourishing of White Supremacy in India both as a practice and philosophy, this seems a good place to start in terms of examining the Indo-European/Caucasian cultural model for gender relations.

The Law Code of Manu

The Law Code of Manu or Manava Dharmasastra (MDh) is without doubt the most celebrated and best known legal text from ancient India. The historical data suggests that this legal treatise was compiled somewhere between the 1st Century BCE to the 2nd Century CE, however Manu was not the first author of a legal code in ancient India and there exist texts which predate his work by two to three centuries. It should also be noted that Manu is not actually the name of the author of MDh. Manu is the eponymous name given to the author (whose identity seems to be unclear). Manu was viewed in ancient India as both the first human being and lawgiver and according to some traditions as the first king. What is most important about this text is that it gives us an insight into the ancient Indo-European mind which created the invidious caste system and brought its patriarchy as well as its racism to ancient Black India which it mutated into its own hate-filled image.

Patrick Olivelle (2004: xvii) describes how "Manu became the symbol of oppression"for women and low-caste and outcaste individuals" in India. He goes on to note that "The first conference by untouchables at Yeola under the leadership of Dr B.R. Ambedkar in 1935, in which it was resolved to reject Hinduism, passed a resolution with the title 'To the Untouchable Community: A New Message of a New Manu'. Within a month a group of young untouchable men gathered in Nasik to burn a copy of Manu ceremonially." (Olivelle 2004: xvii)

Manu is the defining document of Brahamanical Hinduism and the key source of gender and colour based (which is what the caste system is) oppression in India.

A brief taste of the racism in Manu before we focus on its misogyny. In describing the occupations of the various castes Manu says: 'A single activity did the Lord allot to the Sudra, however, the ungrudging service of those very social classes'. (Olivelle 2004: 19) Those of you familiar with the Biblical Hamitic myth will note the obvious similarity with Ham condemned to being a servants' servant and a hewer of wood and carrier of water.

Although women can occupy all the racial castes their role in relation to the men of their caste was equally servile. Manu tells us that "For females tradition tells us, that the marriage ceremony equals the rite of vedic consecration; serving the husband equals living with the teacher; and care of the house equals the tending of the sacred fire." (Olivelle 2004: 28)

Two things are important here. Firstly, the idea of woman as a kind of adult child which one finds throughout patriarchal cultural practice and secondly, the important role of fire in Hinduism which stems from the nomadic culture of the Indo-European invaders who, as mentioned earlier, transformed Black India and created the racist, sexist Hinduism we see today. Traditionally nomads cremate their dead and sedentary people bury their dead. The Hindu practice of cremation is a culture carryover from the Indo-European invaders which continued even after they became sedentary. If you are a nomad it is easier to keep your dead ancestor's ashes in a jar and carry it around in a wagon rather than visit a burial site.

The following quote from Manu reinforces the idea of the 'woman-child'.

"Even in her own home, a female – whether she is a child, a young woman, or an old lady – should never carry out any task independently.* 148 As a child, she must remain under her father's control; as a young woman, under her husband's; and when her husband is dead, under her sons'. She must never seek to live independently. 149 She must never want to separate herself from her father, husband, or sons; for by separating herself from them, a woman brings disgrace on both families." (Olivelle 2004: 96)

Manu goes on to set out the type of absolute loyalty and obedience to be expected of Hindu women. "Though he may be bereft of virtue, given to lust, and totally devoid of good qualities, a woman should always worship her husband like a god. 155 For women, there is no independent sacrifice, vow or fast; a woman will be exalted in heaven by the mere fact that she has obediently served her husband. 156 A good woman, desiring to go to the same world as her husband, should never do anything to the man who took her hand, whether he is alive or dead. 157 After her husband is dead, she may voluntarily emaciate her body by eating pure flowers, roots and fruits, but she must never even mention the name of another man. 158 Aspiring to that unsurpassed Law of women devoted to a single husband, she should remain patient, controlled and celibate until her death. 159" (Olivelle 2004:97)

When you compare the foregoing to the Kemetic transcripts written at least 2000 years earlier the difference in values and mindset is stark.

Nomadism

A little earlier I touched upon the nomadic lifestyle of the Aryan invaders of ancient India and the link between nomadism and cremation as a cultural characteristic. In looking at the development of the extreme patriarchy that has characterised the cultures of Indo-European/Caucasoid people that great Afrikan scientist Cheikh Anta Diop highlighted its powerful effects upon gender relations and power amongst Caucasians.

"In this existence which was reduced to a series of perpetual migrations, the economic role of the woman was reduced to a strict minimum; she was only a burden that the man dragged behind him. Outside her function of child-bearing, her role in nomadic society is nil. It is from these considerations that a new explanation may be sought to account for the lot of the woman in Indo-European society. Having a smaller economic value it is she who must leave her clan to join that of her husband, contrary to the matriarchal custom which demands the opposite. . ... During a difficult and lengthy journey the woman becomes a useless mouth to feed. This is the only sociological explanation that can be given for the suppression at birth of female children among the nomadic tribes. With the attainment of a more settled existence, this practice lost its utility and was forbidden by the Bible and Koran." (Diop 1989: 23 and 25) Of course we know that to this present day that in India female children are very often provided with less health care than male children by their parents and that foetal scanning is used to disproportionately abort female foetuses.

Marimba Ani also explores the theme of patriarchy and nomadism amongst Indo-Europeans. She examines Mercia Eliade's concept of continuous European imperialistic expansion which he terms "Indo-Europeanization" and seeks explanation for this expansionistic *utamaroho* (Ani 1996). Eliade also identifies these Indo-Europeans as the perpetrators of a devastating period of invasions into the Southern regions between 2300BCE and 1200 BCE. Ani cites Eliade, who says,

"This characteristic process – migration, conquest of new territories, submission of inhabitants, followed by their assimilation – did not end until the nineteenth century of our era. Such an example of linguistic and cultural expansion is otherwise unknown." (Eliade cited in Ani 1996: 172).

Eliade identifies the Tumuli (Kurgan) culture as one of the earliest progenitors of 'Western' culture. He characterises them as the "Proto Indo-Europeans and the Indo- Europeans" (Eliade cited in Ani 1996: 172) and traces the inception of their culture to around the fifth millennia BCE and their westward expansion from around 4000BCE. Starting out from their homelands located in the regions North of the Black Sea between the Carpathian and the Caucasian mountain ranges their expansion in turn took in "Central Europe, the Balkan peninsula, Transcaucasia, Anatolia and Northern Iran (ca. 3500-3000). In the third millennia they reached Northern Europe the Aegean Zone (Greece and the Coasts of Anatolia) and the Mediterranean." (Eliade cited in Ani 1996: 173)

Eliade explores the relationship between this pastoral nomadic lifestyle, a seemingly insatiable expansionistic drive, a love of war and the development of specific religious ideas and values. He identifies "the idea of celestial sacredness, light and height or elevation; the idea of creativity in its immediate meaning, the idea of sovereignty, the sky-god as supreme father, and that fire kindled by lightning is celestial in origin." (Ani 1996:173). As noted earlier in relation to our brief discussion of Hinduism, "the cult of fire is a characteristic element of the Indo-European religions. Whereas, Mother Earth as a religious concept is recent among this group. The Aryans had no cities and knew nothing of writing....Iron began to be used only about 1050 B.C." (Eliade cited in Ani 1996: 173)

It is interesting to note that some Caucasians know their history and their true cultural selves. In the cinema feature film 'Highlander' starring Christopher Lambert, there are a group of men (of course) from another planet who are living on Earth and look like other men, except that they are immortal (save that they can be killed if you cut off their heads). These men know that at some point in time – referred to as 'the quickening' – they will have to fight each other until only one remains. This victorious individual will be imbued with great power to bring either peace and harmony (Ma'at) or chaos (Isfet) upon Earth. In the film the most powerful of these galactic warriors is know as the Kurgan. He enjoys violence and warfare, is ruthless and relentless and determined to be The One. Of course the hero Christopher Lambert is able to overcome the Kurgan in true Hollywood style and so the world is saved from disaster.

The naming of the vicious anti-hero after the earliest known progenitors of Caucasian culture is unlikely to have been by chance since everything, down to the finest detail, is planned out in films. This is probably a joke on the rest of the 93% of the world's population, since of course the children of the Kurgan have long since taken over the world and instituted the law of Isfet.

In her book Yurugu Marimba Ani goes further than Eliade and suggests a link between patriarchy and monotheism. "Clearly, monotheism is related to the monarch and monolith, to forms of power. Who is the monarch? Certainly the European answer would be that the monarch must be male." (Ani 1996: 174)

Certainly one can find a stark contrast in the often genderless words for the Creator in many Afrikan languages and the definitively male God of Indo-European religions. I have always said that 'the Creator does not have balls although it appears that God does'. The 'stars' of the 'Great Religions' are nearly all men because they were created by men. Hence they reinforce, justify and codify male power. The Adam and Eve myth in the Bible which is part of the Judaeo-Christian-Islamic tradition is a classic example of this bringing together of a whole range of Indo-European patriarchal ideas. Man is created first; woman is then created from the man's rib like some sort of appendage (depending upon which of the two versions of creation that appear in Genesis one is reading). Woman is created to keep man company rather than for any independent, autonomous, or special purpose. Woman is presented as temptress and psycho-emotionally weak. Woman is untrustworthy.

This myth also reveals the Indo-European sexual neurosis and obsession with the naked body (which becomes shameful after the 'fall of man' [note the masculine identification] after the eating of the forbidden fruit). This neurosis has taken two sharply delineated paths, both of which are united by their focus upon the female body. The European secular (dominant) obsession is with the woman as sexual object, dissected into sections, breasts, legs and buttocks, from which men can choose their favourite 'joint'. Female nakedness and sexuality has become the dominant method of selling products by linking the ideas that the acquisition of material objects ('status symbols') will enable men to sexually coral prized females, no doubt in the way their Indo-European ancestors once corralled their herds of livestock.

One can contrast the above with traditional Afrikan societies. In many parts of Afrika one used to – and still does today to a lesser extent – find women who went about their daily lives bare breasted. This did not cause men to become uncontrollably inflamed, there was not an epidemic of rape (rape was extremely rare) and breasts did not become highly sexualised within these cultures. Breasts continued to be viewed for their utilitarian purpose of feeding babies and young children. It was only with the introduction of Christianity and Islam and the European and Arab cultural concepts that underpin (and have been inserted into their practice) them that the Afrikan female body became highly sexualised amongst Afrikans and a source of shame/obsessive desire. Nowadays of course one finds Afrikan women more likely to be dressed as Europeans or Arabs rather than Afrikans, depending upon whether they follow Christianity, Islam or European Secular Consumerism as their religion. 'Bootylicious' is a manifestation of the Niggerised 'urban plantation' neo-slave sub-culture and born out of the Europeanisation of the Afrikan mind. It is also a product of the sub-conscious homosexualisation of the Afrikan male heterosexual's psyche.

The Arab male sexual obsession (promulgated through religion) is with the control, prescription and hiding of female sexuality. It is linked to the idea of woman as temptress and Man as uncontrolled sexual beast who cannot be expected to control himself when faced with manifestations of the female form. This desire for control of women is taken to extreme forms, such as in some parts of rural Pakistan where men will not even allow their wives to go shopping in the local markets, not even whilst covered from head to toe, for fear of...men of course. This is classic patriarchal/misogynistic behaviour where the faults of men are projected onto women who are then coerced into ever more restrictive behaviour patterns. It is similar to some degree to situations in 'Western' countries where a virtual curfew is imposed upon women whenever a particularly vicious sexual predator is on the loose and women are warned not to go out after dark, or to travel to isolated locations unaccompanied. Imagine what would happen if men were told not to go out after dark so that women could walk the streets safely!

Religion is central to patriarchy. Marimba Ani cites Rosemary Reuther who says:

"The male is seen essentially as the image of the male transcendent ego or God, woman is seen as the image of the lower, material nature......Gender becomes a primary symbol for the dualism of transcendence and immanence, spirit, matter." (Reuther cited in Ani 1996: 174)

The Christian trinity is a classic example of patriarchal thought in action. Here we have The Father, The Son and The Holy Ghost. Where is the feminine in the divine? Of course Afrikans gave the world a much earlier trinity, Ausar, Auset and Heru – Father, Mother and Son. The reader may also be aware that 25th December was the birthdate attributed to Heru who was born to overturn the evil reign of Set (origin of the word Satan?) who had killed Heru's father Ausar.

The early Christian patriarchs ensured that the Gnostic gospels were omitted from the canonical collections since the Gnostics were considered heretics for; amongst other things, allowing women to teach, preach, enact exorcisms, baptise and also for their belief in a spiritual rather than physical resurrection. It took a long time before the Christian doctrine was cemented at the Council of Nicaea (Turkey) conclave in 325C.E. but the patriarchs of Christianity ensured that their religion reflected their culture.

Whenever one writes about religion you are sure to upset someone and I seem to upset most religious people! However, religion is one of the two legs of culture – Language being the other – and hence is too important to ignore for fear of bruised feelings. I am aware that the foregoing will have little impact, if any, on the truly committed, however I hope it will give pause for thought for the remaining readership when considering why the majority of the world's population (females) are treated so badly, in so many ways, in so many different parts of the world and the role religion plays in this.

Table 2: A summative comparison of dominant Afrikan and Indo-European Cultural Patterns and their meaning with regard to gender relations

Cultural Variable	Dominant Afrikan Cultural Model		Dominant Indo-European Cultural Model	
	Foundational Cultural Practice	Value Meaning	Foundational Cultural Practice	Value Meaning
Where the woman lives after marriage	Remains with her clan	High social value attributed to women	Goes to live with husband's clan	Lesser social value attributed to women
Type of economic exchange upon marriage	Groom's family pay 'Bride Wealth' to Bride's family	Woman viewed as economic asset	'Dowry' paid to groom's family	Woman viewed as economic burden
Group settlement patterns	Sedentary lifestyle	Strong connection with 'Mother Earth' and feminine	Nomadism	Strong connection with 'Sky Father' and masculine
Type of accession/descent	Matrilineal	Value of female line and motherhood	Patrilineal	Strong value placed on paternal line in culture with concept of illegitimacy of children
Economic role of women	Women dominated key sectors of economic activity and could trade widely	Women viewed as independent people in their own right with the ability to acquire wealth	Very limited economic role	Women viewed as property of father or husband
Expectation of woman after husband's death	Free to marry again	Not good for woman or society to have unmarried adults (unless they are elders)	To remain unmarried and live dependently off sons or other male relatives	Woman is still husband's property even after death
View of Female Sexuality	Girls taught about sexual practice as part of their adolescent rites of practice	No shame attached to sex or female sexuality	Sex shrouded in mystery and females remained ignorant of sexual practice until their wedding night	Females viewed as temptresses, sex viewed as 'dirty' and shameful. Female sexuality seen as contaminating
Gender identification of deity(s)	Mix of masculine and feminine deities worshipped along with often gender free language to describe 'Creator'	Recognition of feminine in the divine and respect for women	Male Gods followed by Male God with triumph of monotheism e.g. masculinised trinity	No recognition of feminine in the divine and little respect for women

Use of transition rituals	Important Rituals for both sexes	Respect for women and recognition of their personhood	Key rituals mainly confined to males e.g. Jewish Bar mitzvah	Lack of recognition of female personhood
Response to female premarital sex	Viewed as undesirable but not disastrous	Sexual act viewed as spiritual act to be conducted within marriage	Death sentence for woman. Stoning and other brutal punishments. Still mirrored today with so-called 'honour-killings' amongst some ethnic/cultural groups e.g. Kurds	Based upon view of woman as chattel and keeper of group's morals. View of sex as 'dirty' and contaminating.

Table 2

Now in reviewing the above table it is important to note that it is not designed to be all encompassing and fully comprehensive. Whole books can and have been written on the nature of patriarchy and gender roles and status. This table and indeed chapter is designed to be introductory and the table attempts to summarise some of the key points raised throughout the preceding pages of the chapter. It is also important to note that in comparing and contrasting gender relations and practices between Afrikan and Indo-European cultures there will be variations within these large groups. Therefore one recognises that there are Afrikan nations or sub-national groups (often referred to as 'tribes') which traditionally practice patrilineal accession and where the children take the father's as opposed to the mother's name. This does not detract from the general thrust of the argument, nor does it mean that these people have formed fully blown patriarchal societies. What I am suggesting is that there are very clear Afrikan and Indo-European foundational cultural tendencies with respect to patriarchy and matriarchy and these differences are generally stark and very real.

It was suggested to me by a friend that some Afrikan societies are patriarchal and some are matriarchal and that this does not matter as long as there is a balance. I did not argue the point as there was insufficient time; however I fundamentally disagree with this notion. The whole point of patriarchy is that it is anti-MA'AT. Now one may find elements of patriarchy and elements of matriarchy within the same society, overlapping and co-existing as Ifi Amadiume (2001) suggests in her book 'Reinventing Africa', however she does not suggest that these Afrikan societies are properly patriarchal as described in this chapter, rather that European writers ignore the strong matriarchal elements within them and pick out what they see as patriarchal elements.

True Patriarchy is created out of coercion whilst matriarchy is by nature conceived co-operatively. Why do I say this? Well since men are generally physically stronger and more aggressive than women, they have the capability – and too often the desire – to impose a value system that is to their advantage and to women's disadvantage. This value system is called Patriarchy. Conversely since women are generally physically weaker and less aggressive than men, they do not have the capability – and usually not the desire – to impose a value system that is to the advantage of women and disadvantage of men. They have to negotiate social, economic, political and cultural systems with men to seek a fair and equitable arrangement. This is why so-called Matriarchy is not the opposite of Patriarchy in the antagonistic *'power over other'* sense that Europeans conceptualise opposites and gender relations. This is why I prefer the term Matrifocal (or mother-centred) to describe the many pre-invasion Afrikan societies which achieved a high degree of male/female co-operation and balance. I would conceptualise the relationships between patriarchy, matriarchy and Ma'at in the manner depicted in the diagram below.

Diagram (iii) – Relationship between Patriarchy, Matriarchy and Ma'at

Patriarchy   Matriarchy   Ma'at

What have been described as matriarchal societies achieved a better sense of balance through a process of negotiation and learning.

I would see the journey from matriarchy to Ma'at as one where gender relations move from negotiated balance to 'instinctive balance'. That is to say where the idea and belief in the necessity of recognising the feminine in all aspects of society becomes so deeply entrenched that it becomes natural and instinctive and hence no longer negotiated. Just as the left and right leg do not negotiate over which will take the first step or how fast to walk, but move in accord with signals from the brain to meet the needs of a given situation, so masculine and feminine must move together like two legs carrying the body Afrika on its journey towards Ma'at.

A key factor that must be taken into account in considering the arguments put forward in this chapter – particularly in relation to examining Afrikan cultural practice and beliefs – is the need to sweep away the hard patriarchal cultural residue overlaying traditional Afrikan cultural practice as a result of the cultural and military conquest of Afrika by Europeans and Arabs. What we are searching for is the true Afrikan way i.e. what philosophies, ideas, systems, processes, and practices did Afrikans create independently and which therefore best represent the collective Afrikan personality. If one surveys Afrikans worldwide today one will see many people who are psychologically more European than Europeans and more Arab than Arabs (the madness of many of the Afrikans in the north of Sudan who believe they are Arabs is testament to this). Indeed the great Cheikh Anta Diop himself made this very same point and cautioned against assuming that contemporary – and post enslavement – Afrikan cultural practice reflected a genuinely Afrikan value base.

One must also consider that cultural practice will change with changes in the political, social, economic and physical environment. The descendants of the Tumuli (see earlier in this chapter) are no longer nomads and therefore many now bury their dead as opposed to cremating them. Europeans have created capitalism and this coupled with a male labour shortage following their Second War on the World created the need to send women out of the home in large numbers and into factories and other places of salaried employment. It is important to recognise that these changes in cultural practice were driven by circumstances and context not a fundamental change of philosophy.

Similarly the new 'sexual freedom' created by the 'pill' in the 1960's was not driven by a desire to liberate women, rather it was seen as a potential boost to economic production in that it would allow women to control their fertility and hence become more employable and cement the idea of the two paid worker nuclear family. The biggest 'beneficiary group' were men who felt 'liberated' to engage in emotionless and consequence-less sex with as many women as possible and if the woman did get pregnant it was her fault for not using the pill properly.

If one examines certain sanitised cultural practices today one is given a glimpse into an altogether harsher recent past. For example the custom of the father of the bride paying for his daughter's wedding is a cultural legacy of the bride's father paying the groom's family a dowry as compensation for taking on an economic liability, namely his daughter. The father of the bride 'giving away' his daughter stems from the fact that in patriarchal cultures women were viewed as nothing more than chattel and upon marriage 'ownership' passed from one male to another, from father to husband (see earlier section on the The Law Code of Manu).

With changing circumstances practices change, however before taking up the philosophy and practice of another cultural group one should understand something of that people's history and cultural origins. Therefore before Afrikan women take up Caucasian Feminism they need to understand the history of relations between Caucasian women and men, their shared culture and hence their underlying shared value system. Similarly, before Afrikan men start mimicking Caucasian men's appeasement and abuse of Caucasian women it is necessary to understand culturally who Caucasian men really are.

Better still, why not stop mimicking our oppressors and take the best of what we have from our cultural history and refine, reform, adapt – and in some cases reject – it for our contemporary context since this is the only way to fundamentally change and improve relations between Afrikan men and women.

Overturning patriarchy whilst at the same time rekindling Afrikan male power in the fight against White Supremacy are not contradictory goals, rather they are necessary if tricky compliments. These twin objectives are tricky to develop concurrently because of the befuddled state of too many Afrikan men who have internalised the misogynistic foolishness of Europeans and Arabs and believe that being a man means dominating women. Part of this is a deliberate self-deception of course since many Afrikan men find the prospect of 'taking on' the Afrikan woman less threatening than taking on the Caucasian man who dominates us. Afrikan women who love Afrikan people want powerful Afrikan men, not to dominate them, but rather to work with them to overturn White Supremacy and to create a viable supply of marriageable Afrikan men for our daughters.

What Would We Do Without Them?

You wake up one morning and flick the light switch, only to find no response. You turn the power dial in your shower unit to the On position and after the usual five seconds or so warming up time step in only to be greeted by barely luke warm water. You grab a speedy cool shower. After showering you feel the radiators which have not responded to the timer and are stony cold. You begin to worry. You look out of the window into the early winter morning darkness and notice there are no lights on in the neighbouring houses and the street lights are unlit. You rouse your still dozing partner and voice your puzzlement. "What's going on?", you ask. "Go to work", they advise.

Setting off to work in your car you notice a distinct absence of traffic and pedestrians. Hold on a minute, all the people you can see in cars, waiting at bus stops and walking along the pavements are Afrikan. "What the hell is going on?" You notice that there are no buses on the road.

Your workplace seems desolate. You are relieved to see that the building is open, but then remember that the keyholder is an Afrikan which makes you think of the journey to work as you start to conceive of some strange, weird possibilities. Before you get to your workstation you are greeted by a sister, her face contorted in agony and concern. "Have you seen any White people? I woke up this morning and my husband was gone." You reply in the negative and share your strange journey to work that morning. You note how she didn't seem bothered about the Asians or anyone else. You also note that she was ready to talk to you this morning when normally she did her best to avoid conversation with 'racist Blacks' as she refers to people like you. A mixed race sister greets you and said that she could not get hold of her brother whom she normally picks up on the way to work. You do not think it was coincidence that she was living with an Afrikan man and her brother was living with a Caucasian woman.

All thought of work long since banished, the Afrikans gather together, sharing machine gun rapid conversations, interspersed with attempts to make and receive telephone calls by mobile and land line. Well, no one there to monitor the use of the phones for private calls. Mobiles seem to be working better than land lines.

After a few minutes, during which you have established that there is no programming being broadcast by television or radio, one thing seems clear. All non-Afrikans seem to have disappeared in the UK. Well, at least in the places where your collective bredren live. A few mobile telephone calls overseas establish that this is the case in foreign climes.

A sudden hush falls over you and your co-workers as you all contemplate the meaning of these strange events. The eerie silence is broken by a sudden outburst of wailing from the 'looking for my husband' sister, at exactly the same time as a brother with a fiery reputation starts whooping and hollering and shouting "Thank You Jah Jah. I knew you would answer my prayers." Pandemonium breaks out as Afrikans display emotions ranging from absolute joy to absolute despair and all points in between. Two brothers are pulled apart as the comment "No more pink pussy for you now Mr Coconut" sparks an outraged reaction.

You notice a couple of Afrikans sitting in their chairs arms wrapped around themselves rocking back and forth. One is mumbling incoherently whilst the other, eyes gazing upward, is begging Jesus to 'come to us in our hour of need'. Other Afrikans are exchanging high fives, touching fists, hugging or beaming broadly. A significant number are shaking their heads in bemusement and looking confused. The largest group are gathered together and seem to be organising a search party under the leadership of the Director of Social Services who is determined to find his wife.

You move to one side, smile a wry smile and say to yourself. "Now we will find out what we are made of."

Imagine if you woke up tomorrow to face the above scenario. What do you think would be your reaction? What would be the reaction of your family and friends? What would be the reaction of

Afrikans in the place you live? Could we cope in a world without the people who provide us with food, clothing, shelter, healthcare, education, jobs, heating and lighting, entertainment and for many of us love and/or sex. How would we cater for these needs? What would we do with all the brothers and sisters locked up in penal and mental institutions? How does even thinking about such a prospect make you feel? Is this a vision of heaven or hell or something else?

In contemplating the foregoing scenario you have to take out Asians and other non-Caucasians because of course if Caucasians disappeared Afrikans would immediately look to the nearest and next most powerful group of non-Afrikans to metaphorically provide breast milk and wipe our bottoms. We are like a character in a deeply perverse comedy show – broadcast by the BBC in the UK – called 'Little Britain', who as a grown man in his thirties demands to be breast fed by his mother in public places with the phrase ' bitty.., bitty mummy'. Afrikans have still not been weaned off the poisonous milk of White Supremacy.

In considering the above I reckon there would be a range of identifiable responses from different types of Afrikans depending upon their psychological and emotional need for, and attachment to, non-Afrikans, and Caucasians in particular. Since all Afrikans in majority Caucasian countries have an enormous material dependency upon Caucasians this would not be a determining factor.

The Bewildered and Frightened

These Afrikans would be very scared and anxious. They would be the literal and metaphorical rocking chair wailers. There would be plenty of wailing and gnashing of teeth as they contemplate life without their Earthly masters. They would view the aforementioned scenario as a curse from God for our sins and a revisiting of the curse of Ham. They would blame Black Nationalists and the such like for bringing down this curse on our heads. These people would work themselves into a state of mental illness and would soon need caring for by other Afrikans.

The Searchers

These Afrikans also have a huge psychological investment in Europeans, both personally and in terms of European culture. Their immediate concern would be to form a search party and to gather together as many Afrikans as possible to scour their locality – and eventually the Earth – in search of Europeans. Note that I say in search of Europeans, finding other non-Afrikans would be a small incidental bonus in their search for the great prize. Even after the first few days of searching; such individuals would not turn their thoughts to addressing the need to re-establish basic infrastructure, such as power supplies, transportation, food supply etc, in the places they live. No, in fact the search would simply gather momentum as keenness and enthusiasm turned to desperation and fear.

Eventually, as the lack of food supply begins to bite, these people would, with sad resignation, face up to the awful prospect of an Afrikan world, or to be more accurate, a world without Caucasians. Now, once the basic infrastructure had been established one would find these people pushing themselves forward as the rightful heirs to positions of power and influence. Their argument would be simple. They had been well trained by the people who had previously run the world and therefore they were best placed to take over this role. In fact, so closely do these people associate themselves psychologically with Caucasians that they would not see this as the start of a new regime but rather the seamless continuation of the old one.

Their main priority would be to re-establish Western civilisation/Caucasian culture as the only viable way forward in the minds of the masses and they would soon begin to re-establish European cultural and historical celebrations, be it Columbus Day and Thanksgiving in the US or Morris Dancing and binge drinking and violence on a Friday night in the UK. Every opportunity to celebrate even the most minor of European cultural events or achievements would be grabbed with both hands and yet they would tell the people to forget Afrikan culture and history since it had become irrelevant in a world full of Afrikans.

The creation of monuments to 'those who have disappeared' would be the focal point for vigorous campaigns by the Searchers –

once they had reluctantly given up on the search – despite the frequent reminders of how these same people objected strongly to the creation of monuments to the Mangalize (see glossary).

Many of these Searchers will experience long-term trauma and depression as they are forced to 'settle' for an Afrikan partner – the lightest they can find – and live a life without the source of their inspiration and dreams. Life becomes unbearable for the Searchers.

The Flip flopping procrastinators

These are Afrikans who have lived a life of frustration with White Supremacy. They are pro-Black but harbour deep-seated doubts about the capacity of Afrikans for meaningful independent living. They curse the milk of the White breast which provides them with daily sustenance. The FFP will experience surges of panic accompanied by surges of euphoria as their split European/Afrikan personalities battle for supremacy. Because of this internal war for control the FFP are ultra theoretical and forever developing more detailed and complex plans. All the better for putting off the day of action. Such is their state of confusion that they will sit down to plan even in the face of immediate dire need for action.

The Against-ists

As their name suggests these people have built their persona, reputation and identity around protesting and being against. They have energy, fire and passion, which is all good, but also a tendency to knock things down rather than build things up. They love to respond to crises and march and shout and disrupt. They proudly wear their fearlessness as a badge of honour and are happiest in the eye of the storm. When things are quiet they become agitated and they are quick to mock the efforts of Afrikans engaged in long-term, low-key developmental work in the community. If it is not high profile it can't be any good is their motto.

In the absence of 'the enemy' The Against-ists face a crisis of purpose. They have spent so much time being against that they have spent insufficient time understanding what they are for. Inevitably, these people will become some of the most ardent critics of whatever regime emerges. They will not engage in the rebuilding process since they do not want to become contaminated by any flaws in the process. Rather they will produce detailed and sometimes cogent criticisms of the mistakes being made in rebuilding the social system. The Against-ists will battle almost as fiercely with The Rebuilders (see below) – with whom they notionally share a great deal in common – as with The Searchers and in some instances will adopt the stance of a plague on all your houses. There can be no peace for the Against-ists even when their dreams come true.

The Rebuilders

Rebuilders are opportunists in the best sense of the word. They are action and doing oriented and believe that experiential learning is the most powerful form of learning. They realise that they will never have all the answers and therefore this should not be an impediment to act. In the face of the non-Afrikan disappearances their first instinct is to organise to put in place basic infrastructure. Those who do not have trade or technical skills use their interpersonal and communication skills to rebuild morale, identity and a sense of purpose which they recognise will be essential if the new social order is to function effectively. The soft skill rebuilders will write newsletters and pamphlets, broadcast on radio and television using the infrastructure rebuilt by the hard skill rebuilders. The rebuilders will try to promote consensus and frown upon dissent which they will view as counterproductive in the emergency rebuilding period of the new society. These people will be in a minority, perhaps 5-10% of the population and will experience great frustration at the inertia of many of their brothers and sisters. The Rebuilders will be the first ones to get 'burnt out'.

Now of course the foregoing categorisations are stereotyped pen sketches, but I bet you can recognise at least a few people who fall into each category. Of course the moral of the story is 'what do a dependent people do when the source of their dependency is removed?' Do they sink or swim? And if the source of their dependency is not removed can they ever become independent of their own volition? Afrikan people are as addicted to White Supremacy as Caucasians are. Both are locked in a strange and sad co-dependent relationship. It is just that one of the parties gets a great deal more benefit out of the addictive relationship than the other.

What are you doing to promote Afrikan psychological and material independence?

PART II

LOYALTIES AND
ALLEGIANCES

Afrikan Success and Leadership

LEADERSHIP means everything – PAIN, BLOOD, DEATH
Marcus Mosiah Garvey

"No *amount of individual achievement or the gaining of personal acceptance by Whites on the part of Black individuals, will remove from them the stigma of their membership in a powerless race. It will not truly enhance their personal power or freedom. The fact that they have to deny an intrinsic part of their being and identity to achieve "success" and White approval means that a crucially important part of their full humanity has to be negated, that their authentic sense of power and efficacy, their need to be loved unconditionally remains ache-ingly unfulfilled. It connotes that they are isolated and defenceless because they must reject the ability of their group to protect and shelter them in times of social and personal upheavals; that their power is a counterfeited, delegated power, conditionally, tenuously and arbitrarily based on their willingness to ally themselves with Whites in their genocidal assault against the interests and lives of their Afrikan brethren whose fellowship they disdain. The racially isolated Afrikan individual will learn too late that he cannot aid and abet the destruction of his "former" race without ultimately aiding and abetting his own personal destruction."* (Wilson 1998: 97-98)

"*The oppressor must have some dealing with the despised group, and rather than have contact with individuals he approaches the masses through his own spokesman. In its strides upward a race shuffles off its leaders because they originate outside of the group. They constitute a load that sinks the oppressed in the mire of trials and tribulations.*

"Leadership is usually superimposed for the purpose of "directing the course of the ostracised group along sane lines." This was accomplished during the days of slavery by restricting the assembly of Negroes to certain times and places and compelling them to meet in the presence of a stipulated number of the "wisest and discreetest men of the community." These supervisors of the conduct of Negroes would prevent them from learning the truth which might make them "unruly" or ambitious to become free." (Woodson 1933: 115-116)

The foregoing quotes come from three great Afrikan ancestors, Marcus Mosiah Garvey, Amos N. Wilson and Cater G. Woodson. I thought these quotes from their respective works were worth reproducing due to the absolutely critical importance of the points they raise with respect to 'Black Success' and 'Black Leaders'. This section of the book is about with whom your heart lies when it comes to the crunch, when the two armies face each other across the battlefield. The forces of White Supremacy against those of Afrikan liberation. You have to choose one side or the other. If you sit on the fence you get splinters in your backside. If you stand in the middle of the road you get run over. Because the forces of White Supremacy look well equipped and radiate confidence from their numerous victories over the Afrikan Liberation army, the ranked masses of Afrikans who could tilt the scales in favour of the oppressed, stand on the sidelines, afraid, arms folded, in their heads exhorting the Afrikans to victory, but too afraid to even make a noise let alone pick up a spear and shield for fear the Kurgan should turn their wrath upon them.

After the battlefield is turned red with Afrikan blood the spectating Afrikan masses pick up their chains and return to their servile enslavement. It is often said that it is better to die on your feet than live on your knees; however we all know that most of us do not really believe that. 95% of people will choose their knees every time.

106

Black Success

The earlier quote by Amos Wilson highlights how completely warped and self-negating the Afrikan concept of 'success' has become. It is an ironic, perhaps even bizarre, twist of human psychology that the more the oppressor group rejects the oppressed the more large sections of the oppressed group will desire acceptance by the oppressor. The higher the wall the oppressor builds around his/her house the more the oppressed will scramble to scale its heights, never once pausing to think about the possibility of building their own house. Most Black people believe subconsciously – and for many consciously – that the mark of success is to gain recognition from their psychological reference group, Caucasians. To be honoured by other Afrikans is one thing, but to 'crossover', to gain 'mainstream' recognition, well you have 'made it' then.

A frivolous, but instructive example relates to the host of TV talent contests where mainly young people aspiring to be 'pop stars' perform before a studio audience, panel of critics and TV viewers in their homes. The final outcome is based upon the votes garnered from the viewing audience. Now, I do not watch these programmes, however plenty of Afrikans do and many complain to me about the fact that Afrikan performers rarely if ever win no matter how talented they are. In fact you will normally get some half talented Caucasian usually trying to mimic Black vocal styles and dance moves who will triumph leaving the Afrikan performer and viewers perplexed (as happened to Lemar in the UK). My response to my friends is simple… "What did you expect"? Remember when our parents used to tell us that you have to be twice as good as a Caucasian to get half the results. Why didn't you listen to your parents? Are we really stupid enough to think that the same people who have been oppressing us are going to judge us better on a regular basis, even if we are better?

Caucasians instinctively understand self-interested practice. You don't have to give them a textbook for that, they learn it on the breast milk of their culture. When their geneticists speak of the 'selfish gene' it is themselves they should be referring to specifically although they universalise it. They will always vote for Eninem over Biggy Smalls, Tupac, Public Enemy, Dr Dre or Ja Rule etc. Foolishness may litter much of what they all produce but Caucasians will always choose Caucasian foolishness over Afrikan foolishness.

The beauty of the system is that the rejection only further fuels the Afrikan desire to be accepted and thus further elevates the oppressor in the mind of the oppressed. You therefore get Afrikans encouraging other Afrikans to vote en masse to help the brother or sister succeed. Utterly futile in a country where we represent around 2% of the entire population. I've got better things to do with my phone.

So it is now and so it has been since we first became mentally enslaved. I watched a documentary on the life of Sam Cook on television and they made great play of how he initially flopped at some upper middle class Caucasian variety club in New York. Sam Cook finally knew he had 'made it' when he returned to triumph a few years later. Ironically he triumphed when he was himself and did not try to 'sing white' as he had on his first appearance. Even if they do not like you, Caucasians have a grudging respect for Afrikans who are not ashamed to be Afrikan. No one respects a mimicking clown of any hue although you are happy to laugh **at** them.

A sister once warmly congratulated me on having 'made it' upon hearing that my job title included the word 'Director'. Although sincerely meant I found her comment so sad. In my opinion I have not made anything until I demonstrate the capability to provide for my family without total dependence on Caucasians, which is what I am striving for every day. The best thing about my job title is the money it brings which helps me to save and invest for freedom. My career to date has taught me that Caucasians want some Afrikans to 'succeed', – and will ensure that this happens – indeed they need some Afrikans to succeed to maintain the illusion of Equal Opportunities and that 'racism is a thing of the past'.

However what they really want is Afrikans with Caucasian minds. Afrikans who are Caucasian clones to do their bidding without being bid. That is why certain Caucasians and some confused Afrikans began whispering against me after the publication of my previous book. The racists and self-haters started to say 'I never knew Paul was a racist' and 'do you know he hates White people with mixed race children'. What they never knew was that I know who I am and know who they are. What they never knew was that I could critique their culture based upon research, evidence, theory, hypothesis and experience. They also never knew that I was unafraid of presenting this analysis in book form for public scrutiny.

None of my 'silent critics', because to date none of them has come to me face to face for honest discussion – save one person who was sensible and open enough to ask me about the rumours circulating about me which had been fed to her – has alleged that I have mistreated, abused or discriminated against anyone of any shade in my work. The reason is simple, because I have not and they know it. The problem they have is that I do not share the prevailing orthodoxy and Caucasians, in line with their culture of insatiable acquisition and theft, not only want my labour but my heart and mind as well. I sell them my intellect and skills whilst I have to, but my heart and mind belong to Afrikan people.

Such is our desperation for Caucasian approval that we place no moral or ethical markers along the road to success. It is a case of just get there anyhow. If you have to commit war crimes so be it, you can be a success like Colin Powell and Condoleeza Rice. If you have to kiss arse so be it. Kiss arse good like Ving Rhames and Cuba Gooding Jr. Pucker up but as Bill Clinton demonstrates don't inhale! If you have to act the Uncle Tom/Aunt Jemima clown so be it. Clown away like Ainsley Harriet or Queen Latifah and make even Caucasians cringe with embarrassment. The pay is good.

Is this all we can give our children to aspire to? To be other people's agents of wickedness, footstools, buffoons and sycophants? No wonder our children are not impressed by us.

The notion of Black success has lost all purpose and has no moral imperative behind it. Where once the measure of success was the degree to which a person was able to give service back to our community, nowadays the measure of success seems to be how much distance you can put between yourself and your community. The talk is all about transcending your Afrikaness as if it were some sort of ballast holding you down, preventing you from flying amidst the white clouds of a universal, cultureless, colour blind utopia. The measure of success is a Caucasian yardstick and our Negroes are desperate to be culturally assimilated and for their descendants to be physically assimilated so that they can finally rid themselves of their deepseated shame at being born Afrikan.

These forms of 'success' become a form of prostitution for the Negro minority who know better; as opposed to the promised land for the confused majority who do not know better and really believe that Caucasians want to create a level playing field for everyone. For those who know better but are afraid, the question is... When they drop the soap the next time will you pick it up again?

Black Leadership

"After the Negroes became free the same end was reached by employing a Negro or some white man to spy upon and report behind closed doors on a plan to enslave the Negroes' minds. In case that actual employment as a spy seemed too bold, the person to be used as such an instrument took up some sort of enterprise which the oppressors of the race warmly supported to give him the desired influence in the community. This "racial racketeer" might be a politician, minister, teacher, director of a community center, or head of a "social uplift agency." As long as he did certain things and expressed the popular opinion on questions he lacked for nothing, and those who followed him found their way apparently better paid as the years went by. His leadership then, was recognized and the ultimate undoing of the Negroes in the community was assured." (Woodson 1933: 116)

Why is Black Leadership so frequently worse than useless? Why don't most Black Leaders lead? Why is there almost invariably an inverse relationship between the degree of respect accorded Black Leaders by Caucasian leaders and their practical usefulness to Afrikan people?

I bet the above quote from Carter G. Woodson rang some serious bells in your head. You probably felt as if you were standing atop a cathedral bell tower. You see the truth never withers or loses its potency. Ancestor Woodson understood the role of these 'placemen' hired to undermine the Afrikan's efforts at liberation and the same remains true today. Negroes masquerading as Black people.

For a leader to lead an oppressed people effectively they must be free from dependency upon the oppressor group. If you are dependent upon your oppressor to put food in your children's belly you are not truly free to lead. Look around you. How many of our so-called Leaders head up independent institutions/organisations that are free from dependency upon Caucasian funding. Answer, very few. This is one of the reasons why I paid particular attention to developing independent Afrikan institutions/organisations in my previous book (Grant 2003). Without independent institutions we will not have independent leadership.

The following case study will exemplify the failure of our current Negro leadership to support Afrikan people when push comes to shove.

Case Study – DIVERT Trust and a Jamaican rumpus

Between May 1997 and March 2000 I was employed as Project Co-ordinator for the DIVERT Trust in Nottingham, which initially involved setting up and managing a mentoring project for Afrikan-Caribbean and Dual Heritage children at risk of exclusion and/or academic underachievement. The DIVERT Trust was a Caucasian charity – now absorbed by RPS Rainer – focused upon working with socially excluded young people.

As the project developed I was continually looking for ways to provide the young people with some degree of cultural education/reorientation. Working for a Caucasian organisation I would sometimes have to do things and then report on them afterwards where I thought I might encounter a blockage. For example I knew that the trustees would probably object to me promoting the project and seeking Afrikan mentors using a pirate radio station so I did not tell them until a pattern of use was well established and I could demonstrate the positive results.

Over time I developed the idea of taking the children/young people on a trip to Jamaica. I chose Jamaica since virtually all the young people were of full or part Afrikan-Jamaican extraction. I developed a rationale and plan in which the young people's behaviour at school and with the project would be monitored and those who demonstrated improvement would be taken to Jamaica and sold the idea successfully to the Trustees.

Once I had identified costs and raised the funds to pay for the trip I revealed the project to the young people who were pretty excited. And so over a period of months I corresponded with a link project in Jamaica with whom we had established contact, and who were to be our hosts, in order to finalise all the details. During this time I set the monitoring process in train and the young people received regular updates as to how they were progressing.

Eventually we got to the point of departure and I prepared to take seven young people and two volunteer mentors on what should have been the educational trip of a lifetime for the young people. But, nothing runs smoothly when you try to support your own. A Caucasian worker from one of the funding bodies contacted the local newspaper, the Nottingham Evening Post, to stir up some trouble for us. At the time there was this whole commotion in the UK about 'goodies for baddies' centring on the provision of trips and activities for young offenders by agencies of the state. Now of course my project was a school based project not a youth offending project, however the young people were Afrikans so I suppose that was enough to make them all criminals in the media's eyes.

What resulted from this initial media contact by this worker was the most incredible media frenzy. It started with a front page spread in the Nottingham Evening Post with a picture of a golden beach in Montego Bay, Jamaica. They conveniently forgot to mention that we were staying at a convent in Kingston for £12 per night per person – including breakfast and dinner – about half a mile from the ghetto. No, you see Jamaica is either a gun toting hell hole or a magical paradise isle depending upon what suits Caucasian's purposes. In this case they wanted to implant the impression that we had gone on a beach holiday of the sort they favour.

Following this highly misleading article the story was picked up by the national newspapers the following day. This resulted in me receiving a telephone call at Heathrow airport telling me that photographers representing national newspapers were scouring the airport terminals in search of us. You can imagine me telling these young people to stay out of sight and keep a low profile until we could head into the departure lounge and escape our pursuers. Whilst in Jamaica I received daily press briefings from my line manager and soon found that the story was being covered in Jamaica, although with a more sympathetic slant. I even gave a radio interview for a Jamaican radio station.

For the record, whilst in Jamaica the young people were working from 9.00am to 6.00pm every day. They were visiting museums, meeting Afrikan professionals e.g. a prominent barrister and radio broadcaster, going to places of historical interest e.g. Port Royal and keeping a daily diary of activities. This was no holiday. They were to have Saturday afternoon and Sunday off during the two week trip and that was it.

Unfortunately, we never completed the two week itinerary. On day six I received news from the head of the convent that a newspaper reporter and photographer were stationed outside the convent looking to get photographs of the young people misbehaving. It transpired that the Mail on Sunday, a right wing national newspaper in the UK, had flown a freelance reporter and photographer over from Miami to cover the story.

It is difficult to explain the pressure the mentors and I felt under. We already knew that the British media were carrying out a journalistic lynching and had defamed the young people's character. With the first journalists already in Jamaica and the promise of more to follow I took the decision to cut the trip short and return to the UK. The return journey costing more than the original budget for the entire two week trip.

Back in the UK the DIVERT Trust took an investigative approach as if I had done something wrong, although the Board of Trustees and Chief Executive had raised no qualms when the trip was proposed and planned. It was only after the media assault that they suddenly misplaced their backbones. The result was the Chair of the Board of Trustees publicly praising the tremendous work of the Chief Executive – whose main activity whilst I was in Jamaica seemed to be to constantly tell my Deputy that 'this is going to cost us all our jobs' – at public meetings. Not a word for the young people, the volunteer mentors, my Deputy or myself.

However this lack of gratitude or recognition didn't stop them still calling upon me to bring young people to London to represent DIVERT at conferences etc. since our Nottingham project was doing the most active work with young people of all DIVERT's projects across the country and indeed the DIVERT Trust mentoring handbook – which was disseminated to all Youth Offending Teams in the country by central government – was largely based upon policies, rules, procedures and materials I developed in Nottingham whilst delivering the project.

After this whole affair I decided to leave DIVERT as soon as I could and fortunately found another job and left within four months. Even after I left I found out that certain people in the DIVERT Trust were spreading lies about what I had and hadn't done now that I was not in a position to defend myself. It is funny that the Chief Executive never once raised a single criticism of me whilst I was employed by DIVERT. I guess some backs are made for stabbing.

Anyway, back to the point of taking you through this whole episode. What should have been the response of Black leaders back in Nottingham both during and in the aftermath of this racist media attack on young people aged 13-15 and a project set up to help Afrikan youngsters to fulfil their potential? Now you may have thought that even if some 'leaders' did not agree with me taking young people to Jamaica – although hundreds of thousands of young people go to Europe every year – they would have raised cane about the vicious media coverage including attacks by former Conservative government ministers such as Norman Tebbit and Anne Widdecomb.

But no, not a bit of it. These Negroes wanted quiet, behind the scenes, negotiations with the Nottingham Evening Post to discuss our 'differences of opinion' over the coverage. When it was proposed to hold a march through the city centre to the Evening Post's offices one of our 'leaders' advised me to keep away as it could do my career harm and there was no need for confrontation. I am a placid person, but when someone is licking you in your jawbone you need to do something other than turn the other cheek. Of course when the march did take place our venerable leaders were conspicuous by their absence.

There were meetings with the Evening Post and Diversity training for their (all Caucasian) journalists and the usual crap about improving links with the community and eventually it all petered out as normal. However, the lessons I learnt were valuable and being put in the media fire was not harmful. I tried to use the whole episode as a valuable learning experience for the young people to help them get a better understanding of the beast beneath the mask, however I felt that most did not grasp the full implications.

As for our so-called community leaders they just went to prove once again that a man/woman cannot serve two masters. They are spineless, Caucasian minded stooges whose only goal is to be recognised and attain status from their Masters. The people who should have been publicly denouncing the racism of the Nottingham Evening Post and the absolute silence of Nottingham City Council were as quiet as Negro mice. They are well paid for picking up the soap.

The irony of this whole affair was brought into clear focus when the Parents Group that I co-founded in 1998 received an invitation to attend an event at the Nottingham Playhouse theatre on 10 October 2005 at which pupils from five secondary schools in Nottingham would be showcasing the knowledge gained from their educational trip to…yes you've guessed it, Jamaica!

Looks like I was ahead of my time, or is it that when the Caucasian master sanctions an activity it becomes acceptable in our sight?

Lessons to be learnt about Black Leadership

- There can be no effective independent Black Leadership without independent Black institutions
- Afrikan-centred Institutions are the incubation units, nurseries, schools and universities for nurturing and moulding independent Black leadership

- Be cautious of Black leaders who are favoured and promoted by Caucasians
- Most of our so-called Black leaders are Caucasians in Black face
- Because most Black leaders in 'the West' are directly dependent upon Caucasians for their livelihood they find it difficult to act independently when it comes to the crunch
- Most of what Carter G Woodson said about Negro leaders still holds true today. I would add one caveat which is to say the problem is not that we have too many leaders, but rather that we do not have enough leadership

The Mayor, his Advisor and the Professor

Lee Jasper is one of the most high profile Black people in London, probably in the UK. He is at the time of writing employed as Policies Director, Equalities and Policing, in the Mayor of London's office. He is also chair of the National Black Alliance, was formally the Director of The 1990 Trust between 1995 and 2000, is Chairman of Operation Black Vote and National Secretary of the National Assembly Against Racism. Mr Jasper is a powerful public orator and has been at the forefront of many race based campaigns since the 1980's. He first came to prominence as perhaps the leading figure in the National Black Caucus, a loosely structured campaigning group which formalized and became the 1990 Trust (named after the year in which it was founded).

Always ambitious and eager for the limelight, it was no surprise when Mr Jasper was appointed to his current high profile position by the Mayor of London, Ken Livingston. He has been accompanied on this journey to the heart of London based race politics by other leading lights from within the 1990 Trust. The groups of which Mr Jasper is at the forefront operate on the Black = non White model developed in the 1970's and 1980's which is so beloved by Caucasian 'liberals' and their Black political companions and which is pretty much unique to the UK. This ideological stance enjoys very little philosophical support amongst the Afrikan and Asian communities which these 'Black leaders' claim to serve and hence has very little ability to mobilise the masses of non-White people.

Within this section I have been talking about the price that has to be paid when one seeks the approval of Caucasian power brokers, in whatever field one operates. They demand a price and often the price is very high indeed. As a minimum they will demand a public demonstration of loyalty and allegiance to their values, ideas and principles. The more public and high profile your role the greater the pressure you will be under. Mr Jasper is no exception, he faces these same pressures. It was inevitable that he would be tested; the only question was how he would respond to the test. Well, as you will see below Mr Jasper has been tested and come up short, or proven himself a loyal and reliable servant, depending upon whether you view the world through Afrocentric or Eurocentric eyes.

Below is a copy of an email allegedly sent by Lee Jasper to the Black Directors of Choice FM – a London based radio station which plays Black (which is now probably rebranded Urban) music – which highlights his concern over the content of the talk show hosted by Geoff Schumann, at the time, one of only two Afrikan men hosting talk based shows across the London airwaves.

——— Original Message———-
From: Lee Jasper [Lee.Jasper@london.gov.uk]
Sent: 20 October 2003 16:52
To: Patrick Berry; Neil Kenlock; Yvonne Thompson (E-mail)
Cc: Rosemary Emodi; Sheila Archdeacon; Joy Johnson

Subject: Private and Confidential Addressees Only [Scanned]
  Importance: High
  Directors
Choice FM
Borough High Street
London.
Monday 19th October 2003

Dear All
Re Geoff Schumann show.

I write with some regret in relation to a **formal complaint** about the Geoff Schumann show this **Saturday 17th October 2003**. I would ask that you provide me with a transcript of the show as it was in my view a very unbalanced and disturbing programme. I urge you to listen to the programme and come to your own conclusion. **For my part I have, in the past raised these issues informally with Directors** who have continually assured me that a more balanced approach would be take in future by Geoff. Sadly this has not materialised. I now intend to have the said show screened for balance and accuracy and will be corresponding further with you on this matter in due course. I was informed by Geoff that he had tried to contact my press office on Friday afternoon to get 'my side of the story' I have checked with the Mayor's press officers and there is no record of any such call.

I would therefore appreciate it if you could provide me with the details relating to this.

Given my own commitment to Choice FM and the fact that you are one of our principle media partners for the GLA group I am particularly disappointed that despite several informal attempts to resolve these matters no solution seems to have been found.

I suggest an urgent meeting is arranged between my office and Choice representatives at the highest level to discuss these matters further.

Yours

Lee Jasper
Policy Director Equalities & Policing
Mayors Office
City Hall
London.
* * * * *

N.B. my emphasis in bold

The context for the above email was that during the week ending 17 October 2003 (the date of the broadcast referred to by Mr Jasper) it came to the attention of London's Afrikan community that an invitation that had been extended to the internationally renowned Garvey scholar, Professor Tony Martin, to speak at the Mayor of London's First Voice Conference on 24 October 2003, had been withdrawn by Mr Jasper, apparently as a result of concerns raised by the Jewish community. The "disinvitation" was reported on the front page of the Jewish Chronicle dated 16 October 2003.

The matter was raised by Mr Schumann in his weekly phone-in programme the following day in the presence of the popular edutainer, Leo Muhammad who is a prominent figure in the Nation of Islam in the UK. Mr Jasper telephoned the programme live, and was unable to give either Mr Schumann or Mr Muhammad a satisfactory explanation of his actions.

As those of you who have read Professor Martin's book 'The Jewish Onslaught: Despatches from the Wellesley Battlefront' (1993) will be aware, Professor Martin has been right near the top of the Jewish Anti-Defamation League and Eurocentric academics hit list since he had the temerity to include the book 'The Secret Relationship Between Blacks and Jews' (1991) – which details the prominent role of Jews in all aspects of the European transatlantic slave trade in Afrikans – on his recommended reading list for one of his courses. The Anti-Defamation League (ADL) has long condemned this work as anti-Semitic, not as one might expect due to insults and stereotypes directed at Jews, but simply because the book in their eyes does not present Jews in a good light. They do not say that the book contains untruths or inaccuracies because they know it is a very accurate and straightforward analysis and description of this period of history. Over 90% of the academic references in the book are drawn from Jewish scholars who say what all reasonably intelligent people know, namely that European Jews played a prominent, and in some geographical locations (e.g. Brazil, Barbados, Curacao) a leading, role in this brutal trade.

However the truth presents no barrier to the ADL, who soon mustered the not inconsiderable might of the Jewish controlled/influenced media to orchestrate a co-ordinated campaign to have the tenured Professor Martin removed from his post. With the usual Negro lackeys in tow and sometimes at the head of the campaign, the truth got lost in the need to maintain the image of European Jewry as perpetual victims and never perpetrators.

Professor Martin managed to hang on to his job and produced the aforementioned book providing his account of the turmoil and media frenzy in which he became embroiled. However, since this time the ADL and Jewish establishment have been out to get him. Professor

Martin was disinvited from the international conference which was sponsored by the Mayor of London's office because of his decision to share a conference platform with Dr David Irvine a Caucasian British historian and 'holocaust denier'. In my view it was a mistake by Professor Martin to share a platform with Dr Irvine who is a neo-nazi sympathizer and who hates Afrikans as much as Jews, however to suggest that this decision automatically makes the Professor an anti-Semite is completely ludicrous. It is noticeable that his critics have not produced a single comment or word by Professor Martin that even they could describe as anti-Semitic. Their tactic is to convict him by association with the Nation of Islam (via the book) and Dr Irvine.

Hysteria generated via their media friends is the ADL's modus operandi and it was no surprise when Mr Jasper made his decision to ban Professor Martin from the conference, especially when it came to light that he was part of the Black-Jewish Forum, a group I had frankly never heard of prior to this incident, and which I presume has the unspoken agenda of ensuring that Afrikans know their place, stay in it and never utter a word that could be construed as critical of Jewry.

The truth about the relationship between European Jews and Afrikans is that it has for a long time been a Master/Slave, Landlord/Tenant, Employer/Employee relationship and that is exactly how many Caucasian Jews wish it to stay. Whilst Jews have for the longest time been writing books about Afrikans and presenting themselves as experts on our culture as well as controlling Afrikan artistic production, not to mention defaming the Afrikan image via notoriously racist films produced by Jewish owned film studios (right up to the present), Afrikans apparently have no right of reply even when the subject under discussion pertains directly to our history. This is why Professor Martin had to be put in his place as they would see it. Unfortunately for the ADL and others the Professor did not bend even in the midst of their media storm.

For further information on this affair, please see:
http://www.blacksandjews.com/Martin.UK.Disinvitation.html
Looking back, one of the most ironic things about the banning of

Professor Martin is that in 2005 the Mayor of London, Ken Livingston, who is himself a Jew – and who would have given Mr Jasper the nod in relation to the banning of Professor Martin – was accused of anti-Semitism after comparing a Jewish reporter who works for the London Evening Standard newspaper to a Nazi concentration camp guard. Mr Livingston refused to apologise and the affair eventually petered out. Mr Jasper was noticeable by his quietude during the whole affair, perhaps contemplating the difficulty of balancing integrity with the need to keep his £70,000 a year job.

On 3 March 2004, it came to the attention of the Afrikan community that Mr Schumann had been "sacked" from his role as a presenter on Choice FM. The matter was reported by Blink ("The 1990 Trust's independent interactive site for black communities") as follows:

Choice DJ Geoff Schumann axed by Capital bosses
http://www.blink.org.uk/pdescription.asp?key=3007&grp=1&cat=1 97

The Blink / 1990 Trust report included the following:
*"Lee Jasper, chair of the National Black Alliance, said: "Geoff Schumann's sacking is indefensible and he has my 100% personal support in what must be a difficult time for him." His Saturday morning show **radiated both balance and maturity** in addition to Geoff's sparkling personality. His unique contribution to the intellectual and political debate within the black community in London was without doubt beyond compare. **His presence on London's airwaves will be sorely missed particularly by me.**"* (my emphasis in bold)

This is the same Lee Jasper who apparently authored the email reproduced earlier which was critical of Geoff Schumann and in particular his "very unbalanced and disturbing programme". The National Black Alliance, together with The 1990 Trust, was one of a number of organisations who issued a joint statement on 27 October 2003 endorsing the decision to ban Professor Tony Martin from speaking at the conference referred to above.

(Please see http://www.blink.org.uk/pdescription.asp?key=2654 &grp=38&cat=130).

Also included in the list of organisations issuing the joint statement was Operation Black Vote, of which the same Lee Jasper is Chairman, and the National Assembly Against Racism, of which the same Mr Jasper happens to be National Secretary.

The named recipients of the email apparently authored by Lee Jasper are Patrick Berry, Neil Kenlock and Yvonne Thompson, all of whom were black directors of Choice FM between 1990 and 2004. It does not appear that the note was sent to Choice FM's white directors.

These two separate but interlinked affairs raise serious questions about Mr Jasper's integrity and the role he plays within organisations purporting to work on behalf of Afrikan – and other non-Caucasian – people. It seems clear to me that he is a careerist who will divest himself of responsibilities towards Afrikan people as and when it suits him. Questions also need to be asked about the Black-Jewish forum and where Mr Jasper's loyalties really lie.

When Marsa Comes Calling with Trinkets

I received a bit of a shock in May 2004. I picked up a small pile of letters that lay on the doormat and as I quickly flicked through them to see if there was anything worth opening before I went to work, I noticed an envelope with 'On Her Majesty's Service' printed across the top and marked <u>URGENT PERSONAL</u> above the address window in which was written P. Grant Esq. followed by my address. I thought, this looks interesting and opened the letter to discover that the Prime Minister wished to submit my name to the Queen to receive an MBE (Member of the British Empire).

Now you could perhaps imagine my surprise, even shock, to be put forward for such an award, especially if you have read my first book! My first thought was that it was some sort of intricate practical joke by someone who wanted to test whether I would live up to my rhetoric. My second thought was that none of the civil servants involved in this process had heard of my book and that they definitely needed to tighten up on their vetting procedures! My third thought was whoever nominated me for this award was no doubt well intentioned but clearly did not know me very well. My fourth thought was that I needed to check myself to see what sort of persona I was projecting at work – I presumed the nomination could only have come via someone who knew me professionally, and this seemed to be confirmed by the mention of my job title in the citation that they proposed to publish in 'The Gazette'. However my job at the time of this nomination was not focused upon young people and the nomination was for 'Services to Young People' so it remains a mystery.

All in all quite an amusing mystery. My thoughts as I set out for work that day were all centred upon what I should say in refusing this offer of an MBE and a contemplation of how Afrikans who proudly accept these awards reconcile the slavery which was at the heart of the British Empire with their own tacit celebration of Empire as they bow before the Queen when receiving these awards.

There follows below a copy of the letter inviting me to accept the offer of the award followed by the letter I wrote in reply to this proposed nomination and finally the response on behalf of Downing Street. You may notice how Mr Chapman ceased to be *my obedient servant* once I had rejected the MBE!

10 DOWNING STREET
LONDON SW1A 2AA

SECRETARY FOR APPOINTMENTS

W E Chapman

IN CONFIDENCE   4th May 2004

Dear Sir,

The Prime Minister has asked me to inform you, in strict confidence, that he has it in mind, on the occasion of the forthcoming list of Birthday Honours, to submit your name to The Queen with a recommendation that Her Majesty may be graciously pleased to approve that you be appointed a Member of the Order of the British Empire (MBE) .

Before doing so, the Prime Minister would be glad to know that this would be agreeable to you. I should therefore be grateful if you would complete the enclosed form and send it to me by return of post.

If you agree that your name should go forward and The Queen accepts the Prime Minister's recommendation, the announcement will be made in the Birthday Honours List. You will receive no further communication before the List is published. Recipients will be notified of the arrangements for receiving their award within five months of the announcement.

I am, Sir
Your obedient Servant,

William Chapman

WILLIAM CHAPMAN

X8 XXXX Road
XXXXX
Nottingham
NGX XXG

7 May 2004

William Chapman
Secretary For Appointments
10 Downing Street
London SW1A 2AA

Dear Sir,

RE: Recommendation for submission for appointment as a Member of the Order of the British Empire

Thank you for your letter dated 4th May 2004 in relation to the aforementioned matter.

I am writing to inform you that I do not wish my name to be submitted for consideration by The Queen and have completed the form you enclosed accordingly.

Whilst I recognise that it is not necessary to explain my reasons for this decision, and indeed, they may not be of particular interest to the Prime Minister, I thought your correspondence presented a useful opportunity to convey a message the Prime Minister is unlikely to hear from his coterie of advisers, including those Black functionaries who advise him on issues of Race.

Afrikan (Black) people are suffering in Britain, and indeed all over the world, be it in Afrika itself, the United States and Americas, the Caribbean, India (yes we are there in numbers) or anywhere else in the world we find ourselves in numbers. This suffering is a direct result of the Maafa (misnamed Black Holocaust by some) perpetrated against Afrikans by Arabs and most particularly Europeans. The kidnapping, torture, enslavement and murder of tens of millions of Afrikans was a Crime Against Humanity and the British Empire was at the forefront of this genocidal act. I would therefore be at the least a hypocrite and at worst a traitor if I accepted an honour which glorifies that period of British history which centred around the use and abuse of my ancestors

In order for there to be true reconciliation there must be justice, and justice for Afrikans requires, firstly a public apology by The Queen on behalf of the British Government to all Afrikan people for the aforementioned Crimes Against Humanity committed by the British Government, British private companies and British citizens on behalf of the British people and nation. Secondly, the British along with the multitude of other European nations (including the United States) should pay adequate reparations to Afrikan nations and individuals as a gesture of recompense for the physical, psychological, and spiritual destruction these heinous crimes have wrought over many generations, to this present day.

If the Prime Minister truly wants his Africa Commission to do useful work, the above points would present useful areas for consideration and action.

Obviously, I am aware that these demands will not be met in my lifetime, however the Prime Minister will see in the years to come that the flag of Afrikan liberation still flies high and that I am by no means a singular or unusual voice.

I thank you for considering me for this award.

Yours faithfully

Paul Grant

In the spirit of Ma'at

With the purpose of Auset

10 DOWNING STREET
LONDON SW1A 2AA

From the Secretary for Appointments
W E Chapman

11 May 2004

Dear Mr. Grant,

Thank you for letter of 7 May and for returning your completed form.

The Prime Minister is sorry not to be able to include your name in the recommendations which he will be submitting to The Queen for the Birthday Honours List, but he will of course respect your wish.

I can assure you that your comments have been carefully noted.

Yours sincerely,

William Chapman

WILLIAM CHAPMAN

Now what is the purpose of this chapter? Is it an indirect act of boastfulness; to say look at me, I get offered awards even when I don't want them, as some readers may be thinking? Is it an attempt to 'prove' my Afrocentric credentials, as another group of readers may be thinking? Well, my purpose was to provide a concrete example of how Caucasians offer carrots and inducements to make us psychologically indebted to them and to show us that there is an easy path along which they have laid out material rewards and status if only we will come over to the 'pale side of the force'. It was also to explore the question of the appropriate response by Afrikans – who feel any level of commitment to other Afrikans – to these trinkets offered by 'Marsa'.

The psychological relationship between the oppressed and oppressor is complex and full of contradictions and ambiguities. The oppressed has strongly ambivalent feelings towards the oppressor, both loving and hating them simultaneously. The oppressed often scorns other members of the group who nakedly kiss arse, but yet spends a great deal of time unconsciously mimicking and copying the values, mores, philosophy, speech, mannerisms, physical appearance and general ways of the oppressor.

The oppressed who try to resist psychologically often end up fighting the oppressor in their heads from sun up 'til sun down. They can become experts at what they are against, but some have little idea what they are for, having not taken the time to relearn what it is to be Afrikan. The oppressed often end up doing exactly what the oppressor wants, which is fighting amongst themselves and not against him/her. The oppressed uses the oppressor as his reference point and group, as her yardstick, barometer and compass, the only valid measure of worth and achievement. The oppressed comes to yearn affirmation from the oppressor even as s/he complains about the oppressor's oppression.

The corollary to this is the need of the oppressor for the oppressed. The oppressors can only obtain the ego gratification they need as a 'superior' if there is an 'inferior' to be looked down upon with contempt and scorn. In order for there to be a first there has to be a last. The oppressor also experiences feelings of ambivalence in relation to the oppressed. On the one hand experiencing feelings of disgust, loathing and contempt when the oppressed is in close proximity, whilst contrarily feeling a tremendous surge in self worth and pride as s/he observes the pitiable condition of the oppressed. In many senses the oppressor is lost without the oppressed who becomes their wanted/unwanted shadow. The lowliest members of the oppressor group experience these feelings of ambivalence to the greatest degree since they often live in closest proximity to the oppressed and hence feel the greatest degree of resentment at their presence, but also 'need' the oppressed the most since they are at the bottom of the Caucasian pile and need someone to feel better than. This is why the Caucasian working class get so angry and resentful when they see non-Caucasians with 'flashy cars' and other signs of material wealth.

The oppressor cannot bear to observe let alone acknowledge even the slightest sign of development, creativity or innovation amongst the oppressed and hence adopts a standard routine of, Condemn, Copy, Co-opt, Steal (Grant 2003). Contrarily the oppressed is honoured and reacts with almost childlike glee at any sign of acknowledgement, or blatant copying, of their cultural production by the oppressor, feeling that this recognition bestows legitimacy and credibility upon their efforts. The oppressed will gladly handover their cultural legacy to please Marsa. So, for example Negroes have no problem with Black Music becoming Music of Black Origin and Music of Black Origin becoming Urban Music. As long as Marsa is pleased Tom and Gemima are happy.

The Caucasian oppressor knows the value of his/her trinkets and crumbs in maintaining control over the oppressed group and they generally award them to three types of people. The first are the *Confirmed Negroes* who have been happily picking up the soap for years and who need to be rewarded for their treachery. The second are the *Misguided Afrikan Resistors* who although they have been fighting White Supremacy – though they may not always acknowledge it as such – for years, still cannot shake off the 'brotherhood of man' rhetoric that Caucasians have been pumping into our heads for years. These Afrikans are often Christians or

Christianised. The third group are the *New Resistors*, people who have recently come to the attention of the Establishment and whom they hope they can 'buy off' and groom with the right inducements.

Caucasians know that having 'successful' Afrikans clamouring for their awards and hence their affirmation, is an act of voluntarily handing over psychological power from Afrikans to Europeans. They know it reaffirms Afrikan inferiority in the mind of the Afrikan **and** the Caucasian. It says the only judgement that counts is the Caucasian judgement.

When you look at film and television awards you see the points I have raised set before us exquisitely. Let us take three examples: Halle Berry, Ving Rhames and Denzel Washington.

Halle Berry, who seems to think of herself as that strange creature 'A Woman of Colour'; produced, even by Hollywood standards, a ridiculously over the top wailing and gushing performance in which she acknowledged all those Afrikan actresses who had gone before her and whose sacrifices had made it possible for her to be standing before the assembled glitterati in receipt of an Oscar for Best Actress. What she failed to acknowledge, and probably even consider, was that Caucasians are happy to acknowledge and celebrate Afrikans playing roles of self-denigration, such as Hattie McDaniel in 'Gone With The Wind'.

Similarly, Berry was 'recognised' for her part in the film 'Monster's Ball' in which she plays a woman who falls in love with a racist redneck prison guard played by Billie Bob Thornton (very appropriate name) who has put her Afrikan-American death row prisoner husband to death. Ms Berry engages in some graphic sex scenes with Mr Thornton – which is one of her specialities – just to put the cap on her performance. Through her love – and pum pum – she redeems the racist Thornton and enables him to see the error of his ways and they live happily ever after whilst her Afrikan husband rots six feet under. Any messages in this plot do you think? Do you think she would have been recognised if she played a proud sister who wreaked revenge on racist Caucasians?

There is a clear reason why Ms Berry was 'honoured' for her role in Monster's Ball and it has nothing to do with racial acceptance or progress.

What can you say about Ving Rhames? Does the man know no shame or have no pride.

One of Rhames' 'classic' roles was in the Quentin Tarantino – now there is a Caucasian who hates Afrikan men – film 'Pulp Fiction' where he plays a tough gangster whose Caucasian girlfriend Uma Thurman takes a shine to one of his hired hitmen, John Travolta. Near the culmination of this film as Rhames searches for Bruce Willis, whom he intends to kill, he enters into a shop owned by a Caucasian redneck who with an accomplice ties up Rhames at gunpoint and takes him down into a cellar. Rhames, unable to move or cry out is then raped by a leather clad Caucasian moron. During the rape Bruce Willis enters the shop and kills Rhames' captors. In gratitude Rhames promises to cancel the 'hit' on Willis if he leaves town and does not tell anyone about the rape.

Now apply 'The Law of Flip'. When was the last time you saw a Caucasian gangland boss played by a physically powerful ultra-masculine looking Caucasian male raped by Afrikans and then saved by an Afrikan hero? Tarantino knows the impact of depicting a physically powerful Afrikan male being raped by Caucasian males. Rhames does not care as long as it 'helps' his career. Also if you know your history you will know that *buck busting* , the process of breaking the will of enslaved Afrikan males, often involved the public rape of the most powerful and resistant Afrikan male on a plantation.

Rhames' true Negro status was highlighted by his pitiful behaviour when accepting an award for his part in a television show. Upon hearing his name announced Rhames proceeded to genuflect and profess shock and disbelief. To my utter amazement he refused to accept the award and insisted that Jack Lemmon, who was also nominated, come up on stage and jointly accept the award with him. Lemmon initially smiled with mild embarrassment thinking that Rhames was simply acknowledging his reputation as an eminent actor, however as it became clear that the Negro Rhames was grovelling for real, and truly believed that he was not worthy of winning the award, Lemmon began to squirm with embarrassment. Eventually Lemmon was forced to go up onto stage and accept the award with Rhames. By this stage I was hiding behind the sofa in utter embarrassment. It was a truly cringe inducing moment. With such displays of his inferiority complex Caucasians will always leave crumbs – and even some crust – from their table for Rhames.

In his book 'Why Black Men Love White Women' (2004) Rajen Persaud comments upon both Rhames' rape scene in Pulp Fiction and Halle Berry's role in Monster's Ball.

"…This was the most talked about sex scene in Black America until Ving Rhames was cinematically sodomized in *Pulp Fiction*. One interesting note about *Pulp Fiction*: both Blacks and whites invited me to see this movie because of the Ving Rhames "pound in the ass sex scene". But they had different reasons. The whites thought it was an amazing scene and Brothers thought it was racist. (It is also truly important to note that many Blacks "loved" this movie. Some still call it a classic).

Today, at the height of another very desirable sister's career, she is sexually exploited on a nine foot screen while her desirability was destroyed in the eyes of many Black men. Halle Berry's performance in the film *Monster's Ball* further degraded the image of the Black woman. I was also invited to see this film based on this sex scene. Everyone who told me about this movie said I had to see it because of how "*she played herself*". The scene had the beautiful Berry volunteering her vagina to the man who executed her husband. She tore her clothes off, positioned herself "doggie style" and was banged on screen for what seemed like an eternity.

Unlike Pulp Fiction most Black People who saw this film were shocked, disappointed and disgusted. These portrayals depict the false erosion of the Black woman's emotional and sexual discretion. They show beautiful Black women desperately seeking sexual salvation in white men." (Persaud 2004: 36)

Whilst I would not automatically take as read Persaud's belief that his circle of Afrikan-American friends provide an accurate barometer of the views of the whole of the Afrikan-American community in New York, let alone the United States, he does make some cogent points; some of which I touched upon in my previous book (Grant 2003) and which lead into the broader examination of miscegenation later in this book (see chapter 'The Race is Over'). One also has to ponder why Caucasians would consider scenes depicting an Afrikan man being raped as 'amazing'.

Now back to the Oscars. Why did Denzel Washington finally get an Oscar as Best Leading Actor for the film 'Training Days'? Denzel Washington has produced many excellent screen performances, so what was different about Training Days? Was it a far superior film to any he has starred in? Was his performance clearly better than any he had produced previously? Well, the answer to the latter two questions is No and No. However, what was different about this film is that Washington was playing the Baddie. He was playing a cold, cynical, corrupt individual as opposed to the heroic type figures who the Academy of motion pictures usually like to honour as leading actor at the Oscars. When you compare the film Malcolm X with Training Days there is no logical reason – if you are naïve enough to believe in Caucasian objectivity and colour blind approach – why Washington was recognised for the latter and not the former. Of course everything in life is political; it is just a case of whether it is with a big 'P' or a small 'p'. Caucasians understand instinctively the meaning of self-interested practice.

I think it was no coincidence that Halle Berry, Denzel Washington and Sidney Poitier (who received a lifetime achievement award) were all recognised in the same year. I believe the subconscious Caucasian drive was to pull Afrikan-Americans back into the fold with the offering up of some high profile crumbs in the aftermath of September 11th. Also the roles of Berry and Washington were the type of roles Caucasians feel comfortable in recognising – as exemplified by the Academy's previous recognition of that full blown 'Tom', Cuba Gooding Junior, who responded appropriately with a proper kiss arse acceptance speech – and Sidney Poitier has long proven his Negro credentials, including getting rid of his Afrikan wife to marry a Caucasian.

Everything people do has a motivation, whether that motivation is consciously recognised or unconscious. Caucasians, as stated earlier, are the masters of self-interested practice. Awards should never be taken at face value and should always be viewed as, to a greater or lesser extent, politicised.

So what am I saying? That Afrikans should never accept awards developed by Caucasians? Well, perhaps, but the real point is that some awards should never be accepted by Afrikans who love Afrikan people and all others should be considered with extreme caution before acceptance. Afrikans have to break the habit of seeking and valuing Caucasian recognition. When you are at war you don't worry about persuading your enemy to recognise you ...do you!

Afrikan Students – Assets or Liabilities

There was time in the UK – and it is still true in many parts of the world – when students were at the cutting edge of radical protest in this country. Traditionally, the participation of the relatively small Afrikan student population in the UK in such protests has always been limited, informed by an innate wariness of the pseudo-liberal politics of their fellow Caucasian students. However Afrikan students in the UK have often organised independently and of course the first Pan-African Congress was organised by Afrikan students based in London in 1945.

Overall, the level of general student activism seemed to decline markedly during the 1980's whose zeitgeist was perhaps best captured and epitomised by the film 'Wall Street' starring Michael Douglas, with its famous 'Greed is Good' speech by the lead character, Gordon Gekko, who represented the extreme capitalistic, individualism of that period.

The '80's were all about me, myself and I and getting one over your fellow citizen in order to get ahead. Student life reflected this social shift – within an already capitalistic, individualistic and greedy culture – and the radicalism of the sixties and seventies disappeared rapidly. It was time to party and as a student during the mid eighties I have to admit that is what I and many others did. There were still smatterings of political education – our African/Caribbean student society invited speakers from the PACM and ANC in South Africa and some people volunteered at the local Saturday school, however we were best known for throwing the best parties. To be fair I am aware that there were groups such as the Black Action Group at the University of Central England that were quite politicised.

The foregoing overview is written to contextualise my concerns regarding our current crop of university undergraduates which were crystallised by a long conversation I had with a conscious young woman who was completing her undergraduate studies.

The young woman in question met up with me to purchase a copy of my first book and we got onto the subject of the relative level of consciousness of her peers. She informed me that she had given up on her peers, who as far as she was concerned were only interested in parties and displayed an almost total absence of consciousness.

Whilst sympathising with her plight I had to qualify my remarks with the aforementioned admission that I was probably more like them than her during my own student days and that if she were to meet many of them in ten years time she would, in some cases, be pleasantly surprised at the change in thinking that had taken place. Afrikan consciousness – just like anti-Afrikan consciousness – has to be nurtured and supported. It does not just happen naturally. If our young people are raised without an explicit and directive Afrikan purpose how can we blame them when they seek to meld and blend into the dominant European culture. They know no different and are left to find a way home by themselves. In these cases, some of them will whilst the majority of them will be lost to the struggle.

To be culturally European, or to adopt; for want of a better phrase, Negro/Nigger culture, is the path of least resistance. Hence, this sister bemoaned the fact that the African/Caribbean society summer ball, which she did not attend, was headlined 'Pimps and Virgins'. It seems the sisters must have been a little more reticent about being labelled 'whores' than the brothers were about being pimps.

Now, obviously this was all meant to be a bit of fun and equally obviously there was a total lack of awareness or deep consideration about what they were saying about themselves or Afrikan people in general. They were just following fashion and mimicking the worst elements of 'street culture' as promoted by morons like 50 Cent et al. I am sure that none of the male students really think of themselves as misogynists who exploit women and readily use violence to control women, 'qualities' which are the trademark of the pimp. Some of the awards on the night included, Best Dancer, Best Looking Male, Best Looking Female, Best Weave, Worst Weave.

Let's finish with a challenge to our Afrikan students:

"This is the task now before you, Black student. Put your
people before yourself. Forsake individualism for
peoplehood, me for us, individual aspirations for community
aspirations. Make the sacrifices necessary to struggle for
your people. You owe your education to the masses of your
people, no matter which field of study you choose. Doors
open to you today are cracked only because Black people
sweated, bled and died yesterday. Do not betray your
history by failing to acknowledge this debt....To put your
people before yourself is only the beginning of your
responsibilities as a serious Black student. You must
learn to define, determine and represent Black interests as
well. To perform these tasks properly, you must liberate or
free your mind from its mental slavery and develop an
Africentric consciousness. By Africentric consciousness,
I mean the world view that recognizes the legitimacy and
validity of Black or Afrikan interests, goals, objectives,
values and culture and utilizes a Black frame of reference.
Developing an Africentric consciousness is no easy task,
but a task that must be done if our students are to be
assets rather than liabilities."

Zak A. Kondo
The Black Student's Guide to Positive Education

PART III

RELATIONSHIPS

Making it Work

Building Productive Afrikan Male/Female Loveships

Introduction

It is generally perceived that there is a crisis in Afrikan male/female relations in the 'West'. Apart from the seemingly exponential rise in Afrikans choosing non-Afrikan partners – a subject covered in greater depth in the chapter entitled 'The Race is Over' – where Afrikans do choose to engage in intimate relationships with other Afrikans these relationships seem to be increasingly fraught with difficulty, conflict and recrimination.

Now obviously there are a whole range of 'macro factors' such as the prevailing economic conditions, which will have a direct impact upon Afrikan female/male relationships, for e.g. by increasing or decreasing the numbers of economically viable Afrikan males available to Afrikan females, however there are also important personal psychological factors which come into play in determining the likely success or otherwise of a relationship. The following chapters aim to focus upon both of these dimensions, the broader macro factors and the narrower micro factors and to provide ideas and suggestions as to how readers can improve their existing relationship – if they need improving – or for those still searching for their soulmate, how they can increase the chances of making the right choice and decrease the chances of making the wrong choice. This section will also hopefully help parents to provide their children – particularly adolescents – with a framework for understanding the adult relationships they will form.

My credentials

I believe that if one is going to attempt to give advice on any subject, and particularly one as sensitive and important as male/female relationships, then one should be able to demonstrate a reasonable track record of success. There is the cliché of the unmarried marriage counsellor and whilst I value the benefits of theoretical knowledge, when it comes to relationships a bit of positive experience goes a long way.

What can I bring to this subject? Well, I think I am old to have sufficient tested experience to draw upon in giving advice and young enough to be able to relate to the pressures facing Afrikans who are embarking upon new relationships or who are a few years down the line.

I met my wife Beverley on 1st October 1989. We began living together in April 1991 and got married on 9th September 1995. I should make it clear that I am not suggesting my relationship with my wife is the perfect model for Afrikan relationships. Rather, based upon our experience I will attempt to highlight and pinpoint critical issues in building a productive long-term relationship and how we have worked together to strengthen our relationship in the face of the inevitable ups and downs of life.

Section 1

The Broader Context

Relationships do not exist in a vacuum, just like any other aspect of human life. Your relationship with your partner is not just influenced by your personal psychological make-ups and personal interaction, or even just the slightly broader social milieu encompassing your families, friends and local community. Our intimate relationships, just like our social, work or business relationships are influenced by the broader social, economic, political and cultural context. Let us look briefly at each of these areas in turn to exemplify and clarify the point I am making.

The Social Context
In the 'West' we live in a fast paced pressurised social system. With the psychological and geophysical fragmentation of families which accompanied the need for ever increasingly mobile labour following; first, the industrial revolution and then, and even more significantly, the post-industrial revolution, there has been a move from extended, to nuclear to post-nuclear/atomised family structures. Where once family elders – even in the highly individualistic Caucasian world – were intimately involved in selecting spouses for their children, this extended family influence has declined to the extent that even patriarchal cultural remnants such as the prospective groom asking the father of the bride for her hand in marriage have all but disappeared. Indeed it is quite common nowadays in 'the West' for parents to be absent from their children's weddings.

Where once divorce was unusual and frowned upon it is now common and unremarkable. Women are now more likely to initiate divorce proceedings than men as they refuse to endure the ill-treatment of previous generations, but also respond to the ever increasing culture of consumerism in which everything is a commodity – including relationships – that can be replaced with a newer, shinier, higher spec model. As soon as the fire is out the solicitor is in. Marriage is still reasonably popular, but increasingly from the view of participating in a memorable event rather than entering into a solemn commitment. The ever increasing rise of alternative sex styles (see later chapters in this section) as part of the Caucasian notion of sexual progress means that it becomes increasingly difficult for those immersed in this cultural mess to find satisfaction in one person. Serial monogamy is often touted as the best realistic lifestyle of the future.

For Afrikans in search of an Afrikan partner, the landscape – particularly in the UK – looks increasingly grim. Where once mixed relationships in the UK were frowned upon by Caucasians, they are now viewed as normative by a majority of the younger Afrikan population (under 40) and unproblematic by the majority of Caucasians in the UK. The media presents mixed relationships as the progressive social ideal and perpetuates the myth that they act as some sort of barometer of racism within the society.

As Afrikans become ever more acculturised into the UK Caucasian culture, Afrikan female/male relationships increasingly founder under the combined weight of foolish European romanticised relationship concepts, increasing female/male economic disparity and the loss of joint purpose in the absence of a purposive cultural vision. The seemingly ever decreasing supply of marriageable Afrikan men only adds to the pressure and increasingly drives Afrikan women in the UK into the arms of Caucasian men. In the US one sees the slower, but definite, reproduction of this scenario in the one area of Afrikan social development where the UK is perceived by liberal and Negro commentators to be 'ahead' of the US.

The Economic Context
'Classical' capitalist economic theory used to hold that labour was more mobile than capital. Changes in the world economy and

particularly the lifting of restrictions on the movement of capital have rendered this theory completely redundant. Companies have no qualms about moving their sites of industrial production to regions/states or even countries offering lower labour costs, and where these lower labour costs can be combined with a skilled workforce, such as in India, one sees huge movements of money and production.

Where once it was the movement of industrial production and manufacturing in industries such as steel making, ship building, car making and coal mining that decimated the employment prospects of large numbers of poor, low skill males, in mainly urban centres across the rich Caucasian world, now as the *industrial age* has been superseded by the *service age* – in the rich world – the 'replacement jobs' – which have come in lower numbers and at lower wages, and many of which have been taken by the wives, daughters, mothers and sisters of these obsolete males – are also now being exported to cheaper centres of production, as advances in telecommunications mean your local bank's telephonic representative is now as likely to be based in Delhi as Derby.

We live in a so-called *'information age'*, which should be clearly distinguished from a *'knowledge age'*, let alone an *'age of wisdom'*. The gap between the rich and poor is increasing dramatically after a period of around 80 years of significant decreases. The ability to move capital and also to 'produce' and sell with fewer and fewer employees means that the 'information haves' are leaving the information 'have nots' far behind. Even middle managers in large corporations have seen their increase in earnings over the past ten years massively outpaced by the corporate elite in their companies who sit on each other's remuneration panels and award one another massive bonuses, share options and golden handshakes for success or failure. The so-called man and woman in the street with little formal qualifications is reduced to a lifetime of insecure minimum wage jobs and the prospect of a longer working life (as the impact of an ageing population begins to bite) and a longer – with better medical technology – and grim retirement on the breadline. Even many of the so-called middle earners are no more than one or two paychecks from the street.

Unsurprisingly, from an Afrikan perspective, these structural and cultural changes to the economy have had devastating consequences. Where jobs have stayed in the country they have tended to move from urban centres, to the suburbs, to lily white semi-rural enclaves as middle class Afrikans chase their Caucasian reference group for psychological and economic reasons and Caucasians run from their subordinate group for psycho-cultural reasons.

In the US, just as in the UK, Afrikans tend to live disproportionately in the most deprived areas and consequently the economic impoverishment of urban centres has had a disproportionate effect upon Afrikan economic wellbeing. In the 1960's and 70's an Afrikan-American car production line worker with no more than a high school education could earn enough money to maintain his family and send his children to college (university). If we skip forward thirty or forty years we now find that the jobs which have replaced those car production line opportunities have an hourly pay which is less in not only inflation adjusted terms but in actual hourly rates of pay than those manufacturing jobs of the 1960's and'70's. Expanding sectors such as leisure and tourism and hotel and catering generally have a relatively small number of well paid jobs and a large number of low paid, part-time and seasonal posts. These are pin money jobs not breadwinner jobs whatever one's gender and yet increasing numbers of people are forced to subsist on this type of work.

Afrikans in the US and UK have been squeezed from all sides. First Caucasian women came out of their homes to claim second incomes for their families in their quest for self-actualisation and equality with Caucasian men, or so they thought. Given that there are far more Caucasian women than Afrikan men in both countries and that on average Caucasian women have higher levels of qualifications than Afrikan men and that they sleep with their oppressor to boot – although some brothers want to get in on this as well – brothers were bound to end up holding the economic blade. The bottom end of the labour market has been further suppressed by newcomers from all around the world who are prepared – in many cases – to work for less than minimum wage in order to get their foot on the ladder. With the middle rungs taken out of reach and the bottom rungs overcrowded, brothers are struggling to find a place on the economic ladder.

What has been the effect of this economic marginalisation upon Afrikan relationships? Well, one of the starkest effects has been the removal of the Afrikan man from the family home. At the beginning of the 20th century 90% of Afrikan-American men lived with their children. By the 1930's this figure had fallen to 80% a level which was maintained into the 1960's. By the 1980's this figure had fallen to less than 50% and today it is around 35%. In the US 65% of homes with children are headed by a single female. In the UK a similar pattern has been played out over a shorter time span with over 50% of homes with children being headed by a single female. Financial difficulties and the consequent psychological fallout is one of the biggest causes of relationship breakdown.

In the press release promoting his book 'The Integration Trap The Generation Gap', Oba T'SHAKA highlights the profound effects of this economic restructuring.

"With the loss of these jobs, Black men with a high school education or less have been deprived of the ability to support their families, leading to a greater erosion of the Black family between 1968 through the present than between 1619 and 1968." (T'Shaka 2004)

Afrikan women have always had to work hard both within and outside the home, but nowadays too many return to a home without an adult male presence, and tired, frustrated and lonely, are left to raise children, with; if they are lucky, the support of female relatives.

The combination of Afrikan male un/underemployment producing feelings of psycho-social impotence has devastated Afrikan family life in the UK and US.

The Political Context

'Everything in life is political and politics is life.' Politics is about Power and Processes of Decision making. The former allowing one to determine the latter and the latter allowing one to gain and reinforce the former. Why should, and how can; one consider intimate relationships, which most people consider as private and personal, political? Well, families are the foundation block for society. There is an Akan proverb that says that children are the gift of life and that the ruin of a nation will begin in the homes of its families. With whom and how people mate and raise families, or not raise families for that matter, is of vital importance to any nation and is the subject of social, economic and political policy.

Throughout the 20th century the leaders of the majority Caucasian countries, with the possible exception of the Soviet bloc, have been increasingly pre-occupied with birth rates and who is having or not having children. There have been two contexts for this pre-occupation, the internal (national) and the external (international). In this section we will mainly deal with the internal context. When considering issues of birthrates and fertility from a national perspective, there are two primary and inter-related drivers of political policymaking and these can be described as psycho-cultural and economic drivers.

The Psycho-cultural driver

If one says the word eugenics to the not so average man or woman in the street, one is likely to either get a blank expression or an immediate association with Nazi Germany and their genetic experimentation under Dr Mengele. Caucasians in their tried and tested fashion have relentlessly sought to present Nazi Germany as an inexplicable aberration in the smooth and inevitable upward progress of 'Western' civilisation, and an aberration from which no broader lessons can be drawn about the worldview and mindset of Caucasians as a whole. The Germans are left to carry the cultural can and even then their time in the European doghouse was comparatively short when compared to the long-term and vindictive victimisation of nations such as Vietnam for the 'crime' of standing up to 'the greatest nation on earth'. Then again, when one looks at the history of a nation such as Haiti one sees that even the terrible punishment wreaked upon the Vietnamese was as nothing when compared to the punishment meted out to an Afrikan nation which did not do as it was told (see earlier chapter 'Do you remember 1804').

What am I trying to say? Nazism was culturally compatible with the Caucasian worldview. Hitler and Winston Churchill shared a common belief in the Caucasian invention of a hierarchy of 'races', with Caucasians on top and Afrikans at the bottom. They believed in the natural rulership of Whites over Blacks, hence Churchill's deep resistance to Britain 'giving up' its colonies – a move eventually forced upon them by the US, who wanted to own the whole world – after the second European Tribal War on the World. Where Churchill differed from the Nazis was with regard to the question of European Jewry who Hitler regarded as of non-Caucasian origin.

The Belgians under the psychopath Prince Leopold had killed around **20 million** Afrikans in the Congo between around 1885-1910. You won't hear Caucasians talking about this genocide too often, and sadly since most Afrikans get their information from Caucasians, most will not be aware of the unimaginable brutality that took place in the Congo, and which made even the rulers of other European imperialist nations blush with embarrassment and call for restraint – but not act.

The Germans had warmed up for their European internecine aggression by slaughtering 100,000 Afrikans in Namibia during the early part of the 20th century as punishment for the killing of less than a dozen German invaders during an anti-colonial uprising. As I said in the first section of this book Caucasians operate a 'life worth ratio' that is skewed heavily in their favour. In the case of Namibia 1:10,000.

The problem Churchill – who had used chemical weapons to slaughter the Kurds many years before the second European tribal war – and the Caucasian world had with Hitler, was that he turned his aggression inwardly on other Europeans and not outwardly towards non-Caucasians. This is why he is so vilified. If Hitler had gone around the world killing Afrikans he would have become a small footnote of history just like King Leopold.

So what has this all to do with eugenics and relationships. Sorry about the historical detour, but the point is that eugenics was not a

Nazi aberration. Like racial genocide, it was part and parcel and compatible with the European cultural asili. Eugenics really got off the ground in the USA in the 1920's. It was linked to the development of theories around human intelligence which strongly favoured nature (genetics) over nurture (social environment) and were strongly 'race' and gender focused. The upshot of these pseudo-scientific ideas was the belief that poor people were poor because they came from inferior genetic stock and that women were less intelligent than men and that different 'races' had different natural levels of intelligence, and you can guess who was at the top and who was at the bottom of the intelligence ladder.

Well, with this body of scientific 'proof' now accumulating, Caucasians only had recourse to one course of action. They had to stop poor Caucasians from reproducing, since given that the poor tend to have more children than the rich this would have a long-term degenerative effect upon the 'stamina of the race'. So this is what Caucasian governments did. In the US they got the ball rolling and systematically sterilised and locked up in sanatoriums thousands of 'poor white trash' who scored below 80 on IQ tests or showed signs of being mentally defective. The also sterilised their children based upon the logic that they would inherit their parents' faulty genes.

As the USA leads so the rest of the Caucasian world follows and eugenics was picked up enthusiastically, not just by Nazi Germany, but also in bastions of Caucasian liberalism such as Sweden and Canada. So firm were these beliefs entrenched that it was not until the early 1970's that this practice ceased in Sweden and Canada after public exposure by journalists. The revelations of the active practicing of eugenics for more than 40 years led to a wave of public revulsion and the usual apologies from politicians. However, eugenics never died. Eugenics is the father of the science of genetics and whilst the children of the poor are being offered the contraceptive pill as young as 14 without their parent's knowledge the middle classes are being offered ever greater incentives and public subsidy to reproduce in countries such as Germany and Italy where there is a birthrate crisis.

Meanwhile, all over the world, wherever Afrikan women find their fertility in the hands of non-Afrikans one finds disproportionate levels of hysterectomies carried out on Afrikan women by non-Afrikan doctors (Trinidad is a good example where Indian doctors predominate). The destruction of the Afrikan family has always been high on the White Supremacy agenda since the family is the most basic unit of resistance and continuity for a people. From a political perspective it is clear that if the men and women of a group cannot form workable relationships they will have little or no capacity for effective resistance against their oppressors. This will especially be the case if they choose members of the oppressor group as their partners.

Too many Afrikans fail to realise that their relationships – if they are with other Afrikans – have the potential to be powerful centres of resistance and renaissance for Afrikan people. In the UK, where to seek a Caucasian partner is presented as the normative and progressive thing to do, positive Afrikan relationships stand out like beacons of hope and resistance. They send a powerful message to single Afrikan adults, who may be feeling disillusioned in their search for an Afrikan partner, and most importantly to Afrikan children of the viability and unmatched beauty of Afrikan love.

The economic driver

All *over the* Caucasian world populations are ageing rapidly through a combination of people living longer and people having fewer children. In Italy the average birthrate is 0.77 children per family leading to villages literally dying and other towns and villages offering cash incentives for families with children to relocate. This birthrate crisis has also led to the looming spectre of a pensions crisis in countries such as the UK as economists calculate that in the not too distant future the diminishing proportion of the population of working age will be unable to support the costs of providing a state pension for the growing army of people of pensionable age. This has led to a dramatic reversal of government policy as the quite recent trend of reducing the age of retirement and access to a state pension – along with promises of a prolonged and comfortable retirement – has ended with a commitment to increase the state pension retirement age to 70 within the next 15 years and the public recognition that with the current levels of contributions into private pensions most people in the UK can look forward to a retirement with income levels barely above the poverty line.

The Government has introduced incentives and subsidies such as Working Families Tax Credit – on the face of it an anti-poverty measure – which are available to even middle class families with income up to £54,000 per annum (equivalent to nearly $100,000 at the time of writing) to incentivise work for both partners and to encourage couples to have children. In Germany they are also offering tax incentives for women to have children. There are virtually no incentives for women or men to stay at home with their children since whilst they want more children they also want more workers.

Afrikans, with our outlandishly high – but not surprisingly so – rates of single parent households are at a great disadvantage. It is well known that households with the greatest numbers of working adults are the least likely to live in poverty, whilst conversely households with only one or no working adults are most likely to live in poverty. Therefore groups with large numbers of single parent households are much more likely to have large numbers of children growing up in poverty than households with relatively low levels of single parent households. Of course, as alluded to earlier, Afrikans are in a bit of a Catch 22 situation since it is the economic disablement of Afrikan men that has played perhaps the most significant part in creating so many female headed households.

Similarly, Afrikan children growing up in stress riddled and fractious homes are only to keen to fly the family nest – often before they are pushed out – and thus contribute to the further weakening of the Afrikan domestic economic infrastructure as they pay money out to landlords from alien groups rather than contribute that portion of their incomes that they would have paid in rent to the family income with a portion set aside for savings and investment as they build a 'war chest' for their future independent lives. There is absolutely no sensible reason for children to be leaving the parental home to move into – often semi-squalid – rented accommodation at the age of 18 as is often the case. This only happens because so many of our domestic relationships are in a mess, or our children have become acculturised into the selfish individualism of this society (which often but not always stems from the first point).

Financial problems are one of the biggest causes of relationship breakdown in the Caucasian world and any people as economically weak and financially illiterate as Afrikans-Americans and Afrikan-Caribbeans are bound to experience serious repercussions to their relationships.

The Cultural Context

European culture militates against stable, loving, respectful, productive relationships which are free of dominative power. This is the case for Caucasians and even more so the case for Afrikans if we add Afrikan-centred to that list of relationship characteristics. As has been highlighted throughout this text, at the very heart of European culture lies the insatiable need for Power and Control, the European cultural asili (Ani 1996). This cultural drive infects all aspects of European activity, be it cultural, political, economic or social. They must hold the handle and we must hold the blade. Relationships are no different and conform to this cultural rule. When this need for power and control is combined with the ongoing European need for manifestations of newness, progress, change and breaking boundaries, the pressure upon relationships becomes enormous. Add in a strongly patriarchal culture and you have the perfect ingredients for a 'Battle of the Sexes'.

European culture is about me, myself and I. European culture tells you that 'I am because I am aware that I am'. Afrikan culture tells you that 'I am because we are'. These are fundamental philosophical differences and lead to fundamentally different approaches to and behaviours in relationships.

The European culture of individualism is fundamentally antithetical to any notion of Afrikan liberation. Afrikans who have unwittingly bought into European culture have a pronounced tendency to exhibit high degrees of selfishness (individualism), jealousy (control) and to play mind games (power) in their relationships. Afrikans living through Europeanised minds will also tend to privatise their lives and hence their relationships, removing them from the struggle for Afrikan liberation.

Professor Maulana Karenga in 'Crisis in Black Sexual Politics' (Eds. Hare and Hare 1989) clearly identifies that "...social conditions create both social consciousness and social conduct and failure to recognize this can lead one to see racial defects where social ones are more real and relevant....Analyses of the major defects in Black male/female relationships clearly reveal their social rather than genetic or purely personal basis. Thus to understand the negatives of our relationships, we must understand the negative characteristics of society which have shaped them." (Karenga in Hare and Hare 1989: 47)

Professor Karenga goes on to identify "three major structural and value systems: capitalism, racism and sexism" (Karenga in Hare and Hare 1989: 47) that he believes are the source and cause of the major social defects in US society – and no doubt the UK and other majority Caucasian countries as well.

In describing the effects these structural/value systems have on relationships Professor Karenga says "Capitalism then, turns relationships and parts of relationships into commodities and utilitarian arrangements. Racism engenders self-hate, self-doubt and pathological fixation on the white paradigm. And sexism encourages artificial personal power over women as a substitute for real social power over one's destiny and daily life.

Flowing from these structural/value systems he describes "four basic alienated arrangements around which Black people build their lives" (Karenga in Hare and Hare 1989: 48). He describes these as:

1. the cash connection
2. the flesh connection
3. the force connection
4. the dependency connection

"A connection is a short-term or tentative association which is utilitarian and alienated and is designed primarily for the mutual misuse of each other's bodies" (Karenga in Hare and Hare 1989:48). To misuse of bodies I could add misuse of each other's minds, souls and wallets.

Each of these connections has a natural root in European culture. The cash connection is rooted in European capitalism and materialism. The flesh connection is rooted in European cultural despiritualisation and hence valorisation of the physical (seen) over metaphysical (unseen). The force connection is rooted in European patriarchy/sexism and view of male ownership of women. The dependency connection is rooted in European selfishness and individualism. It is a parasitical leach like dependency, the dependency of an addict looking to satisfy their individual needs and has nothing to do with the mutual support inherent in a healthy relationship.

Afrikans who believe their mission in life is to think like, walk like, talk like, act like Caucasians, as well as those who simply and unwittingly think like Europeans, will not have the capacity to contribute to our people's struggle through their relationships even if they maintain a long-term relationship with another Afrikan. Their adopted culture will not allow it.

The novel 'THE CELESTINE PROPHECY' by James Redfield (1994) highlights how well Caucasians know their culture but seek to universalise its traits in order to both disguise and normalise them. This book was a No. 1 bestseller which received rave reviews across the US and sold enormous numbers of copies, initially by word of mouth, as news of the Insights into human nature it contained spread like wildfire. The book describes the Caucasian hero's journey across Peru in search of an ancient manuscript which contains "the nine insights the human race is predicted to grasp as we enter an era of true spiritual awareness" (Redfield 1994 from foreword). These insights together comprise the meaning of life.

One of the 'insights' is that people use 'control dramas' to suck energy from one another and conversely to prevent others from taking their energy. There are four types of control drama, usually with one style predominating in any individual, and these are: Intimidator, Aggressor, Aloof and Poor Me. I do not have time within the restrictions of this book to describe in detail the dynamics of each control drama persona, however they can all be summarised as utilising different forms of psycho-emotional manipulation to exercise control over and gain power (described as energy in this case) from another human being.

Now whilst the later insights offer means of overcoming these control dramas, this conceptualisation of human relations is absolutely typical of European culture. It demonstrates the separation of the subject and object, the knower and the known as conceptualised by Plato. It demonstrates dichotomisation (in this case a Win/Lose relational dichotomy), it demonstrates selfish individualism, it demonstrates the need to exercise control over others and the need to take and exercise power from and over others. It also demonstrates the fundamentally alienated nature of European culture. All these cultural characteristics are classically European and Redfield either deliberately or unwittingly, but in either case typically, attempts to universalise this conceptualisation and turn what is European and parochial into something human and universal.

Redfield also cleverly weaves European evolutionary theory into this as he suggests that human beings must undergo an inevitable parallel emotional evolutionary journey just as Darwin suggested that we must undertake an inevitable biological evolutionary journey. To camouflage the ethnocentrism of his ideas Redfield mixes in a bit of Eastern philosophy to soften the hard edge of Eurocentrism

An Afrikan who had read the book spoke to me excitedly about its contents and the insights and asked me what my control drama was. To be honest I could not remember the control dramas and so the conversation petered out. What was interesting for me when I went back through the book was the wholesale acceptance of these ideas by this Afrikan as if she were a dry cultural sponge ready to absorb whatever cultural ideas she was immersed in. As the proverb says 'If you don't know where you are going any road will do' and if you do not know your culture any culture will do. I do not mean to be hard on this sister, she is like most Afrikans. Our tradition is intrinsically open and xenophilic and without a thorough grounding in Afrikan culture and philosophy most of us are culturally naked and defenceless.

Let me be clear, I am not saying that the Celestine Prophecy is not an interesting book. It is very interesting and the insights certainly struck some chords with me. However, it is written by a European and the world is framed through his cultural glasses. The conceptualisations and characterisations are based upon his experiences, understanding, perceptions and ideas which have been formed in a European cultural crucible. Therefore what he describes and how he describes it should not be automatically accepted as universal truths, and even if his work contains universal truths, perception and viewing angle can change reality. The control dramas probably represent a very accurate description of some human relational interactions and given that most Afrikans are thoroughly immersed in European culture they may well reflect accurately on many Afrikan relationships, both romantic and platonic, however this is a very different thing to saying they represent a universal relational truth or norm.

The fact that the hero is a Caucasian male is a reflection of who the author is and what he knows best. There is nothing wrong with that unless there are attempts to pretend these things are not significant.

Mr Redfield also demonstrated that he is highly tuned to his capitalistic culture by bringing out the following products for sale just when you thought you had discovered everything you needed to know:

The Celestine Prophecy: An Experiential Guide
The Celestine Prophecy: A Pocket Guide to The Nine Insights
The Tenth Insight
The Tenth Insight: An Experiential Guide
A Pocket Guide To The Tenth Insight
The Celestine Vision
The Secret of Shambhala

This is what is known colloquially as 'rinsing it out' good and proper.

Section 2

The Personal Psychological Context

Introduction

In my opinion there are some key questions that need to be posed and answered by any Afrikan seeking a lifelong loveship. Preferably these questions should be posed before commencing a new relationship rather than afterwards. These questions are:

- What do I want out of a relationship?
- What do I need out of a relationship?
- Do I really know the difference between the first two questions?
- What can I give to a relationship?
- What am I prepared to give up in order to make a relationship work?

If you can answer these questions it does not mean that Mr or Ms Right will suddenly pop up out of the ether, however what it does mean is that you are in a good position to make sound judgements about the suitability of potential partners. You will be able to politely dismiss the unsuitables and gently encourage Afrikans with the right credentials.

It is my opinion that many of the ill-judged to downright disastrous relationships that so many brothers and sisters engage in could be prevented if each party had taken the time to pose and answer these questions honestly and thus put themselves in a position to assess the suitability of their prospective new partner. However in a culture that emphasises the physical, material and sensual above the emotional, psychological, intellectual and spiritual, the main criteria for selecting partners is too often 'do they look good and make me feel hot'. These hormonal surges are then interpreted as True Romance or even Love and off the ill starred couple trot, down the road to relationship ruin. Of course once the sexual fire dims a little and they get to know each other a lot more, doubt replaces passion and the grass is no longer verdant green, but fades to the colour of straw.

In my opinion there are some key ingredients to building successful relationships and two of the most important are Commitment and Sacrifice. One needs a lot of the former and some of the latter to make it work, however in this get it quick society people want to cut corners and avoid hard work. Good relationships take time to create and need hard work to be maintained, however the rewards make it all worthwhile.

In this part of this section I will deal with some fundamental but practical issues that individuals need to address to improve their chances of building healthy, productive loveships. These thoughts and ideas will not change the broader context highlighted in the first section of this chapter, however they will hopefully help Afrikans to make the best of the circumstances in which we find ourselves.

Sisters let go of 'the list'

Most single sisters I know have a list. For some the list is short e.g. the brother must be able to walk and talk at the same time, for others it is broken down into chapters, however most sisters have a list. This list details the qualities and characteristics they deem 'essential' in a suitable mate. Now it may sound harsh for me to say let go of the list, after all most brothers have their own criteria so isn't what's good for the goose good for the gander?

Well, what I am really saying is revisit and revise the list and if you keep it use it with caution. Now of course most of these lists are kept in the head and not committed to paper, however the effect is the same. Take my experience as an example. I met my wife outside a nightclub at about 2.30am on 1st October 1989 when I was 23. I did not go out looking for a wife and a partner. I went out to have a good time, listen to some good music and catch the odd slow dance with a nice sister! That was the agenda for the night. Instead I met a young woman who was to change my life. Not bad eh. The only thing I was sure about in terms of relationships aged 23 was that I did not want to get involved in a serious relationship before my late twenties – I thought I would be grown up by then! Now, over the years a lot of people have expressed surprise that I met my wife at a nightclub because they believe that you cannot meet decent people at a nightclub or dance.

It is interesting, we have all these Afrikans who think of themselves as 'decent people' who go to nightclubs but who believe that there are no other decent people who go to nightclubs! Am I saying go out to nightclubs to seek your soulmate? No. What I am saying is be open to possibilities in places you may not expect to find them. Turn down your nose and open your eyes. If you can't meet decent people at nightclubs had been on either of our lists my wife and I would have rejected each other out of hand on a false premise. If I had stuck to my 'I am too young to get serious' criteria I would have lost the love of my life. Afrikans cannot afford to be rejecting good possibilities on the basis of spurious criteria.

How did I know she was the one? Well, firstly I do not believe that there is only one person in the world you can find true love with and you have to search high and low to find this one person. What I do believe is that there are certain types of people you can find true love with based upon your personality, psychology and worldview. I saw my wife in the nightclub before I met and spoke to her outside. I saw that she was beautiful and was immediately physically attracted to her. I did not have the nerve to go up to her for fear of rejection and was cussing my cowardice as I left the club. As things transpired through the conduit of a former friend I was able to meet her and speak to her. A group of us we went to the Blues together and danced away a very special night. I know, decent people don't go to the Blues!

Over the next few weeks we spent many hours speaking on the telephone, me in Leicester and she in Nottingham. This is where I grew in Love with her. I cannot tell you exactly how I knew, however there was a beauty to her spirit, a tone in her voice and a grace in her eyes which overwhelmed me and made me feel glad to know her. Most importantly, despite 'the rush' we took our time. It was over a year before I introduced her to my parents. I always said to myself that the woman I brought home to my Mum would be the woman I married. It was over a year and a half before we moved in together and nearly six years after we met that we got married. Now of course in your early twenties you can work to this sort of timeframe. The important point is to be governed by your head and your heart working in unison. There are all sorts of reasons my wife and I could have chosen to deem each other unsuitable, however how many of these were really important? Not many.

So what to do with the list? My advice would be cut the number of criteria in half and then bin it?

For those who cannot be separated from the list let's look at some of the 'usual suspects'.

Looks

"...as in the society-at-large Beauty structures one's opportunity and life chances, especially for women, as to be the most powerful predictor of status, wealth, self-esteem – even freedom – for the Black individual. ...In fact, after race and gender, one's physical characteristics are the most determinant of access to the society's privileges and values." (Staples in Hare and Hare 1989: 69)

We are all familiar with the reality of the above quote – especially in relation to Caucasian women – which is taken from a book, 'Crisis in Black Sexual Politics' that I would highly recommend to all Afrikans interested in the nature of our most intimate relationships. It is well established that people who are generally regarded as physically attractive receive better treatment than those considered unattractive. It is also considered a truism that men place a higher emphasis on physical appearance in selecting a partner than women who tend to seek out the most 'socially adaptive' males. Hence the beautiful blonde with the elderly millionaire cliché. However something is afoot in the Afrikan community. As Robert Staples goes on to point out in his chapter on 'The Role of Physical Attraction In The Black Community'

"Black Women demonstrate a stronger preference for a physically attractive man than their White women counterparts. When the Roper organization asked Black and White women what qualities they admired most in a man, twice as many Black women listed sex appeal than did White women. In a *Jet* magazine survey of Black women in Chicago, Black women ranked the ten things they notice about men in this order (1) dress/grooming (2) personality (3) eyes (4) mouth/smile (5) money (6) physique (7) thoughtfulness/walk (8) intelligence/handsomeness (9) chest and (10) buttocks... Unlike their male counterparts skin colour is comparatively unimportant." (Staples in Hare and Hare 1989: 76).

As Staples notes only four of the desirable qualities are non-physical in nature. To what can we attribute this greater emphasis on physical attributes upon the part of Black women? Are sisters as shallow as brothers and more shallow than Caucasian women?

Staples suggests that with high status Black males in short supply

Black women may be in effect saying if I cannot have a socially adaptive male I may as well have a good looking one. This is compounded by the fact that Black women are less likely to be economically dependent upon a Black male than Caucasian Women are likely to be economically dependent upon a Caucasian male. Hence it is a case of butt over bucks!

I will let Robert Staples finish off this sub-section on Looks with his sad but profound conclusion.

"Unfortunately, Black women seem to be heading in the same direction as Black men: rating a person by their physical features rather than the content of their character. It is tragic in the sense that it is similar to the racism that has victimized them as a people. When personal characteristics that are genetically influenced make such an important difference in a person's status, that is a genetic determinism that is very similar to the operation of White racism. Since the standards of physical attractiveness are set and dominated by Euro-Americans, it can only presage an increase in group self-hatred. Such a trend can only give validation to the saying: "we have met the enemy and the enemy is us." " (Staples in Hare and Hare 1989: 76)

Lyrics and Self-Confidence/He has to make the first move

'Pssst,.. princess you look sweet'. Brothers love to run lyrics and plenty of sisters love to hear them. Apart from looks, the ability to woo, flatter and seduce with lyrics has always been a critical part of the Black mating game. There is nothing wrong with having the gift of the gab and the confidence to turn a sister's head with your words. However, from a sister's viewpoint one needs to consider how and where did the brother cultivate such lyrical proficiency?

Robert Staples highlights an important cautionary point. His focus is the 'good-looking woman' however it is an important point for all women to note.

"With all her advantages, the good-looking woman is not without problems. One disadvantage is that many desirable men will not approach her because they fear rejection. If she plays the traditionally passive role, she will only be selecting from the men who have the courage to make the initial gesture. Such men are often the playboy types who fuel their egos on the company of the best looking women in the crowd. While one of these same men will cater to a pretty woman's ego and self-indulgent needs initially, he will ultimately exhibit his own emotional immaturity, narcissism and need for dominance that drove him to her. .. Studies reveal that attractive women have much more difficulty in their relations with men, mainly because of unrealistic expectations." (Staples in Hare and Hare 1989: 75).

What is the enduring appeal of the 'gyalist'? Across many different cultures, but particularly patriarchal cultures; one finds women of all social classes drawn to the charming rogue. A self-confident, often handsome (but not always) male whose sole purpose in life seems to be to accumulate as many 'conquests' as possible. The remarkable thing is that even after his character is well publicised there is never a shortage of women willing to become the next notch on his bedhead. What is even more remarkable is that some of these very same women will in the next breath decry the absence of good men even though in practice, time after time, they have declined the more reticent advances of such men with the dismissive comment that 'he is too boring'. It seems for some women reliability and fidelity are indeed boring.

The saddest thing, particularly with respect to sisters, is that by the time these women tire of the 'excitement' of 'is he coming home to me tonight' or 'why does my best friend's child look so much like him' and decide that boring is not so boring after all, most of the loving, stable brothers have been taken by sisters who were wise enough to realise that in a seller's market where Black women are the buyers the perceptive sister makes her investment early.

The best advice I can give to young Afrikan women is if you find a good brother hold onto him. With the shortage in the supply of marriageable Afrikan men; Afrikan women cannot afford to mimic Caucasian women and wait until their mid-thirties, when they have completed their education and spent ten years or more establishing a career, before deciding it is time to settle down. If they do they will have dramatically lengthened the odds against them finding a good

Black man.

Sisters, sometimes the quiet, slightly diffident brother in the corner is the man you should be looking at and sometimes you will need to make the opening gesture. This does not mean you have to go around throwing yourself at brothers, it just means that sometimes you may wish to say hello first. If you like overtly confident men, just remember it is easier to develop self-confidence in an adult than it is to develop good character. See it deh.

Money and Status

I will touch upon this area in more detail a little later when I look at the issue of the viability of relationships where the sister earns significantly more money than the brother. What I will say initially is that there are too many sisters – particularly those who consider themselves 'professionals' – who place too great an emphasis on how much a brother earns – over and above the need to be economically solvent – and in particular the status of the job he holds. In some cases it does not matter how much he earns if he is not employed in a 'professional position' suitable for the sister to share (boast about) with her equally shallow female friends and Caucasian work colleagues.

Educational Qualifications

It is important to distinguish education from educational qualifications. We have a whole army of 'qualified' fools in our community with letters and pieces of paper trailing behind them. Afrikans need education for liberation and to be of useful service to the Afrikan community and humanity as a whole. Where gaining paper qualification helps in that process they are useful, however they are a means to an end – to develop useful skills and knowledge – not an end in themselves.

Before there were degrees there were educated people and one thing the world is seemingly never short of is fools. I have heard some sisters say they would only go out with – this does not necessarily preclude a little undercover ninja business with 'Joe Grind' – a brother who has a minimum of a first degree. To these sisters I say you are fully qualified for work but what about love? You are eliminating the majority of the Afrikan male population on the basis of your fragile ego and pride. They say pride before a fall and in the future as you while away your middle aged spinsterhood cussing 'no good brothers' you will have time to reflect upon your selectivity. I have yet to be shown how a degree in American Studies, Sociology or any other subject for that matter, ensures a happy loving relationship.

Height

I know some sisters have minimum height requirements and I know it is generally expected that the man is taller than his female partner; however some sisters are literally putting their cap out of reach. Now, I have to admit that I have never gone out with a sister taller than myself; however the harsh reality is that I have never needed to. There is not a shortage of marriageable sisters in the UK and therefore before I met my wife I never needed to consider dating the relatively small percentage of sisters who are taller than my height of six feet.

Unfortunately sisters are not in such a luxurious position. **There is a shortage of marriageable Afrikan men** and therefore a little flexibility helps the cause. I am not saying you have to start dating a man six inches shorter than you if this causes you psychological discomfort. What I am saying is trim away at the edges a bit. For example if you read the dating ads in 'Black' newspapers – which is a tragic-comic experience in and of itself – you will often see 'Attractive sister, five feet eight, seeks muscular brother, six feet plus'. Now, there are a lot of brothers out there who are between five feet eight and six feet tall. You probably get more men for your four inches than in any other height range, so to speak. Why doesn't this sister simply say she wants a brother who is five feet eight and a millimetre and above! In one fell swoop she has added several thousand men – unless her other criteria are too restrictive – to her eligible list. Women generally prefer taller men because height is synonymous with power and status. Men over six feet are far more likely to hold senior executive positions than shorter men, however logically they will be in a minority and in greater demand. Trim the height requirements and reduce the competition.

Shade

Thankfully, as highlighted earlier; most sisters place far less emphasis on skin shade than brothers do. However there are still a minority who view shade as extremely important. One of my friends in London told me about a sister who had been shown a great deal of kindness by a brother who was seemingly interested in her, but had not made any overt moves – perhaps fearing rejection. When my friend asked the sister if she would consider dating him her reaction was one of shock…"Oh no, he's too black and too short, he's only a friend." Apart from being surprised at the complete candour and lack of embarrassment of this sister my friend pondered what messages this sister was sending to her two dark skinned sons and how she related to her dark skinned father. Anyway the 'sister' in question soon had her wish and was very shortly embroiled in a relationship with a tall, light skinned brother who mistreated her and stole money from her. The short (he was in fact three to four inches taller than her), dark brother found a nice sister and at the time of writing this chapter they were enjoying a very happy relationship.

This 'looking for Mr Light' sister, who has dipped more than her toe in several non-Afrikan relationship pools, is still single and apparently appears to have no qualms about going to community events and berating the brothers about running down Caucasian women. Her extreme vanity and over-inflated sense of self worth also appear to be unaffected.

Personally, I have less problems with sisters who restrict themselves to darker skinned brothers than those who exclusively date lighter skinned men since the former is normally rooted in a desire to produce children that are unambiguously Afrikan in appearance whilst the latter is normally rooted in self-hatred and the desire to preserve a pigment – and often features – that is as close to Caucasian as possible whilst still being classified as Black. To the latter group I would say, get some help, to both I would urge you to broaden your horizons, Mr Right may be darker or lighter than you first imagined.

Continental/World Afrikan relationships

It is generally considered that 'birds of a feather flock together' and that dating within your cultural and/or ethnic group is easier than dating outside. I know a lot of Afrikan-Caribbean people would not consider dating 'an Afrikan' and similarly equally large numbers of 'Afrikans' who would not consider dating an 'Afrikan-Caribbean'. Now, one would be foolish to pretend that there are no cultural differences between continental Afrikans and in this case Afrikans from the Caribbean, however what is the real issue underpinning these strongly held views.

It is interesting that Afrikans, be they continental or worldwide seem more than willing to consider relationships with Caucasians from any country in the world without culture being presented as an insuperable barrier and yet when it comes to this Continental/Worldwide Afrikan match up you can almost guarantee an inter-family arms house.

My explanation is based around what I term 'cultural competition'. For example if an Afrikan-Jamaican woman and a Nigerian man propose to get married there will often be inter-family cultural competition even if there is not intra-couple cultural competition. What I mean by this is that each extended family network is likely to contain a significant minority or perhaps a majority of members who will look upon this pairing as unsuitable. A large part of this wariness will stem from the fact that these people will believe that their respective family member is marrying into an inferior cultural/ethnic group and that the children of such a pairing will become 'lost' to this 'other' culture. Now, I am sure that you the reader are more than familiar with all the negative hateful stereotypes that abound from Afrikan-Caribbean to West Afrikan and vice versa and perhaps you believe in and perpetuate them. Therefore I will not take time to rehearse them. Suffice to say each clan wants to ensure that their family member does not become Jamaicanised/Afrikan-Caribbeanised or Nigerianised/Afrikanised.

It is interesting that this high level of 'cultural competition' is much more likely to occur for Afrikans in such 'intra-racial' couplings as opposed to 'inter-racial' couplings, for example when an Afrikan (Continental or Worldwide) marries a Caucasian. The explanation for this is simple. Afrikans are taught to believe they are as good as any other Afrikan and therefore you have 'psychological equals' engaging in 'cultural competition' when an Afrikan-Jamaican and Nigerian families are joined through marriage. However, Afrikans learn that they are culturally – and in all other ways – inferior to Caucasians and conversely Caucasians are taught of their supposed superiority from birth. Therefore when you bring these two groups together through marriage you bring together 'psychological unequals'. Even if there is resistance to the marriage in either clan for other reasons there is relatively little cultural competition.

People do not integrate into groups they consider inferior. This is why Afrikans speak of integrating into British – or other European cultures – and Caucasians never consider integrating into Afrikan culture wherever they live in the world. Europeans recreate Europe wherever they are in the world which is why they speak in positive terms of non-Caucasian countries that are 'Westernised'. Afrikans try to integrate and become pseudo-Caucasians whenever they live in majority Caucasian countries and even in majority Afrikan countries.

If these psycho-cultural dynamics are understood it is perfectly possible for Continental and Worldwide Afrikans to form excellent loveships. The key is to recognise and positively challenge the group self-hatred that lies at the heart of the many artificial barriers that family members will put up. So sisters who are self-aware and strong can delete the 'no Afrikans'/no 'Afrikan-Caribbeans' criteria from the list.

He mustn't have any Children
Being a good step-parent is even more difficult than being a parent in this boundaryless cultural desert in which we find ourselves.

Therefore many people do not wish to embark upon this journey. This 'Western' world is neither child-centred nor adult-centred, it is Me-centred, and hence in such a society people are increasingly resentful of children – even their own children – and the time and resources they demand in order to develop properly. One increasingly finds childless individuals complaining of any tax breaks or subsidies paid to parents to assist them with the costs of rearing children. The cry is 'You chose to have them you pay for them' which has some, if limited, validity and appeals to the selfishness which is endemic in these societies.

Of course it is some of those same children who in future years will be washing the bodies and wiping the bottoms of these very same complainants when they reach old age, and left abandoned by their equally selfish kith and kin, are forced to live out their eldership in care homes as the onset of physical and mental decline leaves them in need of supportive care.

Given this anti-child, selfish environment, together with the inherent difficulties of being a step parent, it is not surprising to find an increasing number of – particularly childless sisters – insisting that any prospective suitor must not have any children. Once again such a criteria is eliminating a whole host of eligible brothers from the picture.

There are a few factors to consider. Firstly, the numbers game. Most brothers over the age of 30 have children. So unless you are looking young you are knocking out a whole heap of men. Secondly, most Afrikan fathers are not the primary carers of their children, so even if he does have children it is most unlikely that the child would be living with you full-time should you form a long-term relationship. Most likely the child will be with you every other weekend or somewhere along those lines. Thirdly, if the brother is the primary carer of his children does not that demonstrate exactly the kind of qualities, such as responsibility and commitment; that you say you are looking for!

Perhaps the most significant reason why some sisters are wary of getting involved with brothers with children, has nothing to do with selfishness or worries about being a step-parent, but has everything to do with *'the ex factor'*, the mother(s) of his child(ren). It is a bit of a dilemma really. You want him to show a keen and loving interest in his children, you would question his suitability as your partner if he did not, however lots of contact with his children means lots of contact with his ex and it is not completely unknown for brothers to be doing a regular ninja with their ex despite the fact they were supposed to have finished years earlier.

This is where a sister's counterintelligence network should come into play. If a man with children approaches you, before you make any commitment, and after you have looked him dead in the eye and asked him what the 4-1-1 is with his ex, you send out your feelers and gather in as much background information as possible to aid your decision making. There is no easy answer to these concerns; relationships are built on trust so you need to take extra care to ensure you are hooking up with a trustworthy man.

I hope the foregoing has made some sisters think about what is really important in selecting a mate and how easily one can get caught up in the superficial value system of others and make it our own, to our detriment. My advice... cut the list in half and then burn it.

Breasts, Batty, Long Hair and Light Skin – A recipe for disaster

Let me start out by saying that this sub-section is not an attack on light skinned women it is an attack on the mentality and superficiality of too many Afrikan men.

Earlier in this chapter I highlighted the characteristics which some research has indicated are most important to Afrikan women in assessing men. As was noted there was a decided bias towards physical characteristics/attributes. In this section I will consider the factors which drive Afrikan men in their search for a partner and what they tell us about the psychology of many brothers.

In his work which was cited earlier; Robert Staples notes that "Given that many Black men prefer their women light or White, the supply of such women is limited for a number of reasons. ...When the Roper organization asked Black and white men what qualities are most admired in a woman, the Black males ranked sex appeal fourth – White males ranked it sixth. When *Jet* magazine surveyed Black males in Chicago on the ten things they most notice about women, they listed in this order (1) face (2) legs (3) bust (4) eyes-hair (5) personality (6) dress intelligence (7) smile (8) buttocks (9) walk (10) hands-feet-conversation-sincerity." (Staples in Hare and Hare 1989: 72)

Staples goes on to suggest that "...the first four physical traits are generally most common to white women. The face should be light and keen in features, legs and bust should be big, eyes round, hair long and straight." (Staples in Hare and Hare 1989: 72)

So there we have it, what we have known for a long time. Many Afrikan men with Afrikan partners on a subconscious psychological level are simply seeking Caucasian women with a bit of skin melanin. Of course, nowadays, particularly in environs where there is a ready supply, many more are dropping the pretence and simply opting for the real McCoy i.e. the Caucasian woman.

As suggested earlier, this preoccupation with the physical over the mental is one of the primary causes of failed relationships in our community. A brother will find that even the most beautiful sister's looks will appear less breathtaking over time, as other initially overlooked qualities, become more important in maintaining the relationship. And of course as time and age take their toll if there is nothing aside from looks to commend her the relationship will end as her body sags and her looks fade.

Since men know that most men are driven primarily by looks the husbands or partners of attractive women, unless emotionally secure and mature, are also likely to experience greater levels of insecurity and jealousy – in the perhaps correct belief that their wives/partners will be the subject of sexual attention from other males.

One of the other negative repercussions of this looks oriented approach of Afrikan men is the tendency to keep trying to fish in the same twentysomething pool as they go through their thirties, forties and even fifties. Men have a great advantage over women in this respect. A man who has acquired the trappings of wealth and status or even just a worldly wise persona, can still attract much younger women despite his advancing years and expanding waistline. As noted earlier, women are generally strongly attracted to the most socially adaptive males and many will gladly overlook their male agemates in preference for an older, wiser, more experienced and most importantly, wealthier man.

Unfortunately, because many of these older men are still using the same criteria for assessing women that they were using twenty five years earlier, they are very likely to continue to choose immature, selfish, narcissistic young women purely on the basis of a pretty face and Coca Cola bottle shape. With little in common and nothing to discuss, even the trade off of good sex for money/status soon becomes tiresome for the older man who craves some companionship and mental stimulation to go with the fit body. The younger woman may be happier to stick with it since it is harder to find an economic patron than a stiff dick in the Black community!

These brothers are like *'relationship lemmings'* seemingly doomed to endlessly climb to the top of the relationship hill, throw themselves off the cliff edge onto the rocks below, heal their broken bones only to climb right back up the hill to repeat the process. They will bemoan the absence of good Black women, but will not modify their criteria or behaviour patterns and hence are doomed to endlessly repeat this cycle of failure until time dampens or removes their sex drive. At this point they may seek a companion nearer their own age to see out their old age.

The need for Drama Queens

A sister expressed her frustration to me at the too frequent difference between the sayings and doings of a large number of Afrikan men. We were discussing what it is that people really want in relationships as opposed to what it is they say they want. She was of the opinion that whilst a lot of brothers say they want a mature, independent sister who has her own interests and will give them 'their space', what they really want and often end up with are clingy, jealous, emotionally erratic drama queens. She speculates that whilst these drama queens may be very hard work they give these brothers what they want, which is to feel needed and adored. Many people have a tendency to confuse jealousy for love, whereas jealously is most often a symptom of immaturity, insecurity and often in men a need to exercise power over women. I had never really considered the drama queen angle before, however when I look around I do believe that she has a point. There are some brothers in relationships with some extremely 'highly strung' sisters, for want of a better phrase, and I have always wandered what was the glue that kept these couples together.

Moving Beyond the Physical

If we take as a given that physical attractiveness will play a greater or lesser role in male mate selection, we can still say that looks are necessary but should not be sufficient as the basis for any man seeking a relationship beyond the physical and given that it only takes one sexual coming together to produce a child; and hence a lifetime's connection, looks should not be sufficient for sex. Notwithstanding that in our current state of development the latter point is largely entering the realms of fantasy, it is still worthwhile considering some of the issues that will impact upon the likelihood of a brother being able to form a stable long-term relationship and some of the non-physical characteristics Afrikan men should be looking for in a potential Afrikan partner.

What is your relationship model? – I have expanded upon this issue later in this section (in the chapter 'What have you witnessed Loveships or Survivalships?'), however it is worthwhile pre-empting this fuller discussion with the simple observation that what one has observed – or increasingly not observed – in terms of the nature and healthiness of the relationship between your parents and other significant adults will have a profound effect upon one's approach and behaviour in one's own relationships, especially where one has experienced dysfunctional relationships and this has not been consciously addressed. This is another one of those cycles that needs to be broken, unfortunately too many of us underestimate the deep psychological impact that the nature of these parental (and other significant adult) relationships has had upon our own approach to finding love.

Age at which the brother commenced sexual activity and number of sexual partners – There is an unspoken belief that because, particularly in the Western oversexualised culture, males are obsessed with losing their virginity as early as possible, that no harm results to males who engage in early sexual activity. Whenever stories emerge in the press of schoolboys having sex with adult women, the general tone is one of 'lucky so and so' whereas when it is a case of a schoolgirl having sex with an adult man the tone of the media coverage is much more one of sexual abuse. This response relates firstly, to the patriarchal nature of society, secondly the reality that males are generally physically stronger than females and hence it is deemed that the male adolescent is better able to defend himself against unwanted adult female sexual advances – forgetting that the power exerted is psychological and not physical -, and thirdly to the wide admiration amongst males and females for men who can garner a large number of sexual partners.

Males are encouraged to be sexually predatory given the aforementioned status attached to achieving many sexual conquests. For the male who physically matures at an early age and who is handsome and/or has the gift of the gab, sex will become readily available. What is the downside some brothers are no doubt wondering? Well, they may say that *variety is the spice of life* however I feel there are two often interlocking downsides.

In terms of the age at which an Afrikan male commences sexual activity, there is the reality that physical maturity does not necessarily go hand in hand with psychological/emotional maturity. Just because a boy wants sex it does not necessarily mean that he is emotionally ready to deal with it. Boys can be sexually exploited by older women just as girls can be by older men. A boy who engages in sexual activity at an early age is likely to have much more trouble in later life in viewing sex as something more than a merely physical act and hence is likely to have trouble in fully engaging emotionally in a relationship.

In terms of brothers who are sexually promiscuous – which often but does not always goes hand in hand with commencing sexual activity at an early age – they are much more likely to have trouble in settling down and committing to a long-term monogamous relationship. The reality is that far from satisfying their sexual thirst, their large number of sexual partners simply increases their appetite for sexual variety. Even though these relationships are likely to have been tenuous and at best fragile, they will still feel the urge to mow the neighbour's lawn so to speak!

Sex can become addictive like many other forms of activity and as with all addictions the craving for the next 'fix' tends to increase in intensity and decrease in terms of the interval between fixes; over time. That is to say each fix becomes less satisfying (the high gets lower) and the high lasts for a shorter span of time.

Dealing with past Hurt – One of the things that we as Afrikans have become very good at is universalising the deficiencies of an individual across the whole race. For example, we receive bad customer service from an Afrikan shopkeeper so we immediately cuss all Afrikan shopworkers as wotless and rude. Naturally we immediately boycott that shop. On the other hand when we receive bad customer service from a Caucasian or Asian shopkeeper we may condemn the individual and pledge to boycott them, however very often within a few weeks we are back giving them our money and in all cases we never associate their poor service with their race.

As it is with shops so it is with Love. I tire of hearing brothers with their litany of reasons why Afrikan women are 'too much hard work'. Upon investigation you normally find their discontent centres around the behaviour of one or two sisters whom they loved a little too hard, a little too quickly. On the flip side I have known brothers who have been burned by Caucasian women and never once did they think to generalise the traits of an individual across the whole race.

Of course this is part of the deepseated group self-hatred that lies at the core of so many of our problems. We find it almost impossible to forgive each other or even to see the hurt caused by an Afrikan individual as just that, an individual act rather than our whole people turning against us. Too many brothers shut themselves down emotionally and present a hard face to the world, and sisters in particular, for fear of being hurt. This approach works, however it also guarantees that you will never experience real love.

The Desire to Dominate – In a patriarchal society men subconsciously learn that they should exercise power over women and the degree to which they can control a woman is the degree to which they epitomise true masculinity. Now; most men do not fully act out this Patriarchal masculine cultural imperative to its full extent, however most men act it out to some extent. Remember, this type of controlling behaviour does not always; and in fact does not usually, involve physical violence or even the threat of violence – although that is one aspect of this type of behaviour -, it is more about the use of coercive and controlling psychological techniques to control, prescribe and restrict a woman's behaviour.

The greater the degree to which brothers act out this patriarchal masculine ideal the less they are able to create a long-term loving relationship based upon mutual respect and involving genuine emotional intimacy. As I discussed in the earlier chapter ' Patriarchy

– The Father of Misogyny', Afrikan men have to make a real and concerted effort to rid ourselves of this cultural indoctrination and this involves a process of checking ourselves in our interactions with all women – and our loved ones in particular – and finding the courage and humility to say what for many of us is the hardest word to say..Sorry.

What should we be looking for?

OK. So I should have driven home the point by now that Afrikan men need to move beyond the physical in mate selection, however we still need to consider what type of characteristics we should be looking for in a prospective wife/partner. Below I have set out a list, which I do not claim to be exhaustive, but which hopefully provides a good starting point for reflection, particularly for those brothers whose relationships always seem to come unstuck and who think it is always the sister's fault.

Emotional Maturity – Earlier in this chapter I touched upon the attraction of some brothers for what I described as *drama queens*. These are emotionally immature, jealous, possessive women who experience a high degree of insecurity and consequently anxiety. Because they are insecure and needy they will tend to stick like a limpet to any man they are involved with and show him a lot of possessive attention. This can be misinterpreted as love. It is not. Brothers need to recognise that a mature sister will not act in this way since she will have sufficient self-confidence and self-regard; to value her time, appreciate her own company and respect all people's need for some personal space in any relationship.

Shared Values – This area merges and touches upon the next which is Shared Religious/Spiritual Beliefs. It is vital that a couple have shared values. This is not only important in making the one-to-one relationship work but also in the raising of children. Children require consistent messages from their parents to aid their emotional development. You both need to have a similar worldview, similar views on what constitutes normality, similar views on questions of morality and ethics. You will not agree on all such questions, however you need to be in the same ballpark. Values are the bedrock of culture and one's culture determines to a large degree how one thinks and acts. Many Afrikans are culturally confused or suffering from cultural amnesia and therefore it is important to realise that even those we love can convey anti-Afrikan values, beliefs and behaviour.

Shared Religious/Spiritual Beliefs –This is an important area for consideration since one's religious/spiritual belief is a core part of one's worldview and culture (see later chapter entitled 'Standing on Our Cultural Feet'). When I met my wife I was an atheist and she a lapsed Christian. Since that time I have gone through agnosticism to my present position where I believe in the Creator but do not follow any religion. I pour libation to give thanks to the Creator and to venerate my ancestors and seek to develop my spiritual life. My wife remains a Christian at heart, even though she rarely attends church. Our relationship works because neither of us is 'fundamentalist' in our view and we seek 'progressive compromise' (Madhubuti 1991) in our relationship. However it is better if you share the same belief system and I think it is almost impossible for a relationship to work where the two parties are both strongly committed to different –and particularly proselytising – religions.

Afrikan Consciousness – From my point of view a strong identity based upon the notion of Land, History and Culture and bringing together Colour and Culture, which Europeans transformed into the idea of Race; is essential, however the key issue is compatibility and congruence. Therefore two people who may have what I would consider a Negro Consciousness can make a very good match and enjoy a very happy, and from their viewpoint, productive relationship. Whatever the case both parties need to be singing off the same identity page especially since these ideas, as with Values and Religion, will be transmitted to any children that may come out of the relationship.

Personality Compatibility – It is sometimes said that opposites attract, however they do not always stick. In general terms birds of a feather flock together which is why the massive and increasing rejection of Afrikans as potential partners by Afrikans is a clear signal of our 'functional mental illness' (Grant 2003) and spiritual dis-ease.

Similar personalities tend to make the best match. Of course there are always exceptions and people often think that personality compatibility is all about extroverts vs. introverts, however this is only a part of personality and there are other traits such as self-confidence, self-esteem, determination, resilience, compassion, aggression, passivity, calmness, anxiety etc which are important to consider.

Family Orientation – By family orientation I am simply referring to whether each party wishes to have (any more) children. It is a very straightforward, but crucial issue which cannot afford to be fudged.

Stable family background – In our tradition, which is still extant on the continent, the question of family background is crucial in mate selection. There would be no question of two young people entering a serious relationship without elders, often a senior maternal aunt, carrying out investigations into the family background of the proposed partner. A marriage or serious long term relationship brings together (or should bring together) not just two individuals, but two families and therefore Afrikans who follow our traditions are serious about such matters and questions such as the honesty, solvency, mental health and reputation of the proposed partner's family will be considered. In the 'Western' environment and on many parts of the continent, these practices have broken down or been lost and people now wish to 'fall in love' and 'let nature take its course'. Of course nature often leads them to the divorce courts where there is time to ponder the rashness of decisions based upon hormone charged lust and physical attraction.

Brothers need to understand the crucial role that their partner's mother is likely to play in their lives and understand that this is a 'buy one get several dozen family members for free deal'.

Friendship circle – It is often said 'show me a person's friends and I will tell you about that person'. So, when looking for Ms Right check out her friends. As all brothers know, *the sisterhood* will check you out from the get go and their verdict will have an important bearing upon your survival prospects! However, this is a two way street and you need to realise that not only do you inherit the family you also inherit the friends. Get to know these friends and you will get an insight into your new partner. Let's hope you like what you see!

Conclusion

Part of the problem facing some Afrikan men who claim they cannot find the right sister is that they want a different type of relationship to that which they have experienced to date, however they are not truly prepared to fundamentally change their behaviour or their selection criteria. Part of this change may involve making some hard decisions, so rather than risk the inevitable short term pain that will ensue from making tough decisions they stick to the unhappy status quo; which will never bring them happiness, but which allows them to stay in their comfort zone.

As Na'im Akbar says in his book 'Visions for Black Men' "There are problems with "boys" who think they're men – who enjoy playing games, who enjoy riding in fast cars, who enjoy listening to loud music, who enjoy running after women, and who enjoy running real fast rather than being steady and directed as men are." (Akbar 2003: 43) The only thing guaranteed for these players – unless they make real changes to their lives – is a sad and lonely old age with their memories of the time when they were the 'Don Dada' their only companion.

If Afrikan men would place at least as great an emphasis on the mental as they do on the physical they would make far better relationship choices and would find that for an Afrikan man who is reasonably sane, economically solvent and of even moderate attractiveness the world is truly your oyster given the disproportionately large number of highly eligible sisters out there just waiting to exhale.

When the Sister Earns More Money

Money is not everything, but money is necessary. Old orders are being overturned and the evolving relative socio-economic positions of Afrikan women and men in the UK and US are creating new tensions and difficulties in Black relationships.

As has been oft repeated throughout this section of the book, it is a crude, but historically generally accurate truism to say that men go for looks and women go for money/power in selecting mates. However, times are a changing. If one looks at the UK for example, where Afrikan-Caribbean women are the highest hourly wage earners of all women and Afrikan-Caribbean men are the lowest hourly wage earners of all men, one sees that socio-economic reality will change cultural practice. Combined with the fact that Black women in 'the West' have never really been trained to rely on the Black man for their economic wellbeing – given his position of relative economic weakness – as attested to by the contemporary Afrikan Americanisms 'Do for yourself girlfriend' and 'What have you done for me lately' – one finds that as a large minority of Afrikan women make economic headway and many Afrikan men get left in their financial slipstream, more and more Afrikan men and women are having to contemplate relationships where the traditional economic order is inverted.

Whilst these relationships may be contemplated they still seem fairly rare – in the UK at least – and when they do occur they often seem to founder on the rocks of pride, ego and misunderstanding. I will attempt to unpick some of the difficulties people experience in such relationships in order to help Brothers and Sisters make them work.

I will start by firstly relating my own personal experience of life in the economic doldrums. Though comparatively brief in duration my six months of unemployment at an early stage of my working life left an indelible mark in my mind. In early 1991 I was forced to close my recruitment consultancy business as the effects of the Nigel Lawson (then Chancellor of the Exchequer) inspired economic recession began to bite. I was in limbo, seeking employment in London, where my parents lived and the East Midlands where my partner (now my wife) lived. We had decided that wherever I found work we would eventually both settle given that my long-term earning potential seemed the greater. However I found getting a job rather more difficult than I had imagined. After several weeks of commuting between Leicester where I was living and Nottingham where my partner lived, I moved into my partner's flat.

I did not have any qualms about this since we loved each other, planned to get married in the future and I anticipated finding a job pretty quickly. However as days turned to weeks and weeks to months I experienced the closest thing to depression I have ever felt. Without realising it I retreated into a world within the walls of the flat, apart from going out to sign on, shopping, or going out to engage in job search activities. I felt acutely embarrassed, actually ashamed of my position, which was compounded by the fact that I was living with my partner who was working and in effect supporting me. I did not want to meet anyone who knew my partner for fear they would ask that dreaded question, "so what are you up to then?"

I remember one occasion when I refused to attend the Christening of the child of one of my partner's relatives. I simply could not bear the thought of having to say "actually I am unemployed at the moment" several dozen times to my partner's relatives, friends and acquaintances and risk looks ranging from pity to scorn. I had seen those looks some Black women give to brothers whom they hold in low regard and I definitely did not want to be on the receiving end. So I stayed in the flat and asked her to make excuses for me.

It was not that I was particularly old fashioned or macho; it was just that I could not bear to feel useless and unproductive.

I was very lucky in the sense that I had an extremely supportive and loving partner, who sought to understand how I was feeling and never once complained or criticised me for being out of work and was sensitive in how she handled issues around money during this period. I was also fortunate in that during my sixth month of unemployment

I found a job. I always say that getting a job never has and never will make me as happy as when I got that job. I was floating on air all day after I got the telephone call to say that I was successful in my interview. It wasn't that it was the job of my dreams – I started my working life in self-employment and that is where I have always wanted to return – it was simply that it helped to restore some of my confidence and sense of self-worth. Since that first job I have never been unemployed and my career has gone along pretty smoothly (until the latter part of 2005 when I ran into some major office politics), however that day was definitely the highlight of working for other people. The next highlight will be when I stop working for other people.

Looking back I am still surprised at how much emotional turmoil I experienced as a result of first losing my business and then experiencing unemployment and it made me realise how much we are conditioned, both personally and collectively to judge men by what they do as opposed to who they are. No matter the ever growing presence of women in the workplace, society still gives legitimacy to women as mothers but not to men as fathers even if a man is the primary carer for his children. Some things have not changed.

What I did not face was the long-term prospect of earning significantly less than my partner and so I cannot comment from personal experience on how I would deal with this situation, I can only hope and believe that I could handle it without too many problems.

The biggest upside from that whole experience was the confirmation that I had a proper, solid gold woman. If your woman will stand by you during the bad times you have nothing to worry about and my wonderful Beverley was as solid as a rock when I was at my lowest point. Hopefully I have proved my worth to her over the intervening years and returned the support in kind.

So having reflected upon my personal story above let's look at some of the general issues that may arise when the sister earns significantly more.

Male Pride and Ego

It is commonly believed that Black women in majority Caucasian countries suffer from a double disadvantage in the economic marketplace. This disadvantage is based upon their gender and colour. In a logical extension of this rationale it is posited that Black men suffer disadvantage in the marketplace based upon colour but because they are male, living in a patriarchal society, benefit from male privilege and hence are less disadvantaged than Black women.

Now whilst there is some truth in this argument and whilst it is the belief that lies at the heart of much of the Afrikan male's anxiety and concern in relation to our relative economic weakness, it is not the whole picture by any stretch of the imagination.

There is an allied and also true argument which says that men fear other men and not women and that the dominant group of men (Caucasian men) will do their utmost to stymie the efforts at self-advancement of all other groups of men, and in particular the men from the group he is, and always has been, most hostile to (Afrikan men). According to this argument the Caucasian man will prefer to have the Afrikan woman, whom he can more easily control, close to him in the workplace rather than the Afrikan male whom he views as prone to unpredictable and aggressive behaviour. There is also the added benefit of the sexual favours he may potentially be able to garner from the Afrikan woman, although once again that situation is changing as well.

There was an interesting study carried out in the 1990's which looked at the employment prospects of Afrikan-American MBA graduates seeking opportunities with Wall Street firms. Sending off different paired bogus applications, one from a male and one from a female, they found that on average the female applicants were significantly more likely to be offered an interview than the male. The researchers had put information in the applications to ensure that the receiving companies could clearly identify all the applicants as Afrikan-American.

Now, as I said I believe there is truth in both arguments. The former being favoured by Caucasian feminists and their Negro followers, whilst the latter is favoured by Afrikans focusing upon the issue of 'race'.

Most Afrikan men, deep in our souls, know and silently acknowledge that we have been conquered by another group of men. The war may not be over, however we have lost so many battles that most of us cannot even remember what victory tastes like (even more reason why we should commemorate events such as the Haitian revolution). This is a bitter pill to swallow, made even bitterer by the reality of having to go cap in hand to your conqueror for the means to survive. Afrikan men feel socially and economically emasculated, hence the reason too many give up and opt to engage in 'compensatory masculinity' such as 'breeding' as many women as possible, 'juggling' and living outside the law and other reckless forms of behaviour.

When an Afrikan man's Afrikan woman – for the same is not necessarily true in relation to a Caucasian woman – earns significantly more money than he does, it is not necessarily the case that he resents her success and is not proud of her that causes problems, it is more that her success presents an unflattering reflection of his own 'underachievement' and reinforces his sense of failure. He does not want her to be 'down here with him' he wants to be 'up there with her'. He is afraid that she will become embarrassed by his relative lack of success and lose respect for him. He wants to feel that his contribution to the home is meaningful, because if he cannot play this role he does not know what other role to play. The fact that the Afrikan woman has her 'double disadvantage' to overcome only adds more salt to his wounded pride.

Immature Afrikan men in these types of relationship may well seek out a 'sister from the street' who looks up to him and will massage his ego and make him feel like a man. He will blame his woman for his straying, with accusations that she is always working and does not pay him enough attention, however it won't wash and if she has sense she will kick his lame backside to the curb.

The foregoing paragraphs represent what can happen; psychologically, to the Afrikan man in these cases, not necessarily what will happen. However, it is important for couples entering, or in the midst, of this type of situation to speak openly and frankly to one another about their feelings and any concerns they may have in relation to their relative economic positions. Now of course the easy thing to say to the man is grow up and get over it, however human beings are far from rational at the best of times and a little bit of understanding and discussion will go a long way. Most mature men will speak with pride of their woman's success and use it as an inspiration to carve out their own niche in the world.

Females who want to impress

One of the problems in these types of relationship is when the woman says one thing but deep down wants another. She says that she just wants a good hardworking man who will love her, respect her and be faithful, but really she wants more, a lot more. Part of her says as long as he looks reasonable it is his qualities as a person that count and it does not matter if he is not a high flyer. Another part of her says she would like a man she could really show off to her friends and speak of in glowing terms to her work colleagues.

This type of woman will enter such a relationship with good intentions but her mixed messages and muddled thinking will soon cause problems. The brother will notice how she directs conversations away from his job when speaking to other people. He will start to get irritated by her constant 'encouragement' for him to go back to college or apply for higher paying jobs. When finally she accuses him of 'lacking ambition' it will be time to send the camel to the chiropractor, since this will be the straw that breaks the camel's back!

This type of sister will be overly concerned with the opinion of others who do not necessarily have her best interests at heart and consequently she will have an overemphasis on wants as opposed to needs. The relationship will end in recrimination and bitterness and both parties will vow never to enter this type of match up again believing that the split was due to something inherently wrong with this type of coupling rather than the specific nature of their partnership.

The brother will most likely seek and find a sister 'on his level' pretty quickly, whilst the sister is likely to be left living with her 'success' for a while unless she turns to Caucasian men or other women as 'the only viable options'.

The economic tide has turned and whilst we should not be fooled that Afrikan women as a whole are experiencing some sort of golden age in the marketplace, a significant minority of sisters have made serious financial strides. These women need and deserve to be loved. For those who want to be loved by an Afrikan man their possibilities will be greatly enhanced if they entertain the possibility of sharing their life with a man earning less than they do. For brothers, there are an abundance of excellent women out there just waiting for a good man if you can master your pride and ego. These types of relationship will become easier with time as they increase in frequency, however for now they require even more maturity and understanding than normally required to make an Afrikan loveship work. Is it worth the extra effort? Of course.

What have you witnessed Loveships or Survivalships?

People often model their emotional responses based upon the interactions they observed amongst those nearest and dearest to them whilst they were growing up. If we are considering how to make our intimate relationships work better, we must ask ourselves the questions: What was the nature of the relationships we observed whilst growing up and what have been the nature of the relationships in which we have engaged? Were we generally surrounded by Loveships or Survivalships? Do we even know what a healthy relationship looks like and could we 'bear' to be in one?

If people are subjected to a high level of dysfunctional behaviour they will begin to think that it is normal. If what you regularly observed between your parents as a child was tension, arguments, anger, despair or even violence then you still probably carry some of that emotional energy with you. Or if what you experienced was the one parent you were living with engaged in a series of ephemeral, intermittent, coming togethers, you need to seriously consider the impact these experiences may have had upon you, particularly if you have had difficulty forming successful relationships.

People have a habit of repeating cycles. Children who were sexually abused are more likely to become abusers. We don't think of living with high levels of negative emotional energy as abuse, however how often do children repeat the behaviour patterns of their parents, even if their parents exhort them not to. For example the daughters of teenage mothers are more likely to become teenage mothers than the daughters of women who delayed childbirth until a later age. The children of smokers are more likely to become smokers than children from non-smoking homes. As they say '*Example is Better than Precept*'.

How many strong, happy, loving Afrikan couples who have been together (continuously) for more than ten years do you know personally where both parties are aged beneath 45? You probably didn't need all your fingers did you – unless you are part of a large church or mosque? If like me you have a few digits left then you need to ask the question. What is my success model for building a successful relationship?

When we engage in a new activity, we normally – if we have any sense – look for a model of success, an example of good practice that we can learn from. When we started out upon our relationships journey how many of us had good exemplars of how to make it work?

University of Washington psychologist John Gottman has been studying the interactions between couples for over 20 years. Observing and recording thousands of couples in conversation in his laboratory he has developed a Spaff (specific affect) coding system that has 20 categories corresponding to the widest range of human emotions that he can conceive a couple expressing during a conversation. Examples include: 1. Disgust, 2. Contempt, 7. Anger, 10. Defensiveness, 11. Whining, 12. Sadness, 13. Stonewalling, 14. Neutral etc. By plotting the occurrence of these emotional responses during an observed conversation and following analysis Gottman has been able to demonstrate – via longitudinal tracking of couples – that by observing just a one hour conversation between a husband and wife he can predict with 95% accuracy whether they will still be together in 15 years time.

Now there is not time to go into how he explains the success of his methodology in terms of psychological functioning, and I am not aware whether his methods have been tested for cross-cultural validity, however what most interested me and confirms my own personal observations was the description of what he calls the Four Horsemen, defensiveness, stonewalling, criticism and contempt. Of these his research indicates that contempt is the most important negative emotion and greatest predictor of relationship meltdown.

Now, his findings are not surprising, but what they do is confirm what we should all know and understand, namely that the most important single component of a relationship is mutual respect. Not

Love, but respect, because without respect you cannot have true love, you can only have physical attraction and lust.

Maybe, if it has not been working for you, you need to go back to the drawing board and look for some new examples to emulate. None of us knows exactly what goes on behind closed doors, however if there are people close to you who have a good thing going, why not sit down and talk to them about what they consider to be the essential ingredients for a good relationship? It cannot be of less use than sitting down with your bredren/sistren cussing the deficiencies of the opposite sex.

Our Elders – as opposed to people who are simply old – are an untapped resource and many of them have made it work over decades and under the harshest economic and social conditions. It would not be a waste of your time to sit at the feet of some of these longstanding couples and drink in some practical wisdom. As one Elder said to me when discussing his marriage "If she cook me wash, if I cook she wash". There it is. Reciprocity, Harmony and Balance, in other words Ma'at!

Monogamy – Is there any alternative?

Introduction

Haki Madhubuti in his seminal work 'Black Men – Obsolete, Single, Dangerous? The Afrikan American Family in Transition' presents a challenge to our ideas as to how to rebuild the Afrikan family in 'the West'.

"Where are we going as a people when we allow a great many Black families to become non-functional units or units composed of only single adults and children without support? It should be obvious that monogamy as the "only" way towards happiness and development has its limitations and hazards (Goldberg 1976). It should also be obvious that as the sex ratio now stands, it is impossible for "every" Black woman to have a monogamous relationship with a Black man (Staples, 1978; Madhubuti, 1978; Scott 1977). And unless Black people boldly and consciously tighten up *their* family arrangements, their future will continue to be uncertain." (Madhubuti 1991: 94)

Now, I can imagine many readers, be they single, married, or in unmarried relationships recoiling in horror. However what is most interesting to me, irrespective of people's view of polygamy, is the matter of fact way that many Afrikans – who would be disgusted at polygamy – happily accept the fact that significant numbers of Afrikan men, be they married or unmarried, already have multiple partners 'on the go' at any one time. There are plenty of brothers spinning nuff relationship plates whilst their wives/partners and others pretend not to notice. And this is not to mention the growing number of sisters in relationships who visit the eponymous 'Joe Grind' for sexual 'topping up' every now and then.

Joseph W. Scott in 'Crisis in Black Sexual Politics' tells us that:

"For many people (and the data would suggest that males more than females exhibit this pattern) a monogamous relationship is impossible. Furthermore, the trend is also that the majority of married males and females are promoting it more than the older generation. One result is that more and more men and women, *without planning to*, are starting the sexual bonding process *outside* of their monogamous marital relationships. In other words, the exclusive pair bonds are declining in popularity and alternatives such as intimate friendships, nonconsensual and consensual adultery, and multilateral marriages which include three or more persons are increasing in popularity. All of these alternative relationships involve sexual bonds with someone other than one's primary mate." (Scott in Hare and Hare 1989: 106)

I can recall going to a house party in London in the late 1980's when a friend of mine had his two 'main girlfriends' and four other sexual partners present. Apart from speculating as to what it was he had going for him given that he did not have a financial pot to pee, it did dawn on me during the course of the night that lots of other people in that house were well aware of his situation and understood why he was flitting from one room to the other with such regularity. Even his four 'subordinate' sexual partners, for want of a better phrase were aware that they 'were not alone'. It seemed as if it was just the two 'main squeezes' who were blissfully ignorant.

This 'undercover' type of sexual activity seems accepted in large parts of the Black community, however if he had strode into the place as bold as brass with even two women on his arm you can imagine the kind of admonishing conversations that would have flowed, including comments as to 'how can they accept it, they can't have any self-respect'. Well, lots of sisters are accepting it, but they and others collude in an 'out of sight, out of mind' self-deluding game.

We will now go on to look at some of the more frequent types of relationship that large sections of our community are engaging in.

Monogamy

Monogamy has traditionally described a one man/one woman form of relationship. It implies sexual exclusivity over a prolonged period. With the rise of alternative sexstyles this definition has been expanded to include homosexual relationships.

For the vast majority of human history the vast majority of the world's population practiced polygyny. As Haki Madhubuti notes:

"As European Christians took the world, the one man/one woman form of male/female relationships became dominant (Awoonar, 1975; Leith Ross, 1965; Beidelman, 1971). The Catholics were especially forceful in this regard, preaching that polygynous arrangements were pagan and tools of the devil (Beidelman, 1971)." (Madhubuti 1991: 95)

He suggests that the fundamental problem being experienced by people with monogamy in 'the West', which is manifested in spiralling rates of divorce and the huge growth in single person households, is the difficulty in one person satisfying the many and varied needs of another. With the cult of 'Western' individualism and the increasing belief in the *right* to instant gratification, be it material or emotional, increasing numbers of people view monogamy as a hill too steep to climb.

Omnigamy

Omnigamy is often referred to as serial marriage and is the West's answer to polygamy (Madhubuti 1991 citing Tiger 1978). This practice could also be referred to as time limited monogamy. Although there is not usually a conscious time period prescribed upon entering such a relationship, as pointed out earlier the culture and society shapes social consciousness and social conduct (Karenga in Hare and Hare 1989), hence phrases such as the 'seven year itch' which reflect a point at which many marriages in 'the West' disintegrate. Madhubuti (1991) points out that Omnigamy is far more common amongst Caucasians than Afrikan-Americans who seem to take the dictum '*once bitten twice shy*' to heart.

Illegany

Is perhaps best exemplified by the situation I described in the introduction to this chapter involving my erstwhile friend. Haki Madhubuti describes it as "....nickle and dime pimping and whoring that lonely and insecure women allow into their lives. The male in this arrangement is busy running bases trying to service and control as many women as he can, and responsibility to the "real" needs of these women and their children is not even part of the equation." (Madhubuti 1991: 97)

In these types of relationships the male may or may not have a 'main woman' however for the rest of the women in his life their relationships are very much centred around his 'needs' and his schedule. Illegany differs from mansharing in two important respects. The first is honesty. In illegany some of the women never know the true nature and extent of the man's relationships, some know all of the time, but it is very rare for all of the women to know the truth all of the time. In mansharing, if there are for example two women they will both be aware of the situation and both know who the other woman is. The second is responsibility. In illegany the man rarely takes any financial or other type of responsibility for 'his women' and their children. In mansharing the man plays an active role in all aspects of the lives of his partners and their children (if they have any) and makes a financial contribution to their households.

Some of the key characteristics of illegany include:

(i) **Disingenuous rationalisation and self-justification** by the male who will often suggest in defence of his actions that he is providing some sort of social service to Black women, 'sacrificing' his energy to meet their unmet needs. According to this line without men like him there would be a lot more Black women without a man or going over to Caucasian men. He will often claim that they are happy with what he has to offer.

(ii)   **The illicit/undercover nature of the relationships.** His bredren know the runnings and perhaps the close friends of the women involved.

(iii) **Lack of financial contribution** to the women's households. The man may even be 'financially pimping' off these women.

(iv)   There is a **high turnover of women** (except where children are involved) since these relationships are not founded upon any deepseated emotional attachment

(v)   **The women order their lives and schedule around the male** who may turn up unannounced or at short notice and still expect 'to be looked after'. The woman knows better than to visit his yard without a prior invitation.

(vi)   **Sex is the bedrock and foundation of these relationships.**

(vii) **The male shows little interest in the woman's children** unless they are his biological offspring.

(viii) Whilst people in the wider community may generally be unaware of whom he is bedding they will usually be well aware of his reputation as a 'gyalist' and the fact that he always has plenty of women 'on the go' at any one time. Despite this **there is little community censure** or negative repercussions resulting from his behaviour.

(ix)   Conversely, **the women will be looked down upon within the community** where people are aware of their situation.

(x)   As well as having his 'regulars' **the man will also fulfil his wider 'Joe Grind' responsibilities** by having one off casual sex with other women – who may or may not be in long-term relationships – whenever the opportunity presents.

(xi)   Participation crosses socio-economic boundaries and is not just confined to poorer women.

(xii) **The two foundations for this type of relationship are sexual attraction and female compliance.** If the sexual attraction wanes the male departs quickly and the same is the case if the female demonstrates any suggestion of significant non-compliance to his wishes.

(Adapted from Haki Madhubuti 1991)

Haki Madhubuti (1991) suggests that illegany is the most common form of male/female relationship amongst Afrikan-Americans, which is an awful indictment of social conditions within that society and indicative of our people's failure to respond creatively and productively to such conditions. I would say that there is no room for complacency here in the UK and the situation is probably almost as bad.

Illegany is basically founded upon exploitation. Males exploit the shortage of marriageable Afrikan men to make hay with lonely Afrikan women who perhaps come to the conclusion that it is better to have a couple of slices of a loaf – even if it is near it's sell by date – than no loaf at all. The men hide behind the women's freedom to make choices knowing full well that that 'freedom' is severely impacted upon by their need for male companionship and the emotionally corrosive effects of perhaps years of enforced (as opposed to actively chosen) singledom.

Some of the biggest losers in this whole mess are the children of these women – and particularly their sons – who are exposed to – though the women may try their best to shield them from knowledge of the full situation – dysfunctional, exploitative relationships which present them a 'model' for relationships built around sex and male emotional detachment. Thus unwittingly, many of these women are nurturing future gyalists to do to others what has been done to them.

Polygyny
Polygyny manifests itself as polygamy – men having more than one wife – with which most people are familiar and polyandry – women having multiple husbands – which is less common and less well known. As stated earlier, polygyny was the most common form of mating in Afrika and much of the non-European world prior to mass conversion to Christianity and Islam (Awooner cited in Madhubuti: 1991). It should be noted that even in polygynous societies not all men/women had more than one wife/husband. In the case of polygamy a man had to be able to demonstrate his capability to provide economically for his wives and children. Therefore one

tended to find that the wealthier a man was the more likely he was to have more than one wife and the more wives he was likely to have.

It has mainly been men who have suggested that monogamy alone will not provide all the answers to the crisis in Afrikan family life in 'the West' and this has raised suspicions that some Afrikan men are seeking to take advantage of the current male/female imbalance to legitimise their slackness for want of a better phrase. And I am sure that when the word polygamy is mentioned there are some brothers who automatically think of sex with lots of women rather than lots of women to provide economic, emotional and spiritual support for.

There are some basics of polygamy in Afrika which would probably deter some of these brothers whose actions are controlled by their one eyed brain. Firstly, polygamy is not something you spring on your first wife when you are getting sexually bored. It is agreed and understood *prior* to the first marriage. Secondly, the woman does the choosing. As Haki Madhubuti notes "In the Gikuyu tribe, the wife initiates the question of another wife after a year or so, especially if she is with child:" (Madhubuti 1991: 100) The woman is likely to be less interested in the shape of the batty and more interested in the strength of character of the new wife she proposes!

Marriage is a social institution first created by human beings in Afrika around 40,000 years ago. Its primary functions are to provide a stable social setting for the raising of children and to positively bind men into society so that they will act responsibly. There is no reason other than the nature of our socialisation in 'the West' why there should be greater hostility to polygyny than to the widespread illeganous relationships which occur in the Black community. The first are open and honest and provide much better environments for the raising of children, whilst the second are covert, illicit and exploitative, creating poor environments for the raising of children.

From a personal point of view it would be great if every Afrikan woman who wanted an Afrikan husband and every Afrikan man who wanted an Afrikan wife could find one. If monogamy is to be the only way then there is some serious work needed to resurrect the Afrikan male so that Afrikan women have some viable choices available to them.

Below I have listed some of the main reasons why polygamy (since this is what the polygyny debate is really about) will not be widely accepted by Afrikans in 'the West':

- It takes a greater level of emotional maturity to make these types of relationship work and if many Black people (and Black men in particular) are not emotionally mature enough to make monogamous relationships work why should we expect them to be able to make polygamy work
- In a patriarchal society any return to polygamy would be presented by White feminists and their Negro acolytes as an attempt to subjugate Afrikan women and there is the very real likelihood that this is how the majority of Afrikans would interpret it
- The vast majority of Afrikan women would not accept it and polygamy would only accelerate the headlong rush of Afrikan women towards men from other groups (particularly Caucasian men) on the basis of 'better to have a whole White man than half or a third of a Black man'.
- Most Afrikans in the 'West' are Christianised if not Christian and therefore accept the highly sexualised Judeao-Christian view of morality and hence would view any attempt to return to polygamy as a carnal or mortal sin.
- Significant numbers of Afrikan men would still 'stray,' even if it were socially accepted for them to have multiple wives, based upon the rationale 'you can never have too much of a good thing'!

Mansharing

Mansharing is undercover polygamy. It is very different to illegany in that – assuming there are two women sharing one man – both women are aware of the situation and consent to it. Some of the key characteristics of mansharing include:

- There is a much greater degree of honesty on the part of the man with the women concerned than in illegany

- These relationships are much more complete than in illegany. They have a strong emotional as well as physical aspect.
- The man will be involved in the life of the woman and her children (if she has any) even if the children are not his biological offspring
- Mansharing is 'presented' to the first partner after their relationship has been established either as a way for the woman to keep hold of him or after he has been found out having an affair with another woman with whom he wants to maintain a relationship
- In mansharing the man does the choosing of the second partner.
- In mansharing the power still very much lies with the man.
- The second relationship is generally kept secret from general public knowledge because of the negative response anticipated by the participants if it became widely known
- The second partner will generally feel happier than the first since it is likely that she was aware of and chose the situation she was entering into. The first partner is likely to feel some element of resentment having been presented with this choice after the relationship with the man was established. She accepts it on the basis that half a Black man is better than no Black man.
- The secrecy involved is not healthy since it inevitably leads to half-truths and deceit in order to keep the secret. It would be far better if these relationships went public.

Conclusions

In this chapter I have set out some of the key aspects of the main types of relationship that Afrikans in 'the West' engage in. It is undoubtedly true that the major cause of the fragmentation in Afrikan family live in the UK and USA, and other similar countries, is the economic and psychic decimation of the Afrikan man. As has often been said, men fear men and the Caucasian man's ongoing assault against the Afrikan man has yielded impressive results. If we want most Afrikan women to have viable chances of finding a loving and caring Afrikan man to share their lives with the solution is simple, but difficult. We need to rear larger numbers of strong, loving, conscious Afrikan men. The resurrection and reconstruction of the Afrikan man must become one of our most urgent priorities if we wish to move from relationship rhetoric and resentment to reconciliation. Nature abhors a vacuum and whilst we have a male/female imbalance something will fill the void. That something may be illegany, mansharing, polygamy, 'inter-racial' relationships or homosexuality, however something will fill the void.

Before we move on to look at some of those void filling 'somethings' in the next chapter, I will close this subsection with a few basic relationship tips.

Some key ingredients for building productive Afrikan-centred partnerships:

1. A shared sense of purpose
2. The ability to engage in *Progressive Compromise* (Madhubuti 1991)
3. Emphasis on the 'We' above the 'I'
4. Shared belief system
5. Understanding that without respect there is no true love
6. Shared meals – families that eat together stay together
7. Low priority on material acquisition (This is different to creating productive wealth)
8. Positive extended family support
9. Talking *to* each other rather than *at* each other
10. *Hearing* each other as opposed to just *listening* to each other
11. Placing sex in its proper context i.e. a small part of the relationship
12. No violence or threat of violence
13. Preparedness of Afrikan men to go through some form of public ceremony to express commitment to relationship
14. An understanding of the 'political' nature of Afrikans relationships
15. Rejection of Eurocentric notions of romance and patriarchal dominance
16. A plan i.e. agree fundamentals before you start e.g. do you want children and if yes how many.

Without Boundaries – Understanding European Sexual Culture

Introduction

The reader should be warned that there are references to some very unpleasant forms of sexual behaviour in this chapter and that some readers may be offended or may not wish to subject themselves to such material. I have only included such references after careful consideration and with the aim of waking Afrikans out of the coma that is allowing us and our children to be sleepwalked into another people's sexual way.

A given people have a sexual culture just as they have a social, political and business/economic culture and all are cultural streams which naturally flow out of the reservoir of the overall culture of that people. During this important chapter I will provide the reader with an understanding of the seemingly unconnected changes occurring in the sexual culture of the sons and daughters of Europe wherever they are around the globe. By the end, the reader should be able to understand the underlying causes of these changes and hence understand their largely predictable nature. By way of a test of my *'theory of change'*, during the course of this chapter I will predict what I see as two of the biggest forthcoming changes, or more accurately 'natural' developments, in European sexual culture over the next 20-30 years. Hopefully, we will all still be around to prove me right or wrong!

Identifying European Cultural Drivers

If we understand that as stated in the introduction above, a people's sexual culture is simply a tributary flowing from the primary cultural source, then we will understand that the overriding ethos or asili (Ani 1996) of the culture from which their sexual culture is derived, that is to say, the 'needs' of the culture, will be the same for its tributaries as they are for the primary source. That is to say if we understand the fundamentals of European culture we will be able to understand any component of that culture, sexual or otherwise.

From what has been written by many of our greatest thinkers, and even by people like me (Grant 2003), we know that some of the most important European cultural drivers are:

- *Power* (particularly over 'cultural other' [Ani 1996])
- *Control*
- *Universalism*
- *Progress*
- *Assimilate/Eliminate Difference*

So let us apply this analytical template to European Sexual Culture.

Power

Europeans must have power and power is not necessarily a bad thing since it simply encapsulates the ability to bring about some sort of change or transformation in, or to; a person, object, or circumstance. Power brings to mind dynamic energy and in European scientific terms power is quantified in terms of Watts which encompasses a component of energy. However this European drive for power permeates all aspects of Caucasian culture, activity and relationships. The power they seek is more than power to change; it is 'power over'. Just as we see that Europeans have spent all of their human history seeking to establish dominative relationships, first amongst their own tribes, and then – with particular relish – over all the non-European peoples they encountered, so we see that this need for 'power over' infects even their most intimate and 'loving' relationships.

We see that violence has been a key hallmark of European sexual relationships right since the birth of their culture. This is exemplified by the descriptions of mainstream ancient Greek homosexual culture where adolescent/teenage boys as a matter of routine were placed under the 'protection' of a 'mature' adult male mentor; who as part of inducting the boy into the ways of Greek manhood would take him away and sodomise him repeatedly as part of his education. The man and boy would return to their village to be greeted with a fanfare by friends and family (Baruti 2004). This raping of boys as part of their rites of passage into adult Greek male society was designed to ensure that they would submit to appropriate adult male authority, since in a culture of extreme individualism, alienation and aggression the fear was always that the sons would want to overthrow the fathers.

Freud accurately picked up on the deepseated sexual violence within European culture when he developed the idea of the 'Oedipal complex'. The typically European mistake he made was in trying to universalise European cultural pathology in order to try to normalise it. For those who are unfamiliar with the Oedipal complex it basically states that at a subconscious level all males want to have sex with their mothers and overthrow and kill their fathers. Like the Electra complex and other European psychological constructs it is based upon cultural ideas contained within Greek mythology which Europeans like to believe offer some universal insight into the human condition, rather than a valuable insight into – in these cases – the sexual perversions underpinning European culture.

As a further example the word 'honeymoon' stems from the practice of Greek men sodomising Greek boys and girls under the moon (Baruti 2004). This is what the ancient Greeks and Romans tell us about the ancient Greeks. This is not some Afrocentric invention. This is Europe's premier 'classical' civilisation self describing its culture of paedophilic violence. We see that practices such as sado-masochism and bondage which are increasingly popular amongst contemporary Europeans have their roots in archaic European culture and contain the elements of Power (over), Violence and Control. As mentioned earlier, European clans used to routinely form raiding parties to kidnap women from other villages or tribes and that is the long forgotten root of the throwing of rice or confetti at wedding ceremonies, which are a symbolic reminder of when Europeans used to throw stones and rocks at those kidnapping one of their women. The image of the European caveman dragging the cavewoman by the hair into his cave to rape her is by no means an exaggeration or atypical in the development of European sexual culture. The foregoing descriptions of sexual violence are all examples of the 'force connection' in 'Western' sexual culture as described by Maulana Karenga (1989).

European sexual language also reflects this connection between violence/force and sex in the European psyche. Words/phrases such as fuck, grind, pump, roger, batter, shaft, jook, give her 'the agony', ride, lick it down, punish etc. etc. speak to either an emotionally detached physical connection or an act of subconscious (or conscious) violence and domination. The fact that some of these words come out of contemporary Jamaican culture speaks to the enslavement and acculturisation of the Afrikan mind.

Control

We have already touched briefly upon the issue of Control in the foregoing section on Power and these two attributes are closely associated within European culture and life in general. *Power over* enables one to exert *control over* and control over gives one a sense of power, gives one a power trip. It is this psychological rush, this ego inflating buzz that Europeans constantly strive for as they act out their God complex on Earth. When Caucasians crow about the US as the world's only superpower, and the US President as the most powerful man on Earth they speak to their collective cultural need to be in control and to be seen and acknowledged to be in control.

It is one of the ironies and strange twists of European sexual culture that many of the men who exercise the greatest control and dominance within their culture have a compulsive desire to be dominated and controlled in their sexual life. It is quite common to hear of judges, powerful businessmen and other power brokers exposed for their bizarre sexual peccadilloes which they often give expression to with prostitutes or women who subsequently sell their stories to newspapers. Being spanked seems to be a particular favourite of many powerful Caucasian men in the UK and there is a well known prostitute in the UK known as 'Miss Whiplash' whose services were used by MPs (Members of Parliament), judges, businessmen etc. I have read of other dominatrix prostitutes who have spoken of how these powerful Caucasian middle aged/elderly men seek all kinds of perverse 'sexual' services including acts such as being dressed up in a baby's nappy with dummy in mouth whilst being dominated, being urinated upon, having their penises rubbed with coarse sandpaper or a vegetable grater until blood is drawn (These latter acts were broadcast in a television documentary about prostitution in New York, featuring a 'dominatrix' prostitute 'punishing' one of her clients who was in his eighties). These acts may not be in the 'sexual mainstream' but they are far from unusual in European sexual culture.

How often do you see depicted in television and cinema films sexual scenes involving one sexual partner tying the other's arms to the bedposts? These types of depictions of bondage are ten a penny in this culture and are a 'natural' development from the violent history of European sexual culture. Indeed they are so commonplace that most people do not regard them as being in the slightest bit unusual. I remember a film in which Madonna was simulating sex with Willem Defoe and after binding his wrists to the bedposts she proceeded to pour molten wax from a candle over his chest in what was apparently meant to be a sexually stimulating act. Being rather naïve at the time I thought there is no way that 'normal' people do these kind of things. Now of course, in one sense I was absolutely right, however my interpretation of normality seems increasingly out of kilter with this 'modern' society and it was not too long before I was reading in a newspaper of a Caucasian man admitted to hospital with second degree burns to his penis and testicles caused by....you've guessed it, molten wax! A bit of sexual experimentation gone wrong apparently.

Universalism

As in all aspects of life Caucasians are hellbent upon proving that the European way is the normal way, the only way, the universal way. The more abnormal an aspect of their culture is the greater the effort they put into normalising that particular practice. Now, we probably need to provide some definitions at this juncture. What is normal behaviour? The best definition I have heard comes from Professor Wade Nobles who says:

> "*Normality can be defined as live giving or life affirming behaviour.*"

Now of course different cultures will still use this definition to come to different conclusions regarding the normality of certain sexual and non-sexual practices, however from an Afrikan-centred perspective this definition should help us to gain greater clarity in our interpretation of normal behaviour. Caucasians are not culturally interested in this type of wider definition of normality since in their highly individualistic culture the only real criteria in making a behaviour culturally acceptable is individual consent, which is why they cannot 'hold the line' in maintaining any sexual taboo around any behaviour that involves individual consent.

As an example, there was an interesting case brought before a crown court in London a few years ago which involved a group of homosexual sado-masochists, many of whom had been arrested and charged by the police with assault, resulting from the extreme sexual acts they had been inflicting upon one another, during what can only be described as; a sadomasochistic orgy. The defence was that even though the sadists had inflicted actual bodily harm upon the masochists, because the masochists had consented, no crime had been committed and their sexual preferences were their business and nothing to do with the police and the state. If my memory serves me right they were acquitted.

In an even more bizarre and disturbing take upon the same theme a German man advertised for a willing murder victim. A young man responded to this advert, visited the advertiser's flat where he was ritualistically killed, apparently with his consent. When the case came to court and the killer was charged with murder, his defence was that the victim had consented and therefore he had not committed a crime. It was clear from the court proceedings that there was a strong sexual motivation underpinning the killer's desire to kill. In the end he was cleared of murder and convicted of manslaughter and sentenced to less than ten years in prison (seven years I think). The powerful European cultural drivers of individualism and progress (see next subsection) 'demand' that this taboo is broken and it will only be a matter of time before defendants in such cases are acquitted if they can prove the victim's consent.

If Europeans did not present their culture, sexual or otherwise, as universal, if they did not impose it around the globe, what would they be left with? They would be left to examine their history of incredible and unmatched violence, theft, material greed, rape and domination as particular and peculiar to them. That kind of charge sheet is not good for the old self image. So universalism is the only way. But why?

Marimba Ani explains that "Mircea Eliade has said that it is "sacred space" that becomes the "center of the world" for religious man" and thereby orients him in the universe; i.e., creates cosmos from chaos. Europeans, we could say are essentially "nonreligious." They therefore become enmeshed in a maze of ontological relativity, lacking a "center" of sacred space. The search for the "universal" is a primary thrust in their attempt to create order, to become centered, and to find their place in the universe." (Ani 1996: 511-512)

Whilst I would agree with the general thrust of this quote I think an important distinction needs to be drawn between religion and spirituality. Therefore I would say that whilst Europeans are often religious they are essentially non-spiritual. When one cuts through all the rhetoric, the religiosity of Europeans is essentially the practice of self-worship. This is why they can conceive of depicting their God as a Caucasian man with a long white beard (as on the ceiling of the Sistine chapel) and see nothing blasphemous about it. This is why it was culturally inevitable that they would create/embrace a religion in which God incarnate would take human form, and inevitably they would present that human form as a Caucasian male. It satisfies their self-worshipping God complex, their philosophy of White Supremacy, their culture of Patriarchy and their hyper-materialist despiritualised Utamawaza (see glossary). Not just three in one but four in one, what a metaphysical bargain!

Marimba Ani goes on to reinforce the point I made earlier when she says "The "world culture" objective protects liberal Europeans from self-examination. It is the method by which these would be benefactors avoid focusing on their own cultural/historical roots, less these same roots be identified as the source and matrix of systematic exploitation in the world. European intellectuals can justify directing their attention everywhere except on that which is peculiarly "European"." (Ani 1996: 539)

Marimba Ani's book 'Yurugu' is a seminal work in the critical examination of European culture from an Afrikan-centred perspective. It provides us with the intellectual tools to tear off the universalistic glove covering the European iron fist.

Europeans are busily exporting and imposing their ever more extreme forms of sexual expression around the globe. This is one of the reasons that I do not share the seemingly widespread Afrikan desire to see ever increasing European tourism to countries in Afrika and the Caribbean. They demand a heavy price for their dollars, pounds and euros. When one sees the massive rates of HIV infection on the Caribbean island of Tobago coupled with increasing rates of prostitution of women and men as well as European paedophiles preying upon children. When one sees the havoc wreaked by Caucasian paedophiles in places like Thailand – where the child traffickers were kidnapping lost and orphaned children in the aftermath of the Tsunami to satisfy this Caucasian male thirst – do we think that this is a price worth paying for foreign exchange? Wherever Caucasians go in the non-Caucasian world they demand to express their sexual culture and poor and weak countries usually cave in. So we see in Jamaica the Hedonism resorts where Europeans and a smaller number of culturally lobotomised Negroes give full expression to European sexual perversion. Tourism is culturally dangerous for countries that are economically weak. Europeans do not respect the cultures of non-Europeans, and most especially Afrikan people. They must be kept under control or kept out.

Progress
I would guess that most people reading this book have probably never questioned the concept of 'progress' in general and certainly not in

relation to sexual behaviour, on the assumption that it is a universal concept that we should all strive for. Well, we need to unpick this idea if we are to understand the nuances of European culture and specifically in this instance why European sexual culture is inevitably 'without boundaries'.

Let us go back to Marimba Ani. She tells us that:

"The critical conceptual leap is that by which action directed toward a concrete objective becomes confused with change that is merely reflexive, i.e., in which the object is change itself. The "progress" toward which Europeans perceive themselves to be "moving" is neither concrete nor reachable- a spurious goal indeed. Why then has the idea such attraction for the European mind.....The answer lies in the fact that this ingenious invention- "progress" born out of the European utamaroho – is ideally fashioned to encourage the growth of the technical order while justifying cultural and political imperialism.

....To Europeans, the universe represents actual physical space into which they can impose themselves. Their movement in this respect is never from place to place (they are no longer nomads): it is not *displacement*, but extension. They expand and extend their possessions, never relinquishing territory they claimed. They migrate, but always conquer and consume. By this process they themselves become "bigger". The idea of progress allows for this kind of movement and extension. Conceptually, "progressive" motion consumes all of the past within it, and "progress" is not merely "different from", it is "more than". The idea is, in this way, essentially expansionistic." (Ani 1996: 490)

All the aspects of European culture tie in together and reinforce one another and this expansionistic concept and drive aids the European need to universalise their particular culture.

What then does progress mean in practical terms in relation to European sexual culture?

A central component of the idea of 'progress' is change and newness. As suggested earlier; this concept of progress goes far beyond the achievement of concrete objectives and is so powerful in the European (and Europeanised) psyche that any change, anything new or different is easily cloaked in the garbs of progress and therefore accorded a measure of respectability and serious consideration. Though these acts of newness or change may initially receive a hostile reaction from the general public, the intelligentsia regard their role as one of educating the ignorant masses and are aware that the drum of progress beats strongly in most European hearts and that the culture will eventually give way to the inevitability of 'progress'.

Within the realms of sexual behaviour the concept of 'progress' places a heavy strain on those Europeans – and other peoples with Europeanised minds – who do not have an insatiable appetite for experimentation. Incredible amounts of media coverage are devoted to making people feel inadequate, frigid, repressed, inhibited and just plain sexually dull if they are not willing to try new sexual positions, techniques and practices to keep their relationship 'alive'. If you read the lurid columns of newspaper 'agony aunts' one will find repeated instances of men – and less often women – writing in to complain that their wife/partner is unwilling to be sexually adventurous and that their sex life is dull.

These complaints usually amount to the desire of the male for the female to engage in acts such as anal sex, bondage, sado-masochism or even wife swapping. It is often the case that female prostitutes say that the reason cited by many of their married/cohabiting clients for using their services is this unwillingness of wives/girlfriends to fulfil the man's sexual fantasies. However, when one observes the rubbish and condom strewn alleyways where many of these sexual encounters with street prostitutes take place it makes you wonder how literally 'dirty' these men's fantasises are, especially when one observes the often wretched and pitiful physical appearance and condition of many of the crack/heroine addicted prostitutes whose services they use.

Europeans have a strange psychological attraction for dirt, grime and filth (Baruti 2004). This longstanding 'relationship' is reflected in the Caucasian male excitement at activities such as female mud wrestling and observing women urinating or even defecating as forms of sexual stimulation for which some pay prostitutes. The increasing extreme presentation of blood, gore and filth is a part of this cultural trait as well as a subconscious (on behalf of the producers/writers) process of desensitising the viewing audience to fully embrace this aspect of the culture. A typical, seemingly harmless, example occurred in a highly sexualised medical comedy 'The Green Wing' which aired on Channel 4 in the UK. In one particular scene a man walked into a bathroom to find the subject of his attraction sitting drunkenly on the floor. He bent down and after a brief conversation kissed her passionately only to be told a few seconds later by the woman that she had just been violently sick in the toilet, which accounted for the 'bits' around her mouth.

In another example of this cultural attraction to dirt and filth I recall an incident related to me by a medical student from Leicester University. He told me about a US student named Brian, whom I had met previously, who had attended an end of academic year party thrown by some medical students. In keeping with tradition; a huge amount of alcohol was consumed and Brian had started to get amorous with a female medic. Apparently he indicated his desire to 'go down on her' only to be told that she was 'on' her period. Undeterred; he told her he did not mind and proceeded to perform cunalingus on her behind some bushes in the grounds of the building where the party was being held. Upon returning to the party Brian was greeted by looks of shock and horror. When he asked what was wrong he was told that his face was covered in blood. Far from being embarrassed he reassured those present that he had not cut himself and explained how he had got himself into such a condition.

Allied to the above I am aware that it is quite common for Caucasian men to have sex with their partners whilst they are on their period.

In another vein, I once met a brother who told me about how a Caucasian male whom he had met through work, had; after several weeks of sharing his perverted sexual history and in conversation – presumably to 'soften' the brother up – invited the brother to come around to his house to have sex with his wife whilst this individual observed the act. He assured the brother that his wife was 'well up for it'.

Now, whilst I am not suggesting for one minute that all Europeans engage in the foregoing types of sexual behaviour, nor that some Afrikans do not participate in these types of behaviour, what I am suggesting is that these types of extreme and perverted forms of sexual behaviour naturally flow from the European cultural well and that the reader should be clear that these types of sexual preferences are not as rare as one might imagine.

So, the European cultural sexual drive is for newness and change. Change is progress, progress is good, and hence any changes to sexual behaviour must be good. As mentioned earlier, the only bar on new forms of sexual behaviour is the question of individual consent. If consent is given by an adult who is deemed mentally capable of giving informed consent then any sexual act is acceptable.

Part of this process of sexual progress involves the need to sexualise new parts of the body as boredom inevitably sets in with the 'traditional' sexual organs. Once Caucasians had gone through all the orifices, which was very early in their history they had to make do with such innocuous parts of the body as the toes. Of course we know that the 'shoe fetish' is a well established part of Caucasian sexual culture, however they needed to continue to progress and so the feet and toes became inevitable targets for their sexual attention. In one of the most famous examples of this bizarre behaviour, the Duchess of York – estranged wife of the Queen of Britain's son Prince Andrew – was captured in photographs having her toes sucked by one of her lovers. This just reiterates what I am saying that these types of outlandish behaviours become viewed as 'normal' or at the very most 'a little odd' when viewed through the lens of European culture.

So, Europeans having exhausted the orifices and limbs of the human body, have brought a whole range of tools, devices and implements – vibrators, dildos, bullwhips, cucumbers, riding crops, belts, chains, ropes, masks, hoods, bottles etc. etc. – to their sexual practice but still cannot find the ultimate sexual fulfilment and so are running out of new sexual lands to 'discover' and taboos to break. Animals (see later) are slowly moving centre stage and may the Creator help any aliens they may 'discover'!

As a brief interlude which demonstrates the corruption and

breakdown in Afrikan sexual morality I will share the experiences of a friend who works in London. She works for a voluntary organisation and goes into secondary schools where she works with Afrikan girls, focusing upon their personal and social education. During 2004/2005 she was working with a group of girls aged 13-16 at one particular school and after a few months built up enough trust to enable the girls to feel confident to share their personal experiences. During the course of these discussions it became apparent that all were sexually active and one had been sexually active since the age of 11.

This particular girl who was aged 13 at the time left my friend in a state of shock when she revealed that she regularly patronised a particular nightclub which was the haunt of Jamaican 'bad man'. She explained that these men would buy her alcoholic drinks and she would then willingly go to the toilets with them where they would engage in unprotected anal sex. She would have anal sex with perhaps three or four of these men in one night. When my friend asked why she did this, the girl explained that "you can't get pregnant by anal sex". My friend explained all the negative health implications of unprotected sex with multiple partners and the dangers of anal sex; however this seemed to have little impact upon the girl in question. Perhaps I am naïve; however I was utterly shocked when these activities were related to me as well as being deeply saddened. How much further can we fall? Apparently as low as the alien culture within which we live since we seem unwilling to embrace the ways of our ancestors.

So let us now look at the journey of European sexual progress. The following chart is simplified and made linear for ease of understanding, however what needs to be understood is that all the sexual practices described (with the exception of transsexualism, since they did not have the technology) have been present in European culture since there was first an idea named Europe and a people described as European.

European Sexual Progress

Heterosexuality

Bondage/Sadomasochism

Homosexuality

Bisexuality

Transvestism

Unisexualisation

Transsexualism

What Next?

Incest?

Bestiality?

Paedophilia?

Now some of you may think that the last three types of sexual behaviour are beyond the pale even for a people as obsessed with the idea of 'progress' as Europeans. However by taking the concrete example of Transsexuals I will demonstrate how two of these behaviours will move towards much greater acceptance in European culture over the next 20-30 years.

Transsexuals and their supporters would have us believe that they were born into the 'wrong body' in some tragic twist of fate and that 'gender reassignment' surgery (creating new euphemistic language is part of the process of propagandising for acceptance e.g. gay and lesbian as opposed to homosexual) or sex change surgery frees them from this living hell. Now whilst there are a very small number of people born of indeterminate gender – which is likely to increase with the pollution of the food chain and natural environment – this is not the case for the vast majority of people seeking to change their sex.

With widespread public scepticism over this spurious 'wrong body' argument the transsexual propagandists changed tack to more fertile cultural territory and began to emphasise their individual human rights to live the lives they wanted to live. This proved a wise move and with no cultural argument to rebuff this claim the tide began to turn decisively and transsexuals are well on the way to gaining every form of legal and social recognition they could have wished for.

Now let us look at the reaction of the medical profession to this issue. As part of the scientific community the medical profession are highly esteemed as keepers of European society's highly rationalistic, logical and 'objective' ethos. Based upon this idea one would expect the opinion of the medical profession to be impervious to social forces and based purely upon scientific evidence. But, of course this is far from the case. Scientists are part of human society and subject to changing social mores.

In the 1970's and 80's the Caucasian medical establishment was firmly of the opinion that people seeking to undergo sex change surgery – and those experiencing other less extreme forms of gender disidentification such as transvestism – were mentally ill and required counselling. Where the surgery was carried out it was on the basis of relieving mental distress not an acceptance that the individual in question was really born into the wrong body.

Slowly throughout the late eighties and through the nineties and into the 2000s this view of the medical profession has changed. Not based upon any credible scientific evidence, but based purely upon changes in first liberal elite and then wider public opinion, in response to the individual human rights argument cited earlier.

Now, some would say that doctors have overcome their prejudice and are now making an unbiased assessment of transsexuals. Well in order to test this argument we need a parallel test case involving a very similar process. It so happens that there is an excellent test case, namely people suffering from extreme body dismorphia. In these cases the individual in question rejects a part of their body, for example their foot, and will go to extreme lengths such as attempting self-amputation to rid themselves of this part of their body they say does not belong to them. It should be noted that in these cases there is normally absolutely nothing wrong with the limb in question.

I remember reading of two such cases treated by the same doctor in the UK in the 1990's. Eventually after the failure of psychotherapy to relieve the hostility of the patients to their limbs, and after the failed attempt of one to cut off his leg with a knife the doctor granted the patients' their wish and surgically amputated their respective legs (one each). It should be noted however, that even though both patients were apparently much happier and more mentally stable after the operation the doctor was quite clear that both had been suffering from a mental illness that had manifested itself in the rejection of a part of their body. As far as I am aware the medical profession's response to body dismorphia has not changed substantially on the basis that there is no evidence to suggest that sufferers of this condition have any rational basis upon which to reject various parts of their body.

So, there we see the rub. Two conditions involving the irrational rejection of parts of one's body leading to a desire for surgery to remove the offending limbs/organs. In one case which does not involve the sexual organs the medical profession has maintained a clear line and approach, whilst in the other which does involve the sexual organs it is attempting to rationalise the wholly irrational in order to keep pace with public opinion and the 'demands' of European culture. From an Afrikan-centred perspective transsexuals are mentally ill. There is no sane or reasonable basis for transsexualism. If doctors within this culture want to perform surgical mutilation in order to relieve transsexuals mental suffering then that is their business, however Afrikans need to understand the basis for the normalisation of transsexualism which is cultural and has nothing to do with 'Western science'.

I am sure Europeans will soon claim the discovery of the 'transsexual gene', – just as they did with the 'homosexual gene' –

genetics being the new 'silver bullet' to magic away any difficult social and cultural arguments with the unbiased hand of science. It is interesting though that the vast majority of transsexuals are men wishing to become women, however I suppose 'western' science will soon find a genetic reason for this lopsided gender confusion.

Be sure of one thing, Europeans are determined to have their cultural way. On the very day (30 January 2005) that I began writing this piece on transsexualism I listened to BBC Radio 5 in the late morning and heard a commentator suggesting that there should be a lesbian, gay and transgender history month similar to Black History Month to build the self-esteem of members of these groups.

At the beginning of this chapter I promised you predictions for the future of European sexual 'progress'. The three possibilities posed were Incest, Bestiality and Paedophilia. In my opinion paedophilia will not move significantly towards public acceptance (although it has always been widespread in European culture, see reference to the meaning of 'honeymoon' earlier in this chapter). The main reason for this is the question of consent. Whilst children are viewed as being unable to give fully informed consent to sex the culture cannot openly embrace paedophilia. Obviously moves can be made to lower the age of consent. For example in the Netherlands the age of consent is 13. I also recently saw part of a documentary on television in which British children were demanding their 'human rights' to have sex before the age of consent, which is 16 in the UK. However it is unlikely that the age of consent will be lowered to a pre-pubescent age and therefore paedophilia will remain a strong public taboo.

So, what about incest? Well, Europeans have a new euphemistic name for incest, which is always an encouraging sign for the advocates of 'sexual progress'. Apparently incest is now 'genetic sexual attraction'. It must be true; I heard them say so on television in a documentary on the subject. Documentaries and other 'serious' investigations of a subject are also another sign of the process of normalisation. This programme depicted amongst other characters, the story of a man who was reunited with his biological mother, who had given him up for adoption as a child, only to find that she was exhibiting signs of strong sexual attraction after the first couple of meetings. Having cut off contact in disgust he went to a counsellor only to find that she was sympathetic to his mother's 'plight' and encouraging him to be understanding and not too harsh. The programme went through the usual Caucasian rationalisations for the indefensible, laying the foundations for future programmes which will no doubt continue to 'unravel the mysteries' of 'genetic sexual attraction'.

Adult consensual incest fits very well into the pattern of behaviours that should be acceptable within European culture. The problem with incest is its close association with adult sexual abuse of children and hence paedophilia. It is a well known fact that most sexual abuse of children takes place within the family or its immediate friendship circles. However, when (and not if) a test case is brought before the European court of human rights by a consenting incestuous couple demanding recognition of the legitimacy of their relationship the culture will have no defence. This type of relationship will meet the cultural tests of consent and doing no (immediate) harm to others (Caucasians do not understand the concept of harm in its broader cosmic sense) and therefore can only be resisted for a matter of time.

As I mentioned earlier the linear schematic depiction of European sexual progress depicted earlier in this chapter is not strictly accurate since all of the sexual behaviours/practices shown have always been widely practiced to a greater or lesser degree in various European cultures – with the obvious exception of transsexualism for which they have only recently developed the medical technology. The point of the diagram was to show how, over time, these practices have all moved centre stage within the culture of the Caucasian.

Similarly, incest has always been there. Nathan and Julia Hare in their truly excellent book 'The Endangered Black Family' note that "...two San Francisco sociologists claimed that their two-year study indicates that the practice of incest is not harmful psychologically and may be beneficial to your health. In a paper, "The Final Taboo," delivered to a sociology convention in Los Angeles, the incest sociologist was defended by the New York Times columnist Anthony Lewis, Washington Post columnist Mary McGregory, Bryant Gumbel of the Today Show and Carl T. Rowan, syndicated columnist, as well as Tom Brokaw. Even Walter Mondale, on "This Week with David Brinkley" and Senator Robert Dole, R-Kansas, on "Meet the Press," saw fit to hedge on the issue. When Ronald Reagan, shooting from the hip, spoke out against it, he received so much flack that White House Chief of Staff James Baker, in a rare press conference, said the President "obviously misspoke" and that he meant that it is "not the pragmatic thing to do." (Hare and Hare 1983: 176-177)

You see, I am not saying anything they have not already said. It is just that you believe it when they say it! Eventually their culture must embrace adult incest.

Last but not least is bestiality. Not to be left out; bestiality also has a shiny, odour free, new name. Bestiality is now Zoophilia! Bestiality has a long history within European culture and Europeans' strangely intimate relationship with animals, and in particular dogs, has long been a source of fascination combined with repulsion for many Afrikans.

There are many depictions in European art dating back several centuries B.C. of men having sex with goats, sheep, dogs and other animals. These pictures can be found on vases, pots etc. Bestiality was quite widespread amongst Europeans in the pre-Christian period and only became a strong taboo in around the 3rd century B.C.E. In the Middle Ages men or women found engaged in bestiality were hung along with the poor animals. These points were highlighted during a documentary broadcast on Channel 4 in the UK entitled 'Animal Passions' (2004).

This programme highlighted both the irresistible cultural drive amongst Caucasians to tear down all forms of sexual taboo and the shockingly widespread nature of bestiality in the US. It should be noted that this was not the first programme on bestiality broadcast by Channel 4 who are well known for their 'firsts' in UK broadcasting. A few years earlier they had broadcast a programme about a man in the USA and his 'love' for his donkeys. This programme was presented as an examination of the bizarre in human behaviour; however there was a qualitative difference in the nature of 'Animal Passions'. This programme was an insight into the 'zoophilic community' with the participants presenting themselves as everyday normal people who just happened to have sex with animals.

It turned out that there is a thriving and growing internet community of animal sexual abusers as I prefer to refer to them. They seek each other out over the internet not just to share their sexual experiences with animals, but also to seek out human sexual partners with the same sexual proclivity. There was an example of a married couple who met over the internet. They described their first meeting. The woman invited the man to her farm and upon his arrival took him straight away to the barn. In the barn was her favourite pony stallion and she described how she proceeded to perform a sexual act upon the hapless pony to 'break the tension' as she put it. She explained that she knew that the pony wanted her to do this by his state of sexual excitement. Her husband described how this act 'turned him on' and they went on to fondly describe the rest of that evening's sexual activities. It turned out that the pony stallion was at the centre of their sexual lives and the husband relayed to viewers how he often allowed the pony stallion to anally penetrate him in an act which he claimed did not give him particular sexual pleasure, but where he drew his satisfaction from the pleasure derived by the pony.

There was another couple featured who met each other as already practicing sexual abusers of animals. Everything was fine until they started having children. After a while the wife persuaded the husband that they had to stop having sex with animals for the sake of the children. This agreement seemed to hold up until one night the wife awoke to find her husband absent from their bed. Intuition took her down to the barn where she found her husband *in flagrenti* with one of their fillies. With the husband adamant that he could not keep away from the horses the couple agreed to an amicable divorce.

The wife told the journalist how she visits her husband's new home every couple of months to 'see' their pet golden retriever who was her longstanding sexual partner. The husband, happy to be unrestricted in his sexual behaviour, readily confirmed that if given the choice between a good looking woman and a pretty filly, he would choose the filly every time.

In this insight into the sexual underbelly of the USA there were further tales of men and women who had sacrificed their marriages and children for the 'love' of various animals.

Now you may be thinking that these were a few strange people in a vast country of over 260 million people. However apart from the many thousands of people who regularly use the various websites devoted to bestiality what most struck home with me during this programme was excerpts from a church service, full of seemingly ordinary Caucasians in a rural part of the United States. During this service, at which children were present, the minister urged his flock to adhere to the instructions of the Bible and quoting a specific biblical passage urged his congregation 'not to lie down with animals' as it is a mortal sin. The camera focused in upon various members of the congregation who did not seem surprised or shocked by this advice. Why would a preacher make such a statement unless such practices were fairly widespread in his community?

In a strange twist one of the contributors to this tale of absolute debauchery suggested that people engaged in bestiality were not strange, they were just "different, like gay people". (Animal Passions Channel 4 2004)

On first reflection it seems absolutely extraordinary that such a programme could be broadcast on terrestrial television in the UK. However, upon consideration, and if one returns to the analytical template utilised during this chapter – and book – one recognises that it was always just a question of when, not if, such a programme would be aired. The European's need for newness enshrined within their conceptualisation of 'progress' makes it inevitable. Sure there will be intra-cultural battles and divisions; however the European progressives will always win out in the end.

Some Afrikans seem to think that if they strategically concede cultural ground to Caucasians on matters sexual and accept that which they find unacceptable, that Europeans will be satisfied, however they sadly misjudge the nature and character of their reference group and oppressors. Whilst Afrikans are accepting European sexual progress in one area, Caucasians have already moved on to the next taboo to be dismantled. There is no appeasement of Europeans in the arena of sex just as there is no appeasement of them in any other cultural domain. It is their way or the Afrikan highway.

In another illustration of how, step by step, Caucasians are dismantling this taboo, I watched a television interview on a respected news programme, *Newsnight,* broadcast on BBC2 in 2004. The programme's most well known host, Jeremy Paxman, was interviewing Edward Albee the highly regarded Caucasian liberal playwright (who wrote 'Who is afraid of Virginia Woolf') about his latest play that had just opened in a theatre in London's West End.

The play was entitled *'The Goat – Or is her name Sylvia?'* and was about a Caucasian architect who 'falls in love' with and then engages in a sexual relationship with a goat. In what I at first thought must be some sick joke Albee proceeded to explain to Paxman how this was a 'morality play' exploring fundamental human values and that he felt that bestiality was a good vehicle to allow this exploration. So here we had two elite, highly intelligent Caucasian males discussing the fundamental lessons to be gleaned about the nature of human values from the story of a man having sex with a goat!

Even more recently I came across the following report that appeared in the Observer newspaper on Sunday 17th July 2005 and which reinforces my point regarding the slow, inch by inch, almost imperceptible embrace of bestiality within Caucasian mainstream culture. I am absolutely convinced that the following story would not have been deemed newsworthy even ten years ago and this is perhaps the most important aspect of the story, not the depravity and perversion of the person involved, but rather that a respected national newspaper in the UK would deem such a story worthy of coverage.

Man dies after horse sex

"A man has died after apparently engaging in anal sex with a horse at a farm in Seattle, Washington. An autopsy revealed that the man, who has not been named, died due to perforation of the colon, said Sgt John Urquhart of the King County Sheriff's department. Washington is one of 17 US states where sex with animals is not illegal, though sex with smaller animals can be deemed to be a form of animal cruelty which is a crime. A police spokesman said the horse

involved in the incident was not harmed."

It is interesting to note that many states in the US have deemed it necessary to legislate against such activity which would perhaps indicate the fairly widespread nature of such activity. After all why would you legislate against the inconceivable? It is also just as interesting to note that despite this widespread legislative activity 17 US states have decided not to make such activity illegal despite the obvious evidence that bestiality is common in the United States.

It is important for me to re-emphasise that these activities and sexual proclivities are not new to European culture; rather it is just that they have reached a point where they feel dominant enough to reveal their full cultural selves to the rest of the world. For example, bestiality has featured in pornography, which has always featured in European cinema, right from the very beginning of cinematic history, towards the end of the 19th Century. From the very inception of cinema; Europeans immediately began making illegal pornographic films. An infamous example was *'Le Canard'* made in 1895, which apart from large amounts of gratuitous human sex, features several instances of bestiality, including a man having sex with a goose or similar large bird. Much later the film 'Animal Farm' gained cult status and I can remember that back in my student days during the 1980's a Caucasian housemate invited me to stay in one evening to watch Animal Farm with the lads. I politely declined the offer. There are some things best left to other people's imagination.

Sexual progress is everywhere; in February 2005 the British Board for Film Classification gave an 18 certificate rating to the film 'Nine Songs'. This certification allows the film to be shown in any run of the mill cinema in the UK. What is extraordinary about this is that this film has prolonged scenes of the two stars engaged in real sex. There is no simulation, the couple in question had sex on camera as in any pornographic film and it has been granted a certificate for general release. Even the film's director admitted that he never expected the film to get an 18 certificate. The reasoning for this decision was that apparently the British public are not shocked by seeing sex on screen any more. And why would they be when sexual imagery and language is fired at them constantly via all media forms.

European sexual 'progress' is a road to nowhere. It leads to ever more bizarre, alienated and despiritualised forms of sexual practice. Participants are forever reaching for the stars and coming up empty handed. It can only lead to ever increasing levels of relationship break up, emotional isolation and social fragmentation. Europeans want to throw their cloak of sexual culture over the entire planet to normalise their madness. For them the outlandish soon becomes normal. For rightminded Afrikans this is sickness and we need to keep well out of it.

Assimilate/Eliminate Difference

Diversity is one of the great cons and great paradoxes of our time. When Europeans speak of celebrating diversity they are being genuine, if you understand what they really mean by diversity. Since we are 'over here because they went over there' Caucasians have had to come to terms with an increasing range of complexions and features – at least in urban areas – adorning their day to day encounters. Like their Roman ancestors they have decided to grant some of the 'barbarians' citizenship, but just like Rome this citizenship is conditional. It is contingent on demonstrating certain characteristics, qualities and values – Western values.

The citizenship of which I speak is not the citizenship of the British, French or US passport, although in Britain they are bringing in moves – as in the US – to get new immigrants to swear allegiance to the Crown and demonstrate an understanding and positive acceptance of British history and culture, it is the citizenship of cultural inclusion, the citizenship which allows one to join the mainstream, or more accurately Whitestream of these societies.

Caucasians want a diverse society of one hundred different shades and one European culture. They want a world of over two hundred nation states and one European culture. That is the meaning of diversity, the celebration of surface difference as long as there is a unitary, monolithic European cultural core. So yes, within the realms of sexual practice, Europeans celebrate diversity. You can fully participate in the sexual madness I have described above and be embraced within Western civilisation. What diversity does not mean is that you can have views, opinions and beliefs that are contradictory to European culture without facing censure.

You cannot be clear in your unwillingness to join in their sexual 'progress' without facing accusations of being, backward, hateful, or some form of *phobic* or *ist*. The accusatory prefix will depend upon the nature of your refusal to culturally bow, please pardon the pun. It does not matter if you accept that these diverse forms of sexual expression are 'normal' for Europeans and are happy for them to get on with it. No, you must accept these practices as universal, the implication being that since Europeans are the most 'evolved' and superior human beings it is natural that they should be the most sexually evolved and it will take time for the more backward, underdeveloped peoples on Earth to culturally evolve into these newer/'higher' forms of sexual expression.

Biological evolution has proved such a useful and powerful European theory that it is now applied to virtually every aspect of life. Hence those of us who refuse to join the European sexual party are characterised as flat-earthers standing against the course of nature itself, when ironically it is we who advocate the upholding of the laws of nature.

Diversity is the new stick to beat us into submission. Caucasians aim to use their difference to make us all the same. Already Caucasians are using their economic power to direct social policy in Afrikan and Caribbean countries. Mwalimu K. Bomani Baruti (2004) notes how a minister in the Trinidadian government complained about the pressure being put upon him and his colleagues by the EU to adopt more 'liberal' policies towards homosexuality if they wanted to continue to receive favourable aid donations. Similarly the high profile attacks on Jamaican dancehall artists such as Elephant Man, Beenie Man, Vibes Cartel etc. for their sometimes violently anti-homosexual lyrics; is I predict simply a precursor for a full blown assault on Jamaican social policy with regard to homosexuality. Of course the irony is that the Jamaican Prime Minister PJ Patterson has been surrounded by ongoing rumours that he is a homosexual.

In matters sexual, as in all other areas of life, the Caucasian message is simple: culturally assimilate or be eliminated, physically, economically or both.

What Europeans choose to do, Europeans choose to do. What Afrikans choose to do, Afrikans choose to do. This could be the basis for diversity, respect and tolerance. However since Europeans have a universalistic mindset and proselytising desire this is not how things are, and this is not how things can ever be. Just as in every other area of human activity until Afrikans have sufficient power to resist Caucasian power, Europeans will continue to forcefeed us the hemlock of Western civilisation until we believe it is the milk of life. Afrikans have to get off the White cultural breast and stand, culturally self-sufficient and strong, asserting our right to live the Afrikan way.

The 'Race' is Over – Ethnic Cleansing, UK Style

"Practice is Theory Made Manifest"
Professor Wade Nobles

Why would a people engage in 'voluntary' ethnic cleansing? This is a question that must be posed and answered when one examines the issue of Afrikans engaging in 'inter-racial' relationships in the UK. One must also explore the meaning of the word 'voluntary' in this exploration and in the end produce a theory that has credibility in relation to the behaviours people are engaging in, the sociological trends that can be imputed from these behaviours and the outcomes or impact that will ensue from these behaviours.

The theory must not – although this is the most popular 'mainstream' (Caucasian or Caucasianised) approach – be based on an individualised and isolationist approach centring around personal choice and individual psychology, and devoid of political, sociological and historical context.

In my previous book (Grant 2003) I provided a theoretical framework for understanding differential rates of miscegenation between Afrikans and Caucasians in different geographical locations with different Afrikan:Caucasian population ratios. To briefly summarise. The greater the Afrikan population (relative to the Caucasian population) the greater the level of Caucasian hostility to miscegenation. The lower the Afrikan population in relation to the Caucasian population the greater degree of acceptance and active promotion of miscegenation. In the former case it is all about protecting the Caucasian gene pool, whilst on the other hand in the latter case it is all about eliminating the Afrikan gene pool through integration/assimilation.

I previously demonstrated the validity of my hypothesis by examining patterns of miscegenation in Australia, UK, USA, Brazil and South Africa and I shall now examine the current trends in Nottingham, here in the UK, to further validate my ideas and set out in stark terms, for those Afrikan ostriches amongst us, the reality of how White Supremacy promotes, fosters and inculcates psychological dispositions and social policy directives and ideas that are self-destructive to its victims.

Why would a people engage in voluntary ethnic cleansing or ethnic euthanasia? They would do so if they were politically, historically, culturally and sociologically unaware, combined with an individual (often subconscious) psychology that perceived nothing special or unique about their group that was worthy of special effort to preserve and develop. Add in a dose of individualism, loneliness, desperation and in too many cases racial self-loathing and you have the key ingredients.

Let us now look at the Nottingham data and then examine the explanations and implications.

Table 3

	Mixed		Black or Black British		Mixed:Black population ratio
	No.	%	No.	%	
All People	8,370	100	11,562	100	0.72:1
Age					
0-4	1,465	17.6	653	5.6	2.28:1
5-15	3,042	36.3	1,800	15.5	1.69:1
16-29	2,297	27.4	2,176	18.8	1.06:1
30-49	1,250	14.9	4,417	38.1	0.28:1
50-pensionable age	135	1.6	971	8.4	0.14:1
Pensionable age — 74	106	1.3	304	5.0	0.36:1
75+	49	0.6	399	3.4	0.12:1

Source: *2001 UK Census (Nottingham City Profile)*

N.B. Total Nottingham population currently around 270,000. The mixed population heading was not disaggregated, however given the author's knowledge of Nottingham it is safe to assume that they are overwhelmingly the product of Afrikan/Caucasian relationships.

I hope the above table puts the reality into clear perspective. Given the almost exponential increase in Afrikan/Caucasian sexual relationships I postulate (conservatively) that by between 2060-2070 the Afrikan-Caribbean population in Nottingham will be considered statistically insignificant in social policy terms (less than 1% of the total population and probably nearer 0.5%) and there will be less than 50 Afrikan-Caribbean children in Nottingham aged 0-4.

Let me make a quick but important point. This discussion does not constitute an attack upon people of 'Mixed Race'. They represent simply a staging post, a transition phase in the White Supremacist mindset and drive to eliminate Afrikans in the UK. Miscegenation is not about the *browning* of White Britain to create a mixed race utopia as some deluded (and deliberately disingenuous) Afrikans believe. It is about the *whitening* of Black Britain to eliminate the insoluble 'Race Problem' which is US (including those of dual heritage). A little later I will take you through the six stages in the whitening process and how the 'Argentina effect' (see later in this chapter) works. However before we look at earlier attempts elsewhere by Caucasians to achieve these same goals, let us debunk the hype and myth surrounding miscegenation in the UK for the racial 'flat earthers' who keep telling me 'race' is not an issue in 'modern Western societies'.

Let's first examine the mainstream or 'whitestream' sociological explanation for the huge increase (and rate of increase) in Afrikan/Caucasian sexual relationships. The key points with regard to miscegenation from the viewpoint of this Caucasian sociological paradigm are:

- Mixed relationships are a good thing in and of themselves and represent 'social progress',
- Mixed relationships are indicative of 'colour blind' mating,
- The greater the degree of miscegenation the lower the degree of societal racism (an inverse relationship)
- In the modern progressive society people will mix in accordance with their population ratios. E.g. for Afrikans in the UK eventually 93% should have Caucasian partners since this is the proportion of the population that is Caucasian, 5% should

have Asian partners, 2% Afrikan partners, and so on. This is the utopian melting pot dream.

- Miscegenation is about the 'browning' of White Britain.

Flaws in the Caucasian paradigm

- There is no focus on the outcomes of this type of behaviour and who benefits
- Absence of wider political, economic or sociological analysis
- There is no historical analysis or comparative study (e.g. Australia, Argentina, Brazil) since this would draw attention to the long term outcome in the UK and less altruistic Caucasian goals,
- No real focus on why different non-Caucasian groups miscegenate at vastly different rates in the same country
- No focus on how Caucasian behaviour varies dramatically according to their population relative to other non-Caucasian groups, especially Afrikans
- Focuses upon the individual's story, in keeping with Caucasian's high individualised and individualistic culture, as opposed to the group's welfare which is the Afrikan cultural priority.

Just to reinforce the point about the agenda that is being pushed, take at look at this request for participants in a new programme that was broadcast on BBC3:

From: "Joanne Collins" <joanne.collins@diverse.tv>
Sent: Friday, May 14, 2004 7:14 AM
Subject: Contributors wanted for BBC Three programme on Black relationships

Hi everyone, as most of you know I'm currently working on a programme for BBC Three about black relationships.

As part of the programme we'd like to speak to the following people about their experiences:

NB: we are particularly interested in finding contributors of Caribbean origin

- Black women who don't date black men (age 21-40)
- White women who exclusively date black men (age 21-40)
- Black men who don't date black women (age 21-40)
- Black/mixed children who've grown up without their fathers (age 13-25)
- Black single mothers with children by three or more Black men (age 21-40)

Please circulate this e-mail to as many people as possible. And if any of the above sound like someone you know? please let me know or tell them to contact me on the details below.

Many thanks, Jo

Joanne Collins
Diverse Production Ltd
6 Gorleston St
London
W14 8XS

Interesting that she is making a programme about 'Black relationships' but does not seem to want to talk to any Black people actually in relationships with other Black people! If you think this is all by accident you are kidding yourself. It may not all be consciously directed but it is most certainly culturally directed.

A Blast from the Past – Lessons from South America
In my previous book (Grant 2003) I provided an overview of the concerted, deliberate and explicit attempts by Caucasians in Brazil to 'whiten' that country. This was in the context of trying to get Afrikans to understand what the real deal is in relation to miscegenation and Caucasian motivation in relation to this subject.

The following section on Brazil is taken from my previous book and will I hope assist in this process.

In Brazil Afrikans are referred to as Preto (Black) and those of mixed ancestry – the vast majority of whom would be considered Black in the UK – as Pardo (Brown). By the 1980's these two groups constituted 47% of the total population, however since it is well known that many non-white people in Brazil like to classify themselves 'up' the racial hierarchy it is certain that the majority of Brazilians are from these two groups as classified in Brazil.

Let us take a brief overview of the ethnic history of Brazil in order to demonstrate the systematic attempt to 'Whiten' Brazil through immigration and miscegenation.

"A demographic survey completed in 1798 resulted in the following data:

Table 4

Racial Group	Population Numbers	%
Civilised Indians	250,000	8
Whites	1,010,000	31
Slaves	1,582,000	49
Free Blacks	406,000	13
	3,246,000	

N.B. percentages rounded up to nearest whole figure.

The famous politician Rio Branco indicated that in 1822 the Brazilian population was distributed as follows:

Table 5

Racial Group	Population Numbers	%
Whites	1,043,000	30
Blacks	1,930,000	55
Mulattoes	526,000	15
	3,499,000	

N.B. Rio Branco highlighted a total population of 3,800,000.
The composition of the remaining 301,000 people is unknown.

The above survey information was taken from 'Brazil Mixture or

Massacre? (Do Nascimento 1979: 77)

We see clearly demonstrated a Brazil with a majority Afrikan population. This continued to be the case until near the end of the enslavement period in 1888. Between 1872 and 1890 the Caucasian population increased from 3,787,289 to 6,308,198. This was part of a systematic campaign to 'improve' the racial stock of Brazil.

As Do Nascimento tells us "In the 1920's Brazil was subsidizing by law the immigration of European whites (Celts and Nordic races, Iberians, Slavs, Germans, Portuguese, Austrians, Spanish, Russians and Italians) who flooded the labor market and took jobs from Blacks." (Do Nascimento 1979: 76)

He further goes on to highlight the starkly different reaction of the Brazilian authorities when the President of the State of Mato Gross discovered that Afrikan-Amerikans were preparing to take up the land concessions he was offering to people prepared to settle his wilderness state. When the awful news reached the President he hurriedly terminated the concessions notifying the Ministry of Foreign Relations. In response to the reported possibility of large scale Afrikan-American immigration the noted physician and writer Afranio Peixoto pleaded "Will we have enough albumin to refine all this scum? God help us, if he is Brazilian." (Do Nascimento 1979:77)

To exemplify that the whitening of Brazil was no accident but a consistent and concerted attempt at genocide here are a few further quotes to consider:

Scientist Oliviera Viana noted:

"the ethnic group that contributes the largest portion to the "melting pot" has the potential to dominate the make-up of the population, not only in its morphological type, but also in its psychological and cultural type." (cited in Do Nascimento 1979:76)

Arthur Neiva an intellectual supporter of these genocidal policies said:

"Within a century the nation will be white." (Do Nascimento 1979: 76)

By 1950 Whites officially constituted nearly 62% of the

population, Pardos nearly 27% and Blacks 11%. These figures certainly back up the comment of Clayton Cooper a visiting politician from the USA who in 1917 reported:

"An honest attempt is being made here [in Brazil] to eliminate the Negroes and mulattoes through the infusion of white blood." (Do Nascimento 1979: 78)

The foregoing has hopefully given you a clear picture of White Supremacy in action in a country that has successfully sold the world a picture of a 'non-racial democracy', free from the discrimination and prejudice that blights other European dominated countries. Sadly, many Afrikans have bought into this nonsense despite the absolutely appalling treatment meted out to Afrikans in Brazil over the years. Caucasians in Brazil worked damned hard to get into the majority, which they have lost in recent years, however they realise that as long as they can keep the so-called Pardos racially disidentified they can maintain control. This racial disidentification comes in many forms including allowing non-whites – even those with dark brown skins – to classify themselves as white.

Giorgio Mortaro, the leading Brazilian demographer of his time, is quoted by Do Nascimento on this subject of racial reclassification:

"Those born from unions between brown-skinned and black-skinned people are classified as white: and through the reclassifications the black group loses a great deal and gains but little, the brown group gains much more than it loses, and the white group gains a great deal and loses nothing." (Do Nascimento 1979: 79)

Caucasian Brazilians like to talk of class rather than race, but since most Afrikan-Brazilians are poor and most European Brazilians are not, this is the thinnest of disguises behind which to hide White Supremacy.

You only need to know the history of the Portuguese as a slave trading and colonial power to understand how vicious the system of White Supremacy is in present day Brazil.

Diagram (iv) – Inter-racial relationships where there is a majority Afrikan population

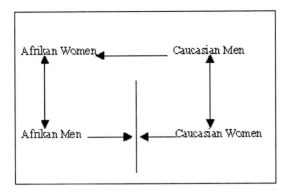

The above diagram shows the dynamics of inter-racial sexual relations under White Supremacy where there is a large minority; or majority Afrikan population. As can be seen, intra-racial sexual relationships are unrestricted. Caucasian men also have free access to Afrikan women. The arrow is one way to highlight the power dynamics i.e. almost invariably in societies such as Brazil or Azania, the Caucasian man is of much higher social class and has the Afrikan woman as a mistress or concubine, whilst maintaining his public relationship with his Caucasian wife or girlfriend. Remember, I am looking at the generality not exceptions.

Sexual contact between Afrikan men and Caucasian women is restricted since the Caucasian woman is needed to produce Caucasian children and the Caucasian man cannot risk her being impregnated by the Afrikan man. Naturally, where the Afrikan population is small this barrier disappears and Afrikan men gain free access to the 'highly prized' Caucasian woman.

Afrikan-Brazilians have been sold a bag of tricks by their Caucasian oppressors who are hell bent on exterminating their Afrikan biological and cultural identity. Unfortunately, due to the language barrier Afrikans in Brazil have been somewhat sidelined in the Pan-Afrikanist movement which is a shame given that if the so-called Pretos and Pardos realised they have more to gain as one, they could take control of Brazil.

Take note, in 1798 62% of the population of Brazil was classified as Afrikan (Black). Today, around 5% of the Brazilian population is classified as Black (although we know that this is a huge underestimation due to people classifying themselves 'up' the racial hierarchy). What do you think will happen to a people who represent less than 2% of their country's population – as is the case for Afrikans in the UK – where the oppressor group is as equally intent on eliminating them as the Caucasians in Brazil were and are? You know the answer already.

The Argentina Effect

I have always wondered about Argentina. From my earliest memories of watching international football I always wondered why Brazil and Argentina, two great footballing rivals from the same continent had such different looking teams. Brazil's greatest teams have always strongly featured Afrikans and other non-Caucasians of various mixed descents. In fact whenever the Brazilians have whitened their football team their results have suffered.

Argentina on the other hand has nearly always been represented by a team of Caucasians with the occasional hint of non-Caucasian blood in a few of their players. Why the difference when we know – or perhaps more accurately, should know – from the historical record that plenty of Afrikans were kidnapped and shipped to Argentina. Where did all these Afrikans go? What happened to them?

There is, perhaps rather surprisingly, an extensive bibliography on the history of Afrikans in Argentina. One example is a book by Francisco C. Morrone 'LOS NEGROS EN EL EJÉRCITO: DECLINACIÓN DEMOGRÁFICA Y DISOLUCIÓN' (1995) which explores the reasons behind the rapid population decline and eventual disappearance of Afrikans in Argentina. In his review of this book Roberto Pachecho of Florida University highlights the active denial of the present day Caucasian population of Argentina of the presence and cultural impact of Afrikans in Argentina (1997).

"Ask the typical Argentine about what he or she knows of Argentina's black population or that country's African heritage and one is likely to receive one of two responses. The first and perhaps most common response, at least according to George Reid Andrews, is the categorical denial on the part of most Argentines of the existence, past or present, of Afro-Argentines. This opinion is especially common among residents of Buenos Aires; ironically, it was the port of Buenos Aires which served as an entry point for African slaves destined for the mines and estates of the Viceroyalties of first Peru and then of the Río de la Plata and eventually the Argentine confederation from the sixteenth to the mid-nineteenth centuries.

Moreover, Africans were especially visible in and around the city of Buenos Aires, whether as domestic servants, day laborers, urban slaves, militia members, or as *gauchos* (cowboys), field slaves, and peons in the countryside. Despite this history, *porteños* (natives of the city) insist on telling themselves and their visitors that "There are no *Negros* in Buenos Aires" (see George Reid Andrews, *The Afro-Argentines of Buenos Aires, 1800-1900* [Madison, 1980], 3).

The second response, while acknowledging the historical presence of Argentines of color, often denies an African component in Argentina's culture. Concomitant with this opinion are questions about the fate of Afro-Argentines. What happened to them? How did they disappear from the population and the national consciousness?" (Pachecho 1997)

Morrone's work clearly establishes that both in the colonial and post-colonial periods the Afrikan presence in Argentina was massively under reported (*en un número mucho más elevado al que se le asigna* [11]).

In 1810 Afrikans constituted around 30% of the population of Buenos Aires. This is an important statistic to remember when one considers that in the UK, the city with the largest, in relative and absolute terms, Afrikan population is London, where Afrikans currently make up around 10% of the population (around 700,000 people) and where around 75% of all Afrikans in the UK live. If the Afrikan population of Buenos Aires could be eliminated so quickly, why not the Afrikan population of London and the UK?

Morrone suggests that the Afrikans in Argentina were reduced to almost invisibility as a result of miscegenation, disease, and warfare

(13-18). Pacheco notes that "It is well-known that throughout the Americas blacks intermarried and "passed" for white. Moreover, nineteenth-century nation-builders favored the whitening of their populations. Thus, positivist politicians and social theorists supported massive European immigration as a means to not only add laborers to nascent industrializing economies but also to whiten ("improve") the Creole populations of Latin American republics. Unfortunately, Morrone does not address these issues at all; instead, he dwells on the colonial practice of buying legal "whiteness" (*gracias al sacar*) and miscegenation during slavery (15-17)." Pacheco (1997)

Pacheco makes some important points. In my previous book (2003) I highlighted the active miscegenation policies of the Australian government during the 1950's when they kidnapped more than 10,000 Aboriginal children in order to 'raise them as white' with a view to psychologically conditioning them to marry Caucasians and aid the genetic elimination of their people. There is a film 'Rabbitproof fence' which depicts these events. The Australian government of that time also enacted immigration policies designed to encourage white immigration.

If we move to present day Europe we see the countries of the European Union building 'Fortress Europe' via policies such as the Schengen Agreement and desperately keen to keep Afrikans out. Similarly in the USA we see the welcome afforded to Caucasian Cuban refugees, in contrast with the so-called liberal President Bill Clinton's illegal decision, during one of his two terms in office, to blockade Haiti during a period of extreme unrest in order to prevent Afrikans refugees landing on US shores. Of course this did not prevent his many Negro supporters from inhaling deeply at the merest hint that he was about to pass wind!

According to Morrone, disease was a second major factor in the disappearance of Afrikan-Argentines. He correctly observes that the lack of medical care severely reduced the numbers of Afrikans in Argentina. Afrikans were especially decimated by frequent plagues throughout the eighteenth and nineteenth centuries, especially yellow fever (1871).

There is a clear parallel here with the contemporary decimation of

Afrika by the AIDS pandemic which was created by Caucasian scientists as the ultimate tool for population control. In the contemporary situation the Caucasian elite sit by wringing their hands as Afrika suffers, just as they did in Argentina. Pacheco (1997) suggests that it is ironic that the health and well-being of Afrikan-Argentines worsened after emancipation, a phenomenon he notes was common throughout the Americas (18); however his surprise, or failure to correctly interpret this phenomenon, is due to his lack of recognition of the functioning of White Supremacy.

During the enslavement period Afrikans had a clear and beneficial function for Caucasians. After emancipation, the Afrikan presence became increasingly viewed as problematic. Afrikans became obsolete, just as the tractor made the horse and plough obsolete in rich countries. What do you do with obsolete equipment? You discard it and leave it to rot. So, naturally this is what Caucasians did in Argentina, Brazil and many other places. This is partly what Haki Madhubuti was referring to when choosing the book title 'Black Men: Obsolete, Single, Dangerous? (1991).

In the UK and USA we have reached this point. Afrikans; and Afrikan men in particular, are viewed as obsolete. The post European Second Tribal World War labour shortages of the 1940's and 1950's, which catalysed the British **requests** for Afrikan-Caribbean immigration; are long over, and just as in the US a service oriented post-industrial society does not need strong Black backs and does not wish to share the spoils of a knowledge based economy with Afrikan men. Therefore prisons are the new plantations and concentration camps, drugs (creating violent destructive crime) and disease (AIDS in particular) are immediate solutions and miscegenation the long term answer to eliminating the 'race problem'.

Returning to Argentina Pacheco notes that "we find that the most devastating factor accounting for the disappearance of Afrikans in the Río de la Plata, however, was the endemic warfare of the nineteenth century. Beginning with the English and French invasions of Buenos Aires in the century's first decade and continuing through the wars of independence, the civil wars, and culminating with the war against Paraguay (1865-1870), Afrikan-Argentines volunteered for and were conscripted into the military. Domingo F. Sarmiento (favorably) commented on the way war diminished Argentina's black population (see *Conflicto y armonía de las razas en América*, 2 vols. [Buenos Aires, 1900]).'' (Pacheco 1997) It is again worth drawing comparative parallels. In the US war against Vietnam Afrikan-Americans who constitute 13% of the US population made up 33% of US troops and 43% of US casualties. When it comes to dying for their causes Caucasians are always willing to make us more than their equals.

Similarly, Morrone notes that about 40% of San Martín's army that crossed the Andes was Afrikan-Argentine [56]). He provides statistics on slave recruits, black troops, and casualty rates. He notes that Afrikan-Argentines were disproportionately killed or wounded in battle (31), correctly suggesting that they were used as cannon fodder (*carne de cañón*).

In his review Pacheco makes a crucial point. He says that "Morrone correctly emphasizes the triple effects of miscegenation, disease, and war as factors in the decline of Afro-Argentines. Unfortunately, he often does not relate one to the other. For instance, when discussing miscegenation he only briefly relates it to the absence of black males killed in war (97). Afro-Argentine battle casualties indeed encouraged miscegenation between black women and immigrant males, since black male-to-female ratios were skewed. Nineteenth and early-twentieth-century European (read white) immigration to Argentina is not even discussed in this study.'' (Pachecho 1997)

I hope you have spotted the parallels again to the current situation in the UK. The supply of marriageable Afrikan males available to Afrikan women has been massively reduced by Afrikan men partnering with Caucasian women, the economic devastation of Afrikan men, imprisonment and capture in their system of criminal injustice, mental illness caused by living as conquered men, drugs and homosexuality (which is being actively promoted to Afrikan men). The Afrikan woman is now alone and lonely and ripe for picking by Caucasian men who twenty years ago would not have stood a cat in hell's chance of being allowed through the gates of heaven.

Everything is in place for the final push to eliminate the Afrikan presence in the UK. The Caucasian policymakers in the US are watching closely and already picking up on the lessons being learned over here.

Where once Caucasians used crude and blatant techniques for eliminating Afrikans, they are now more refined and sophisticated in their attempts at genocide. Certainly wherever they are in the clear majority they have learned the benefits of *killing us softly with their love*. Voluntary ethnic euthanasia is the most effective and efficient method of all and leaves the murderer without bloodstained hands.

Morrone's work amply demonstrates that Afrikans in Argentina were totally marginalized. Afrikan-Argentines were not citizens; Argentina was (is) a racist, colour-conscious nation that excluded Afrikans. Furthermore, Pacheco notes how "the nation's intellectual founders consciously "whitewashed" Argentina's history (what Paul Gilroy has called "strategic silences")." (Pacheco 1997)

In addressing this issue I believed it to be vital to provide the reader with a clear historical example of the successful ethnic cleansing of a significant Afrikan population since; so many Afrikans, particularly those with Caucasian partners, insist on living in this fantasy world where it is believed that you can never eliminate 'dominant Black genes' and where they imagine that in the years to come a significant proportion of 'Mixed Race' people will consider marrying Afrikan people and thus maintain an Afrikan presence. Why they think 'Mixed Race' people will want to marry members of a despised and downtrodden group when most of the members of that group themselves do not even want to marry each other, I do not know. At present in the UK over 75% of Dual Heritage (Afrikan-Caucasian) individuals have Caucasian partners and this figure is rising as fast as for Afrikan/Caucasian relationships.

This fantasy seems to be particularly strong amongst some Afrikan women with Caucasian partners who think that as their children's primary carer they will provide a strong Black identity (for those who have not completely run away from a Black identity) and hence their children will consider taking Black partners. Time will prove the vast majority of them wrong and self deluded.

In the final part of this discussion I will take you through the stages that will occur in the virtual elimination of the Afrikan population in the UK during this century.

Six steps to Whiteness
Stage 1 – Initial contact

This covers the period from the late 1940's through the 1960's. During this period there was still a great deal of hostility to miscegenation – particularly from Caucasian society – however the deepseated psychosexual fascination between Afrikan men and Caucasian women, together with residential proximity, inevitably drew them together, and mixed relationships, though initially uncommon, grew steadily. Afrikan female/Caucasian male relationships were extremely rare.

Stage 2 – First a trickle then a flood

This period covers the 1970's and 1980's. During this period Afrikan male/Caucasian female relationships increased greatly and the media began to slowly recognise this growing trend (although they still felt more comfortable representing Caucasian males with Afrikan females, as in the TV sitcom 'Mixed Blessings'). During the mid 1980's there was a slow but definite increase in Afrikan female/Caucasian male couplings.

Stage 3 – The Dam breaks – The coffee coloured dream

During the 1990's mixed relationships lost all form of taboo within the Afrikan community and began to be strongly represented as a clear sign of societal racial progress and became the norm for Afrikans aged under 30. Virtually every famous Afrikan in the UK had taken a Caucasian partner and large numbers of Afrikan women gave up on waiting for a Black man and decided they just wanted a man. For younger Afrikan women Caucasian men became their partner of preference. In cities such as Nottingham; Mixed Race children came to outnumber Afrikan children during this period.

Stage 4 – The Silent Elimination Begins – Rise of the Near Whites
This stage covers the period 2000 – 2025. As the large, young and increasing Mixed Race population matures they will overwhelmingly choose Caucasian partners and produce a new generation of Near Whites (this term is not intended as an insult). Some of these children will be able to 'pass' for White, however in virtually all cases they will be psychologically and culturally Caucasian. During this stage, outside of London and Birmingham, there are very few Afrikan children being born to Afrikan couples born in the UK and the age profile of the Afrikan population begins to rise rapidly.

Stage 5 – Decline of Mixed Race people, Death of the Afrikans
Between 2025-2050 the Mixed Race population will stop growing very suddenly as there will be insufficient Afrikans in the appropriate age categories to produce children with Caucasians, and since relatively few Mixed Race people enter into relationships with other Mixed Race people their population profile will begin to age rapidly. The Near White population will have reached adulthood in significant numbers by this stage and will begin to produce Caucasian children with Caucasians, thus completing the circle.

Stage 6 – Death of Mixed Race people and Absorption of Near Whites
During the period 2050 to 2070 I predict that one will see only an insignificant number of births of Mixed Race children and a dwindling number of Near White births. The Mixed Race children who were born in the 1990's will be ageing and there will be no one to replace them. Near Whites will continue to have children with Caucasians and by the end of the 21st Century there will be only a tiny number of children of full or part Afrikan descent in the UK.

The only intervening factors that can prevent the predictions set out in stages 4-6 are; firstly, a continued influx of Afrikan immigrants (which Caucasians will do their level best to prevent) or secondly, a change in the psychology and behaviour of Afrikans i.e. Afrikans choosing Afrikan or Mixed Race partners.

Under White Supremacy in the UK there are three relationships to be discouraged and these are:

- Afrikan to Afrikan
- Afrikan to Mixed Race
- Mixed Race to Mixed Race

The foregoing relationships must be discouraged since they suggest or have the potential to create pro Black racial consciousness and increase/maintain the Black population.

On the other hand there are three types of relationship to be encouraged and these are:

- Afrikan to White
- Mixed Race to White
- White to White

These relationships are to be encouraged since they all have the potential to either destroy Afrikan racial consciousness (and genetic presence) or build Caucasian unity.

I hope that my predictions are incorrect; however everything I have seen, know and have read tells me that I am right.

It takes two (Afrikans) to Tango

It is ironic that at a time when Afrikans in the UK are rushing headlong towards oblivion there is a rebirth and flowering of Afrikan pride in places such as Uruguay, Peru, Columbia and Costa Rica where Afrikans have suffered from extreme racial disidentification under a more subtle, but just as insidious, form of White Supremacy. It is also noteworthy and ironic that in Uruguay, which is featured in the following text, this rebirth in Afrikan pride has taken place after the decimation of the Afrikan population in that country over the past two hundred or so years. The following extracts are taken from an article written by journalist Sebastian Rotello that appeared in the Los Angeles Times on 3rd February 1998.

"…..Argentina's black population all but disappeared, decimated in the 1800s by yellow fever, intermarriage and massive military recruitment of blacks, who then died in wars. In Uruguay, people of African descent accounted for about half the population two centuries ago; they now number about 189,000 in a nation of 3.2 million.

Awakening Interest in Recent Years

Traditionally, Afro-Uruguayan culture received little attention—inside or outside the country—except during Carnaval, the festival this month when costumed candomble drummers and dancers take to the streets.

Recent years, however, have brought an awakening. Books and academic conferences on racial themes proliferate. An outspoken black leader—a former maid who has become a writer and activist—ran for Congress in 1996 on the ruling Colorado Party ticket. ....And in a gesture of recognition, Montevideo, the capital, erected a waterfront statue of Yemanja, the goddess of the sea in the African-based Umbanda religion, which has adherents from across the ethnic spectrum.

"There are more and more institutions devoted to African culture, some younger and with international connections and others that are more traditional and conservative," said Ruben Galloza, 71, a painter and candomble composer in Barrio Sur. "They are not always united—they pull in different directions."

.... the region has become a fertile field of study for U.S. experts on African American culture. Although many Americans know very little about Uruguay, African American scholars have shown a keen interest, organizing academic conferences and specializing in themes such as the work of Afro-Uruguayan literary figures.

In contrast to Argentina, where dark-skinned people often are referred to insultingly as negros (blacks), little Uruguay – known as the Switzerland of South America – prides itself on a history of prosperity, social welfare and tolerance. Unlike its conservatively Roman Catholic and class-stratified neighbors, Uruguay legalized divorce long ago, welcomes political refugees and offers accessible quality education to all.

That atmosphere has kept race conflict to a minimum. Many Afro-Uruguayans see no need for racial politics or alliances. ...But there are few black university graduates or government officials in Uruguay. Poor health, housing and job conditions are the result of paternalistic racism, according to Galloza.

'We Allow Ourselves to Be Dominated'

"The racism is not direct like it was in the United States, where black people, upon being rejected, organized and became strong," Galloza said. "Blacks in the United States fought and demanded. In contrast, in Uruguay, we don't demand. We are dominated and allow ourselves to be dominated."

African slaves and their descendants figured prominently in the founding of Uruguay and Argentina. In the late 1700s, Montevideo became a major arrival port for slaves, most brought from Portuguese colonies of Africa and bound for Spanish colonies of the New World: the mines of Peru and Bolivia and the fields and cities of Argentina and Uruguay.

...By 1834, when Uruguay abolished slavery, documents described African dance rituals in Montevideo and the countryside known as tangos, with the accent on the second syllable. The word referred variously to the drums, the dances and the places where the religious rituals were held. Therein lies an intriguing musicological tale about the obscure origins of the tango, one of the best-known Latin American musical genres.

The tango developed simultaneously in Montevideo and Buenos Aires. Although typically regarded as the creation of Italian and Spanish immigrants, the tango's music and the dance movements associated with it were deeply influenced by African dance and music, according to experts.

The modern tango is an offshoot of African dances, the experts say. The new form shed the drums in favor of the guitar and the bandonion, a type of accordion, and melded with immigrant musical influences: habaneras brought by Cuban sailors; Andalusian melodies from Spain; and nostalgic Italian folk songs. The sound and lyrics of the hybrid product combine driving rhythms and blues-like lament.

The beat and the roots remain African, according to Galloza and others.

"The rhythm of the tango, more than the tango itself, was, is and will be black," Galloza said. "It evolved with the lyrics and everything, but the base is black."

Despite the lack of definitive documentation, most Argentine scholars agree on the African origins of the word and the fundamental role of African dances. In the Buenos Aires of the late 19th century, African-derived dances survived in the remnants of black communities in old port neighborhoods. Curious new immigrants from Europe and gauchos from the countryside frequented the dances. Later, they simultaneously imitated and mocked the black dancers, creating a style of their own in waterfront dives and music halls.

"In the brothels, they imitated the dances they had seen," said Eduardo Rafael, a Buenos Aires journalist who is an authority on the tango. "The form of the dance has a very strong African influence."

Nonetheless, the emphasis by white and black Uruguayan connoisseurs on the tango's African aspects has caused a spirited dispute in Montevideo's cultural circles. Galloza accuses critics of trying to "whiten" history.

"There is a lot of debate about this issue of the tango. There are those who say it's reverse racism," he said. "But let those who disagree tell me where it's from. The word is black. It's like saying that the word 'tarantella' is not Italian." ...."

The latter section of the article above concerning the attempts to culturally steal and 'whiten' the tango is an example of an absolutely classic and typical Caucasian response to Afrikan culture, and is highly instructive to events we see unfolding in contemporary Britain and the US. The article in effect describes the cultural piracy that Caucasians have perfected and made their own. In my previous book (Grant 2003) I described the various stages in this process as follows:

- Condemn
- Copy

- Co-opt
- Misappropriate (Steal)

You can see these stages described in the article starting with the mockery (condemnation) and copying through to the latter two stages. It is interesting that we see this same process repeated time and time again and still we see Negroes falling over themselves to assist in the theft of their cultural legacy. In the UK we have the MOBO (Music of Black Origin) Music Awards where already we see the not so subtle attempt in the title to take our music away from us by referring to Black Origin and not simply Black Music. It naturally follows that one of the benchmarks for the success of these 'integrationist' awards is the number of non-Afrikan award recipients. However Music of Black Origin is still too Black for these New Age Afropeans and their Caucasian cultural masters and now Black music is to be totally assimilated under the new nom-de-plume 'Urban Music'.

Apparently there is no 'Sub-Urban Music'; however there is 'Urban Music'. Afrikan cultural creation is now reduced to a description of the type of physical landscape that most of us live in. Of course these processes are all about creating racial/cultural dis-identification under the guise of racial non-identification or racelessness. What Caucasians present as their new 'raceless' cultural agenda is of course the same old tactic of dressing up White Supremacy in universalistic clothing. They tried to steal Jazz – however even their prodigious capacity for lying was overwhelmed by truth – they have stolen Rock n' Roll, they have stolen Rock (they can keep that), now they want contemporary R'n'B and Rap (with their dutty little Eninem). Of course none of this is possible without Negro Gate/House Keepers who are there to mouth the lines and arguments fed to them, like cultural automatons incapable of independent thought.

These processes are all about Cultural elimination/euthanasia which is a necessary corollorary/precursor for biological elimination. Once a people give up their culture there is no reason for them to exist since their culture is what gives them purpose and makes them unique. The world does not need anymore White people in Blackface.

The latest example of this Negro/pseudo-liberal agenda is the Emmas (Ethnic Minority Multi-cultural Awards). The article below says it all.

Diversity awards slammed for honouring Beckham
GG2.NET NEWS [25/05/2004]

Bling enough? How black are the Beckhams?

DAVID Beckham was awarded for multicultural achievement last night, but the honour has been condemned as "insulting" by a leading race campaigner.

The Ethnic Multicultural Media Awards (Emma) gave David Beckham the award for sporting personality of the year.

"David Beckham represents everything the Emmas stand for," the Emma Foundation's Bobby Syed said.

"He's a sportsman who crosses all multicultural boundaries and represents a positive message that all cultures on this island influence our daily lives."

But the decision was criticised by Piara Powar, director of the Kick it Out campaign, which aims to stop racism in football.

"It's an insult to those of us who are from an ethnic minority or who are black," Powar said.

"The way he defines himself, as a young, urban, hip lad, does not make him an ethnic minority.

"I can see how it gives the awards publicity, but I don`t see how it helps encourage youngsters from ethnic minorities. I don`t think he`ll understand why he`s got it."

The award, presented at a ceremony at the Grosvenor House Hotel in London, was given a year after a documentary described the England captain as "Britain`s most famous black man".

The television programme 'Black like Beckham', described the England star as an icon for Britain`s black community because of his taste for designer clothes, his choice of music and his jewellery.

Beckham is a fan of all things "bling", has a tattoo of the dead rapper, Tupac Shakur, and a large collection of hip-hop records.

He shared his award with a biological Black man and then footballer of the year, Arsenal`s Thierry Henry, who of course is married to a Caucasian.

Art Malik and Parminder Nagra won the awards for best male and female television actors while The BBC`s exposé of police racism, The Secret Policeman, was awarded best TV documentary.

It is a deepseated inferiority complex that drives Negroes to believe that any Caucasian who copies the dress, speech or any other superficial 'Black' cultural representation is paying us some sort of homage and therefore must be rewarded and praised. The Negro fool who made the programme 'Black Like Beckham' was of course attempting to be ironic, however it was also indicative of his desperate craving for fame and Caucasian attention and approval. We can be pretty sure that he awakens to the wrong kind of inspiration in the mornings!

Mexican Backlash

We are now moving into Central/North America as we look at the fears of Mexican nationalists that their youth are being damaged by their mimickery of Afrikan-American hip-hop lifestyle. If you look beneath the vicious racial hatred directed at Afrikan-Americans – which in itself is a sign of how deeply acculturised into aspects of

Caucasian culture this individual is – there are some interesting and relevant points made by the author.

It is clear that as cultural nationalists these Mexicans feel their way of life is under attack and these are some of the very same concerns that Pan-Afrikanists express in relation to the imposition of European cultural values on Afrikan people; wherever we are located. The willingness of their youth to embrace a foreign sub-culture is high on their agenda and by the same token Pan-Afrikanists lament the increasing acculturisation of our youth in service of White Supremacy.

Therefore, I have no qualms about the desire to defend and protect one's culture, what I do criticise vehemently is the half-baked analysis which leads the author of the following text to conclude that Afrikan-Americans are making a conscious effort to brainwash Mexican youth and usurp traditional Mexican culture. If only our hip hop stars had such planning and strategic skills and such a sense of loyalty to Afrikan people that they saw their music as a means of waging war on behalf of their people. If only we were so lucky! Sadly this is far from the case. And if this was the case would Mexican youth be a priority for indoctrination? Most of our hip hop stars have only two masters to whom they pledge allegiance, the first is their ego and the second is their bank account.

The hatred towards Afrikans within the following text speaks for itself and speaks to a person who is ignorant of world history and contemporary political and economic affairs. It is clear that this person does not even have a grasp of such basic facts as who controls the music industry and wider media outlets within Mexico and the US.

Subject: Mexican cultural nationalist speaking on Hip-hop Music...
From the La Raza Unida email list:
Ce-Tekpa Toltekoa
Mexican-Jaguar: For Honor and Glory!
Chapter Three:
On the Music of the Negroid
Edited by Lorena O. Ramirez.

"Assimilation, acculturation, melting pot, half-monkeys, and mongrels the methodical and systematic indoctrination of the Mexican youth. God forbid!

Thinking it is completely harmless, African-American hip-hop/rap music is swallowed without a clear understanding that the consequence on the Mexican psyche results in Mexican youth becoming `black' and ignorant and stupid.

This should not be confused as saying that the African-American music is bad, but rather that it is bad for the Mexican people in general. Everything that is Mexican for Mexicans!

......How are we going to proclaim the ways of the ancestors, by rapping? ...If we are to survive as a culture, we must prohibit and persecute and root out all those wannabe Negroid-Mexicans, and seek the formation of a strong cultural Mexican Movement. But why must there be a choice to be made between Negroid and Mexican? Why must we even choose between Negroid culture and Anglo-Saxon culture, as though we lack culture ourselves? Why do we have to be either a Negroid or a Caucasoid? (Black and White? I say stay BROWN.)......

It becomes obvious that Mexican individuals who forsake their race are neither members of our race nor relatives of ours. They constitute a different breed, a community of half-breeds, half-humans and half-monkeys, imps and little chimps...

...Who can guarantee the cultural existence of our nation if we are given as role models a dumb and ignorant people with no tradition, history, culture and language?

.........In observing the Mexican youth of today emulate the Black sub-culture, it is not uncommon for one to witness a lost generation which resembles little chimps in clownish attire throwing their little slogans like: `west side' or `yo yo wad up G'.........

The way I see it, if you behave like a Negroid, then you are a Negroid; therefore, you must be treated like a Negroid (Just the same, if you look like a Negroid and have the Negroid personality, then, you must be a Negroid!)

Exterminate the brutes!

.........Songs conveys ideas. And we interpret these same ideas to mean `something', and the impression that these ideas create in our sub-conscious produce the immediate effects that are visible for anyone to see (violent behavior, change of character, different style of attire, bad English diction, etc), and thus, such African noises actually have more power than people believe. Yet, we are all aware of this.

The fallacy then that defenders of rap and hip-hop make is that such music is universal…Such musical creation gives interpretation to the African-American experience in the United States. It is not music for the intellect, but a burst of African emotions and tribal rhythms. The reactions that it causes to different racial people is not the same as the reactions that it is supposed to cause, to inspire, to the African community (living in the United States)…

…..Hip-hop is not universal……….

We must have a definite ideology, an ideology that is rightfully and truthfully ours. We must write and speak the language of our people. We are bound culturally to our nation. The ideology of the African American is very misleading because it is neither African nor American; it is nothing but a mirror image of the slave consciousness………

There are no choices…… Our race above all else!

We feel instinctively that music moves, disunites, unites, guides, misguides, and influences people…and we find in hip-hop the feeling of powerlessness expressed in their violent behavior and vulgar English diction.………

We must prevent the animalistic, foreign, and barbaric culture to rule us like satraps………

I shall be the first to denounce openly the political-racial of the black sub-cultural movement known as hip-hop in line with the Mexican cultural movements……

Our ideological foundation assumes only one thing: Mexico for Mexicans (and, `Our race above all else!')………At present, I am being pointed at with hatred and hostility because my faithfulness and my loyalty are to my people and my ancestors,…

…If we are to give free reign to the unrestrained and immoral and chaotic African sub-culture, as is presented to us in the United States, then we must be prepared to look at our cultural eradication passively while our enemy grows strong and bold……

But who are behind the mammoth music industry?...Who controls
almost all broadcasting radio stations? Do we own our `own'
Mexican radio stations here in the United States?..... We have
been denied the right to broadcast our sentiments, while Anti-
Mexicans can use the radio for their anti-Mexican
propaganda:........

We have been infected by the constant repetition of
acculturation, assimilation, adoption of foreign ideas,
interracial marriage, and other nonsense.

...Let Mexicans unite and own their own newspapers and
radios so that they can instill in the Mexican the ancient
Mexican warrior discipline (e.g., http://www.aztlan.net)...

The music presented to the Mexican youth on radio and
television is...based solely on capitalistic foreign
principles.

Everything in life is political; thus, to assume that Hip-hop
lacks a
socio-political philosophy is just complete ignorance.

Mexican, we must become an example to other Mexicans!
MEXICAN, STEP FORWARD!

There are interesting parallels between the foregoing thoughts and
those of a 'mulatto' advocate which were set out in my previous book
(Grant 2003). In both cases there was an extreme anti-Afrikan
sentiment conveyed, with both authors having clearly internalised
Caucasian racist philosophies and ideas. In both cases they are quick
to blame Afrikans for their woes, which are clearly due to their
subjugation by Caucasians.

In the above extract the author asks who controls the music
industry? Well you would have to be pretty stupid not to be able to
answer that question. The same people who conquered and control
Mexico. If indigenous Mexicans controlled Mexico they would have
control of their radio stations and would be able to better protect
themselves from the perceived assault of hip hop. Just as if Afrikans
had not been conquered by Caucasians some of our youth (and
adults) would not now produce some of the vile, violent, misogynistic
trash that passes for 'Black music', whether in hip hop, dancehall,

RnB or other Black musical genres. The author targets his/her telescopic lens at the wrong, but easy, target. It is easy to disrespect a people who manifest a widespread lack of self-respect, but much harder to take on the real enemy who runs Mexico and the world.

They speak of a return to the traditional values of Mexican culture and yet the irony is that there is nothing traditional or Mexican about his/her racial epithets directed at Afrikans. By adopting the language and philosophy of the Caucasian racial hierarchy s/he simply places him/herself towards the bottom of the racial ladder along with all the other 'Browns', although s/he may take comfort in feeling that s/he is still above the Blacks. If the author really wants to return to the roots of his/her culture s/he may wish to ponder the giant Olmec heads (see photograph below) which would tell him/her of a different, more respectful relationship between their ancestors and mine.

The Olmec Heads are colossal stone sculptures that came out of the ancient Mexican Olmec civilisation which commenced around 900 BCE. The photograph below was taken at a museum in Barcelona in 2004 where they have lifesized reproductions of the Olmec Heads. As soon as I saw the colossal stone head I was filled with an incredible excitement. I had read about these sculptures but to see and touch and stand against an accurate reproduction was like reconnecting with a piece of our history in a very real and wonderful way.

You will notice that the face does not look like any Mexican whom the aforementioned Mexican nationalist would recognise. This is clearly an Afrikan face. So why would one find huge depictions of Afrikan heads in Mexico? Well, the following quote by Jose Meglar that appeared in the bulletin of Mexican Society of Geography and Statistics provides the answer:

"In 1862 I was in the region of San Andres Tuxtla, a town in the state of Veracruz, in Mexico. During my excursions, I learned that a Colossal Head had been unearthed a few years before.... On my arrival at the hacienda I asked the owner [of the property where the head was discovered] to take me to look at it. We went, and I was struck with surprise: as a work of art, it is without exaggeration a magnificent sculpture... what astonished me was the Ethiopic type represented. I reflected that there had undoubtedly been Negroes in this country, and that this had been in the first epoch of the world." (Meglar cited in Browder 1994: 209)

Naturally, later Caucasian scholars tried to undermine Meglar's honest and straightforward words, however in 1939 a researcher Matthew Stirling excavated the same Olmec head that Meglar had described and which he realised was carved from a single block of basalt. The huge head was around eight feet in height, eighteen feet in circumference and weighed more than ten tons. The following quote from Stirling reinforces and confirms the conclusion reached by Meglar.

"...It presented an awe inspiring spectacle. Despite its great size, the workmanship is delicate and sure, its proportions perfect. Unique in character among aboriginal American sculptures, it is remarkable for its realistic treatment. The features are bold and amazingly Negroid in character." (Stirling cited in Browder 1994: 210)

Tony Browder in his brilliant book 'Nile Valley Contributions to

Civilisation' goes on to summarise some of the evidence of an early Afrikan presence in the Americas and in Mexico in particular. He tells us that sixteen heads have been identified in various parts of Mexico which were sites of the Olmec civilisation and that they range in weight from ten tons to an astonishing forty tons.

At these various Olmec sites a large number of skulls and skeletons were unearthed and "A careful study of them lent support to the theory that there was a significant African presence within the Olmec population. In September, 1974, at the 41st Congress of Americanists in Mexico, Dr Andrzej Wiercinski, one of the world's leading skull experts, announced that African skulls had been found at Olmec sites in Cerro de las Measa, Monte Alban and Talactilco.

Wiercinski's evidence noted that at the pre-Classic cemetery of Talactilco, 13.5% of the skeletons examined were found to be African,...." (Browder 1994: 211)

Tony Browder goes on to tell us that it appears that Africans arrived at the pre-Classic stage of the Olmec civilisation and then over time were absorbed into the general population. He suggests that probably no more than 500 Africans (all of whom seem to have been male) made the journey to the Olmec civilisation and that given that the helmets depicted on the Olmec heads are "identical in every detail to those worn by Nubian soldiers in Africa between 948 and 680 B.C.E." (Browder 1994: 211) as well as the "typically Ethiopian braided pigtails, ending in rings and tassels" (Alexander von Wuthenau cited in Browder 1994: 212) of the colossal stone head of tres Zapotes No. 2 that it is most likely that these Africans travelled to the Americas from the Nile Valley.

For further information on this subject I would suggest the reader obtain the excellent book 'They Came Before Colombus: The African Presence in America' by Dr Ivan Van Sertima.

Now, of course the museum in Barcelona did not mention any of the foregoing facts in their display information especially since it would destroy the myth of their beloved Cristobel Colon (Columbus) 'discovering' the Americas and 'West Indies'. Similarly it seems that contemporary Mexican nationalists are unaware that we have met before under much happier and more respectful circumstances.

So What?

This is the question that has to be posed and responded to, because it is the argument that underpins the pseudo 'brotherhood of man', colour blind rhetoric of Caucasian leaders and policy makers in the UK. It is also an argument implicitly and occasionally explicitly supported by Negro integrationist leaders (most of whom have Caucasian or non-Afrikan partners) such as Trevor Phillips, head of the Commission for Racial Equality who speaks glowingly about his children being part of a coffee coloured future for Britain and who says forget colour we are all British.

The genetic elimination of Afrikans in the UK does not matter if you believe, firstly that Afrikans have nothing unique and special to contribute to humanity that is worth preserving, and secondly if you believe that Afrikans in the UK cannot make a worthwhile contribution to the worldwide struggle for Afrikan liberation. Obviously, many of our people do not even believe there is – or should be – a worldwide struggle for Afrikan liberation.

The second point relating to the contribution that UK Afrikans can make to the worldwide struggle for Afrikan liberation is important, since although we make up only a tiny fraction of the worldwide Afrikan population, in economic terms we punch well above our weight. In worldwide terms we are amongst the richest Afrikan populations and our greatest contribution to the struggle can be made via developing trade and economic links with Afrikans in Afrika and worldwide. So there is a vital global reason to preserve a significant Afrikan presence in the 5th richest country in the world.

Afrikans in the UK have boarded a train without carefully checking the departures board. They think the train is travelling from John O' Groats to Birmingham, where they have friends and relatives, but in reality the destination is Lands End and over the cliff edge to oblivion. When the train sweeps past Birmingham some of the passengers will realise that there is a serious problem, however by then it will be too late unless someone is brave enough to pull the emergency cord to stop the train.

A people without an instinct and desire for survival, do not deserve to survive and will not survive. Since the Afrikan Turkeys in the UK seem intent upon voting for Christmas who can blame Caucasians for killing us softly with their love.

I hope this chapter will have opened some eyes and caused serious pause for thought. If you love your people and have teenage children get them to read this chapter at least, if none other, and discuss it with them. The drive to eliminate Afrikans in the UK is well under way, relentless and some would say irreversible. I also hope this chapter acts as an early warning system to Afrikans in the US where a similar assault is in its earlier stages.

Loving, Raising and Rearing Afrikan Children

There is nothing more important than the development of the next generation of Afrikans. Children are our immortality, hope and reason for continued struggle. Whilst there are enormous opportunities for group development open to Afrikan people on the continent and worldwide, the challenges are also enormous. On the motherland the combination of the AIDS pandemic, economic austerity measures imposed by the IMF/World Bank etc. and corrupt leadership has created an Afrika with per capita income lower in absolute terms than twenty years ago and the scourges of war, poverty, hunger and disease stalking the land. In the UK and USA one finds the Afrikan family in crisis, economic inequality increasing amongst Afrikans – mirroring wider social trends – and increasing alarm at the levels of so called 'Black on Black' crime, mental illness amongst the young, educational failure and to be honest every other symptom of social meltdown. Afrikans in the Caribbean – and parts of Central and South America – seem to be going through a sort of intermediate experience with some of the extreme absolute poverty of the poor world combined with the myriad psychosocial ills of Afrikans in the rich world.

Now of course these are generalisations. There are rich Afrikans in Afrika and desperately poor Afrikans outside of Afrika; however as a broadbrush description I believe the foregoing has some validity.

In this chapter I will be exploring how those of us living in the so-called 'Western world' should be rearing our children. Whilst I will be using Afrikan principles I will generally restrict my discussion to this geo-cultural area because I believe the circumstances of Afrikans in the UK can be readily translated to those of Afrikans in the U.S, Caribbean, Canada and Europe whilst I am not so sure that this is so true with regard to the motherland, apart from in terms of the need to return to (and create anew) the Afrikan way for Afrikans wherever we live.

It is important too for those of us living in the UK to understand that we are living in an anti-child environment. Even amongst Europeans I believe that the British are considered one of the most child unfriendly people around. I have had some experience of other European nations and this is certainly my experience. I have previously briefly touched upon Caucasians' uniquely emotional relationship with animals and nearly everyone must be familiar with the Caucasian saying that 'A man's best friend is his dog'. In accord with this belief the myth surrounding the formation of ancient Rome says that the city's two founders, Romulus and Remus, were suckled by a female wolf. In the UK the charity that provides sanctuary for donkeys receives greater donations than Mencap the leading national mental health charity. Similarly the RSPCA (Royal Society for the Prevention of Cruelty to Animals) receives greater donations than the RSPCC (Royal Society for the Prevention of Cruelty to Children). In all the non-material aspects of life this is not a good place to rear children.

At the time of writing this I am 39 years old. Within the course of my lifespan there have been seismic shifts in the nature of Afrikan family life in the UK. The one thing that has remained constant has been the pattern of negative social, economic and emotional outcomes for Afrikans in the UK. However, as Mari Evans points out, as the implementation of White Supremacy has changed Afrikans have become confused and lost focus and purpose in our childrearing:

"As the society has changed, so have our perceptions of ourselves and of our relationship to the society. And as a result, so have our childrearing patterns. As long as oppression could be clearly identified, African Americans coalesced around the maintenance of values that insured the rearing of what was known then as "race men and women." When, in response to struggle and pressure, the forms of racism changed from overt to covert, the perceptions held by African Americans changed; somewhere along the way we lost our clear view of racist forms and started "hoping more than knowing"." (Evans 1995: 287 [in Moore, Sanders and Moore eds]) The Relationship of Childrearing Practices to Chaos and Change in the

African American Family, African Presence in the Americas, Trenton, NJ: Africa World Press 1995.

One of the ten attributes of the soul that the Kemetic Neophyte (trainee priest) was expected to achieve was 'Steadfastness of Purpose'. What was true then is true today and it is this loss of purpose to which Mari Evans attests and it is this loss of a sense of common struggle that is one part of our childrearing problem.

So let us start at the beginning, but before we look at parenting through the child's ages let us define what we are talking about. I will once again return to the work of Mari Evans who provides a distinction between raising and rearing children:

"[R]aising is "providing for" while rearing is "responding to". Raising can be satisfied by providing the essentials: food, shelter, clothing and reasonable care. "Rearing" is a carefully thought out process. Rearing begins with a goal and is supported by a clear view of what are facts and what is truth (and the two are not necessarily synonymous). Rearing is complex and requires sacrifice and dedication. It is an ongoing process of "preparation"....Obviously, something *different*, some carefully thought out *process*, some long-range *political* view is present when one has a clear sense of one's reality and, therefore, intends to rear presidents, rulers, or *free men and women* (Evans 1995: 306 [in Moore, Sanders and Moore eds]) The Relationship of Childrearing Practices to Chaos and Change in the African American Family, African Presence in the Americas, Trenton, NJ: Africa World Press 1995.

The 'Love' to which I refer in the title to this chapter is not real love, but rather that misguided belief that parental love is synonymous with complying with a child's every request, particularly in relation to material demands, caving in to tears or temper tantrums, condoning destructive or rude behaviour with phrases such as 's/he's tired' and generally giving in to every childish whim and desire. This love believes that its measure can be counted in pounds, shillings and pence and therefore will put the household finances in peril to satisfy their 'little darling'. This love is at the heart of the spoilage of a large segment of a whole generation of Afrikan children. This love is self-indulgent and abrogates its responsibility to draw clear boundaries and make unpopular, but necessary decisions. This love is often an over-reaction to the parent's negative perceptions of their own experience of being parented. Because they feel they were raised under an overly harsh regime they swing the pendulum to the other extreme and raise their child in a chaotic, permissive, boundaryless, over-indulgent and capricious regime. The rotten fruit that is harvested comes as a surprise to no one except the parents themselves. As the saying goes, *'the fruit never falls far from the tree'*.

An example of this type of 'love' was depicted in a TV programme 'Supernanny' broadcast on Channel 4 on 06 April 2005. The supernanny in question is sent in to sort out parents who have children whose behaviour is out of control. In this instance the parents had four children aged 4,6, 8 and 10, two of whom were completely rotten and the other two who were not much better. They were violent to each other, the mother and household objects as well as being extremely verbally abusive. The father was reasonably strict and able to control their behaviour and sanity returned to the household when he returned home from work. The mother who did not have an outside job was weak, ineffectual, indulgent and downright pathetic. She said her husband was too strict and did not want to be like him for fear that the children would grow up not to love her. The way her four year old child rewarded her for her 'unconditional love' was to spit in her face and call her a f—-ki-g b-t-h. Her response to being showered in saliva was to whimper "now that's not very nice is it?", to which the child succinctly replied, "no it's not."

This mother was the epitome of poor parenting. Instead of dealing with her obviously deepseated psychological issues and fear of rejection she was allowing these emotional faultlines to cause her to abrogate her parental responsibilities. In many ways she was as emotionally needy as her spoilt children. What such parents seemingly fail to understand in their emotional immaturity and foolhardiness is that they are not only failing their children but that they are failing the wider community that will have to deal with all the future anti-social behavioural problems that their indulgence is storing up. However, in a society without extended family structure and little notion of reciprocal community obligations there is very little help and support for such parents aside from the few who are scrutinised by such TV programmes or until they are slapped with Parenting Orders by the Youth Offending Team, by which time the behavioural die is usually cast.

Planning your Children

When I tell some people that my wife and I planned how many children we would have, when we would have them and the age gap we wanted, they react with incredulity and say something like 'you can't plan things like that'. My response is why not? People with sense plan all the important decisions in their life. Just because there are factors at play over which you have no control does not mean you should not plan. As was noted earlier in this book: "The plan is nothing, planning is everything" (General Eisenhower).

The decision to have children is the most important decision any adult will have to make in their domestic life and the most important act that any adult will play a part in, in their domestic life. How can something like that be left to chance. I am astonished when I hear of couples who separate because they fall out over whether they should have children or not, particularly after they have got married. How can you get married or commit to a long term relationship and not have discussed and agreed such a fundamental issue. Start as you mean to go on and if you start without a plan, without agreement and without a common set of goals and principles that is how you will parent together...or more likely apart.

Conception and Pregnancy

Start as you mean to carry on. Most people don't pay much heed to the emotional circumstances surrounding the conception of a child.

I believe it was Dr Patricia Newton who developed the term 'post-traumatic slavery syndrome' to reflect her belief in the inter-generational transmission of trauma, particularly with respect to the passing from one generation to another – down to the present generation – of the trauma experienced by our ancestors during the enslavement period. Certainly most people are well acquainted with generational cycles of repeated behaviour and the plaintive cry of politicians, social scientists etc. (when the behaviour is deemed negative) of 'how do we break the cycle'. Now the types of behaviour that are normally under scrutiny are due to family/community socialisation as well as the broader social and economic environment and this applies to post-traumatic slavery syndrome. However one factor that is often omitted is the physiological transmission of behaviour/response patterns from mother to child leading to repeated psychological outlooks.

What I mean by this is that all of the emotions experienced by a woman during pregnancy are experienced directly and proportionately by her child. Different emotions and emotional states elicit different physiological responses including hormone production. If a mother experiences fear or anxiety her adrenal glands will be activated and send adrenaline coursing through her circulatory system to prepare her for 'flight or fight'. There will be an increase in heart rate, dilation of the pupils and all the other symptoms of fear. The child in the womb whose circulatory system is directly connected to the mother's will experience all of these physiological responses even if they are not consciously aware of fear. If the mother experiences repeated exposure to fear, anxiety, anger, frustration and other stress inducing emotions this can have an immediate effect upon the heath and well being of the mother and child, but also the long-term psychological disposition of the child.

A baby that has been carried by a woman who has had repeated exposure to fear/anxiety/anger/frustration inducing situations is much more likely to be clingy, cry excessively even when dry/fed/warm etc. be physically tense and prone to aggression as a child. Every Afrikan woman on a slave plantation would have been repeatedly exposed to these types of negative stimuli i.e. psychologically traumatised and what Dr Newton has been trying to get us to consider are the long-term psychological effects of 20 successive generations of trauma upon a people. How do you think a people treated in this way would behave? Look around you at our communities and you will see the answer.

Unlike the eminent Dr Newton I have no medical, psychiatric or psychological qualifications, however I have eyes to see, a brain to interpret and analyse, and a heart to feel, and I have come to the conclusion that one of the most interesting things that happens to people who are repeatedly traumatised is that they operate out of a state of 'anticipatory fear', that is they are almost waiting for the next exposure to trauma to happen and act as if they are being traumatised even when the traumatic stimulus is removed. These trauma induced responses in effect become their 'normal' behaviour. Since we know that children model their own behaviour from that of their parents and other significant adults it is not surprising that a cycle of traumatised behaviour is established and becomes tremendously hard to break.

It is therefore paramount that pregnant women should be protected as far as is possible from all forms of stressful stimuli and there is a special responsibility upon the husband and/or father to create a protected environment for the mother of his child. Men should avoid arguing with their wives/partners at the best of times, but especially during pregnancy; brothers need to find ways to diffuse disagreements and adopt a conciliatory approach. One of the problems that we have is that our crumbling family structure – leading to a lack of practical and psychological support – and weak economic situation, leading to financial worries, are exactly the right conditions to produce stress in a pregnant woman. This is aside from the inter-generational effects referred to earlier.

The economic stresses referred to above are one of the many reasons why it is advantageous to plan a pregnancy. A planned pregnancy is much more likely to be a budgeted pregnancy with sufficient financial provisions made to cater for the many new and one-off expenses.

One of the most scandalous and despicable of all male behaviours is when men are unfaithful to their expectant wife/partner and use lack of sex as an excuse. To think that a woman is putting her body through the strains of pregnancy and the best way her man can think to reward her is to go and have sex with another woman. If a man will do that to you when you are pregnant he will do that to you anytime.

Plan your pregnancies, plan your conceptions, conceive in love and gestate in love.

Birth – 6 years

Just like pregnancy it is good to have a birthplan, although it should also be recognised that you may need a contingency plan as things do not always work out as envisaged, particularly with the first child. Also with most women in the rich world delaying their first pregnancy until a later age (the average age for giving birth to a first child is now over 30 in the UK) there is a slightly increased risk of complications. The best age; physiologically, for a woman to give birth is in her early twenties.

I think the best advice is to speak to as many women as possible about their experience and consult closely with your doctor about your options so that you are informed and prepared for all circumstances. I would strongly advise both parents to attend ante-natal classes even if the father decides that he will not be present at the birth.

In a fragmented world of nuclear and now sub-atomic families any processes or rituals that have the capability to bring the parents' circle of family and friends together in a spirit of active consciousness must be highly valued and maintained/restored. It is for this reason – as well as others – that the Afrikan naming ceremony is so important, since it offers a time and space to reaffirm the reason for producing children, reiterate the need for and commitment to collective 'community parenting' by all those present and an opportunity to acknowledge our Afrikanity and all that that should mean. There was a time when being a God-parent was perceived as a serious commitment, great honour and position of great responsibility. Sadly, that is all too often no longer the case in our world of ephemeral, fleeting relationships.

One of the biggest mistakes we make is to follow the childrearing fads and fashions of Caucasians. As a rule Caucasians have very little to teach us about childrearing. Despite the material wealth of 'the West' you will generally not find a more rude, arrogant, opinionated, disrespectful and ungrateful child in the entire world than the 'Western child'. These traits are a direct result of the highly individualistic, 'dog eat dog' culture of Caucasians, as the last vestiges of collectivism and communitarianism break down in these societies.

Unfortunately, since most Afrikans do not know where they are going any road will do and since the 'Western' road is brightly lit, well signposted and nicely paved, it is this route of least resistance (in the short run) that is chosen. It is only when the Afrikan lemmings have taken that fateful step over the edge of the cliff that they have pause for thought.

Take sleeping with your child as an example. Caucasians in their strange anti-human way decide that the best thing for a child after nine months in the warmth and comfort of the womb is not only to be put straight into a cot, but to put the cot in another room away from the mother. Stop and think. Don't you see that this must be disorienting at best and traumatising at worst for a baby. Which mammal can you think of that is in any way similar to humans that dashes away its young to sleep away from the mother. The only time a mother in the animal world would leave her young would be to hunt/forage for food and amongst pack animals the young would be left with another adult member of the group. Afrikan mothers have been sleeping next to their babies for time immemorial without problems. Suddenly Caucasians say it is not the modern thing to do so we follow like Black Sheep. They decided bottle was best, so we all went to bottle, then breast was best so it is back to breast. In Afrika you have poor mothers wasting money buying formula milk which is then made up with unsterilised water leading to illness and sometimes death in the baby, all for the desire to copy people in the rich white world who it is assumed know and do best. Companies like Nestlé market formula milk as if it is some high status product in Afrika and other poor parts of the world. Fortunately long-running campaigns by Afrikans in Afrika have led to the closure of Nestlé factories in various parts of the world and increased the awareness of poor women.

A word to the wise. Formula milk is not as good as breast milk and formula milk is better for Caucasian babies than it is for Afrikan and other non-Caucasian babies. Afrikan women have far higher levels of certain key minerals in their breast milk than Caucasian women. Formula milk is based upon the mineral and vitamin make up of the Caucasian woman's breast milk. Therefore Afrikan children are being left with a mineral deficiency when they are raised on formula milk (Afrika 1998). This is not an attempt to guilt trip sisters, this is just simple fact. Many of our health problems are caused by our failure to adhere to the laws of nature which is compounded by the pressures of so-called 'modern' or more accurately 'anti-human' society. Always remember products such as formula milk are created for profit and convenience not to maximise health.

The spoilage of Afrikan children begins young. As parents in the rich world have fewer and fewer children so there is a tendency to concentrate more and more emotional attention on these children. Many working parents, particularly sisters, who are often left to raise their children single-handedly, experience severe guilt over their inability – due to the demands of work – to spend sufficient 'quality time' with their children. For those parents who are not emotionally strong and clear about appropriate parenting this guilt can lead to a tendency to over-indulge their children and give in to unreasonable demands to alleviate a tantrum. A child should get nothing for tears. You see embarrassed parents in supermarkets pleading with their screaming, emotionally overwrought toddler who has thrown him/herself on the floor and all too often some form of bribe is offered to persuade the child to behave reasonably.

Whenever my children threw tantrums I had two responses. In the house, or some other place of safety, I would simply step over them and leave them to it. It is amazing how quickly the screaming stops when there is no audience. In a public place such as a supermarket I would simply pick them up, put them over my shoulder and carry on with the shopping. No matter how hard they screamed or struggled I would keep repeating calmly "I will let you go when you stop screaming and are ready to behave." Since I was a lot stronger than them I always won and it only took a few of these experiences for the tantrums to disappear never to return. Bend the tree whilst it is young and establish the pattern for the rest of the child's childhood i.e. you are in charge not them. The tail does not wag the lion.

When it comes to discipline I do not hit my children. I did hit my son a few times when he was younger, but decided it was not a productive way to discipline him and have never hit my daughter. There is huge debate around this subject and I am not one who believes that hitting your child automatically causes serious long-term psychological harm, however my experience leads me to believe that there are better ways to instil self-discipline – which is the only true discipline – in a child.

Parenting is not a democracy it is a benign dictatorship. Too many culturally unbalanced Afrikans are all too ready to abrogate their parental responsibility in service to Caucasian ideas about giving children choices in almost everything. Too much choice can be even more harmful than too little and when you see parents indulging small children who refuse to eat their dinner and 'giving them what they want' you can see a recipe for disaster, pardon the pun. The point of food is to nourish the child's body and mind and give them the energy to think and grow. Children do not know what is good for them; they only know what they like, which is normally the sugar and salt laden processed food that most get exposed to at an early age. I hear parents saying things like you can't make them eat it if they don't want it. Well, I must be a bad parent in these people's eyes because I have made my children eat lots of food they didn't want because I understand that they are focused upon wants and I am focused upon needs. And the most amazing thing is how they come to enjoy foods they initially used to screw their face up at. The hardest part and key to parenting is knowing how much power to relinquish as the child grows up, as one moves from dictator and instructor to eventually become advisor. However 0-6 is not the age at which to end the dictatorship!

7-12 years

As the world of the child becomes more externally focused to the outside world, as they form strong peer friendships with children with whom they have significant contact outside of school, so the strength of the foundation you have laid for your child will be tested and become clear. They say show me the boy/girl at seven and I will show you the man/woman and this is remarkably true. By seven many enduring behavioural and personality traits have become embedded into the child's way of dealing with the world and the longer any negative characteristics are left unchallenged the more difficult these will become to alter.

This second half of childhood is crucial in shaping and moulding the future adolescent and then adult. One of the most talked about issues facing Afrikan people is the raising of Afrikan boys. Male development is the crucial issue and problem facing planet Earth since men are, and have been for the longest time, wreaking havoc on women, children, as well as the flora and fauna of the planet. When one examines the sheer scale of male violence against women and children across the globe it is amazing how little specific attention is paid to the socialisation of boys.

It is only now as Western societies become ever more fragmented and individualistic and the notion that increasing material wealth automatically leads to increasing human happiness is shown for the fallacy it always was, that there is serious consideration as to why male violence remains so high, why young male suicide is on the increase and why young male mental health appears so tenuous. All these ills are writ large across the Afrikan male community in the UK, North America, Caribbean – and probably whole world – and the question of male development is now high on the agenda.

One of the problems we have had in discussing male development has been the tendency of some Afrikan males with what I can only describe as 'issues' to blame the problematic behaviour of too many of our boys on the seemingly ubiquitous Black single mother. These men are quick to point out that it takes a man to teach a boy how to be a man and yet when many sisters point out that they would be only too glad to see the father(s) of their children take responsibility for teaching their sons how to be men, turn their fire on sisters and say that the fathers keep away because Black women have poisoned their children's minds against them.

Now whilst it is often said that there are two sides to every story – which is not the same as two truths to every story – and whilst I know Black women who have used their children as a weapon to get back at their former partner, there is absolutely no denying that too many men abandon their children after splitting with the mothers and yet are all too keen to start new families – and supposedly take on additional financial and non-monetary responsibilities – when they have not even discharged their responsibilities to their existing children.

The love and support of a **stable** father is of vital importance to rectifying the imbalance in the Afrikan family. Even if the father does not live with his children he can still be a father to them. It is not all about money. Too many women use financial contribution as the benchmark of fatherly commitment and too many men use lack of money as an excuse for ducking out of their wider parental responsibilities. A father should contribute what he can afford. Not what he feels like paying, but what he can afford. Child maintenance payments should be the highest priority after paying for his own food, clothing and shelter. Not money for the bookie, for alcohol, or for entertainment, but money for his children.

In terms of male development, Years 0-6 are mother's time, from 7 onwards it is father's time. What do I mean by this? I do not mean that only one parent has a legitimate role to play during each of these two specific timeframes. What I mean is that when a boy reaches a certain age his father needs to become a more central figure in his development and as the boy develops; introduce him, bit by bit, into the world of men. If the parents live apart and particularly if they have just a single male child, then the parents need to seriously consider whether the boy should go to live with his father. Mother provides a type of nurturance that the father will find difficult to replicate and father provides a type of nurturance that the mother will find difficult to replicate. Put these parenting energies together and you have balance, Ma'at. In the film 'Boyz in the Hood' Cuba Gooding Junior who played the lead role was sent by his mother to live with his father played by Laurence Fishburn when he was about twelve and she was having difficulty controlling him. In the film his mother was wise enough to realise that her son needed male energy and it is important that sisters do not perceive such acts as failure but rather as insightful parenting. As I noted earlier, it is better for this transition to take place at age 7 or 8 rather than much later as a response to problematic behaviour.

Now obviously the biggest problem with this scenario is that even if mothers were prepared to let go of their sons, there are too many fathers who are not prepared to accept their sons. In these cases mothers need to try to draw upon brothers, uncles, cousins, male friends etc. to offer support, guidance and counselling to their sons to help them navigate the road to manhood.

Do we have a problem with single parent households? Undoubtedly yes. Is this the fault of Afrikan women? Undoubtedly no. The problem is that human beings are social, pack animals designed to live in groups, clans or what we may term the extended family. This is the best environment in which to learn how to parent and in which to raise children. This 'developed world' has created under-developed social structures which cannot serve the purpose they were designed for. This is why it is so important to think about whose legs you lie between or whom you allow to lie between your legs. Every sexual act has the potential to create life and parenting can be a pretty lonely business these days, so you need to be damn sure that you wouldn't mind being bound to this person for the next twenty odd years via the conduit of a child.

'Force ripe never good' as my father often told me during my childhood and I now fully understand what he meant. Just like those force fed battery chickens injected full of chemicals during their brief lives – and water after they are dead – too many of our children are force ripe. Children may be physically bigger (taller and fatter) than previous generations, however they are not necessarily more mature. Too many people equate the oversexualised 'adult' behaviour of many children as signs of emotional maturity. They could not be more wrong. There are two fundamental issues as I see it.

The first is that due to what I can only put down to diet, the age at which children begin puberty is falling significantly. There was a report in the Guardian newspaper in the UK a couple of years ago which highlighted scientific research which indicated that the age at which girls were commencing menstruation was falling by six months every 40 years. The report noted that it was not uncommon for girls as young as eight or nine to begin menstruation and that this trend was particularly marked amongst Afrikan-American girls. It was suggested that the increased consumption of meat – which has been injected with steroids and all sorts of other chemicals – in the contemporary diet and the high levels of oestrogens in the water supply and consequently food chain; was another contributory factor.

The second issue is that children are exposed to such a barrage of adult; conversations, images and ideas that they are literally robbed of their innocence. The exposure to media is so wideranging that it is almost impossible for concerned parents to monitor and control their child's media diet. The pendulum has swung full circle and where once there was peer pressure – particularly amongst girls – not to engage in sexual intercourse at a young age, now I hear of Afrikan girls being teased by their schoolmates because they have not lost their virginity at the grand old age of thirteen. Of course the story I related earlier in this book about the thirteen year old girl engaging in anal sex with multiple adult men is indicative of an extreme end of this continuum; as well as the spectre of male sexual exploitation of children.

Too many children are placed in an (warped) adult world, with adult pressures and concepts and simply cannot cope. In a world which is obsessed with the physical and material, it is believed that bigger children equates to more grown up children when nothing could be further from the truth. There has never been a generation of children with less responsibility and more choice. In past generations with much larger families many children had to learn how to look after younger siblings, carry out significant household chores and deal with much greater levels of poverty. Now this is not to say there are not children acting as carers or living in poverty today in rich countries, what I am suggesting is that many of the playstation generation do not understand the meaning of material hardship (although many are emotionally deprived), just as when compared to my parents' generation I do not know the meaning of material hardship. The problem is how do we maintain pro-social communalistic values in the midst of such greed, materialism, selfishness, individualism and alienation.

13-17

The teenager is an invention of the European mind. For the vast majority of human history, including in the European world, there was no concept of 'the teenager'. The teenager, as a social construct, was born in the 1950's and epitomised with the brief but meteoric rise of the film star James Dean who starred in films such as 'Rebel Without a Cause'. However the teenager was socially conceived in the bowels of European evolutionary theory which not only conceived of humans evolving from apes, and which not only conceived of Caucasians as the last human evolution; having evolved from the 'lower races' – of which Afrikans were naturally the lowest – but also conceived of individuals evolving throughout their lifetime.

The teenage years were equated with the period of savagery in human developmental terms – in which it was understood by Caucasians that many peoples (particularly Afrikans) still lived – and it was the job of adults (Caucasian men) to control and guide 'teenagers' (non-Caucasian people) through this period until they had acquired full adult consciousness (become acculturised into Western civilisation). It is also important to note that the teenager is very much a Caucasian male construct about male development.

The book 'Lord of the Flies' by William Golding, which was also made into a cinema film, perfectly illustrates the points made above. In the book a group of boys are stranded on an island without adults. The children quickly descend into a wild and chaotic existence. Inside the front cover of my copy of the book is an excerpt from a review published in 'The Times' newspaper which is highly instructive and reinforces some of the points I make above.

" '...Mr Golding knows exactly what boys are like; he has a compelling imagination; and the vivid realism with which he describes the disintegration of their **untried and precarious civilisation under the pressure of nature** carries the reader to the bloody climax.."

[my emphasis in bold] (*The Times* newspaper review in Golding 1969: inside cover)

The book also has a highly racialised theme to it, even though all of the characters are Caucasian. In the story the boys soon split into two groups, one comprised of those led by boys with light coloured hair who seek to maintain some semblance of order and justice (civilisation), and another group led by boys with dark hair who quickly descend into bloodthirsty savagery. This racial and racist undercurrent to the book was not given much attention at the time, since of course Mr Golding was simply reflecting and reinforcing the ideas of the culture into which he was born.

Of course, I highlighted in the earlier chapter on European sexual culture how the ancient Greeks used to induct teenage boys into adulthood and also how a deepseated underlying fear lay at the heart of this process. This was the fear that unless suppressed and subordinated these Greek sons would join forces with their mothers to murder and overthrow the rule of their fathers – as embodied in Greek mythology by the story of the Greek God Zeus who, aided and abetted by his mother, murders and overthrows his father Chronos to become King of the Gods.

We can clearly see in the UK, USA and other parts of the world infected with the European cultural virus that the culture has come full circle and adults are once again afraid of teenage boys who are characterised as – and whom in some cases behave like – wild and dangerous savages.

What does the foregoing mean for Afrikans trying to bring Afrikan children to a constructive and productive adulthood? Well, it means that many of the difficulties and traumas of the teenage years are either created or greatly exacerbated by the social environment in which our children are growing. Many parents now expect their teenagers to go off the rails, to be difficult, rude, unco-operative, moody etc. It is a self-fulfilling prophecy. Many of us do not seem to understand that this is still not the case in many parts of the world where children and parents have not been socially conditioned to believe that this is 'natural' behaviour for teenagers. Many of us are also sadly lacking in an even cursory understanding of European cultural history which tells us quite clearly that the history of the Caucasian is a history of war, conflict and aggression. Europeans mark their history by wars and conquest and this conflictual mindset infects every aspect of their culture, including the raising of children.

If you watch British television you will see an amazing barrage of programmes about the conflict between parents and their children, with the children ranging in age from toddlers to grown adults. It is the culture (including diet) that is producing the unmanageable children and teenagers, not the children's hormones. Therefore the remedy is to blame and change the culture not to blame nature and attack the child's hormonal system with drugs such as Ritalin. We have a society producing ever growing numbers of children with depression and other forms of mental illness and no one seems to stop to ask why, in societal as opposed to individual terms.

I can recall an Afrikan mother telling me how her teenage daughter has turned against her because she has clear and firm boundaries and does not allow her daughter to hang around 'in town' with her friends. Her daughter says she is horrible and too hard and can't wait to leave home. In an unsupportive culture which emphasises children's rights and parental responsibility, but has little to say about children's responsibilities and parent's rights it is hard to hold the line. But hold the line we must. Let middle class Caucasian parents experiment with their children, we should stick to what is tried and tested and took 200,000 years or so to develop!

For all the reasons stated above, combined with the reality of rapid physiological, emotional and intellectual development, this is without doubt the most difficult period of parenting. During this period there will be a significant relinquishing of power by the parent, to the point where by the time the child reaches seventeen the general balance should have shifted in the direction of parent as advisor with, instruction as much more of a last resort. Both parties know that the parent remains the ultimate source of authority, as in the Jamaican saying '*Two bull can't reign in one pen*' however the wise parent will gradually increase the range of issues over which the child can exercise choice knowing full well that the child may be leaving home to go to University at 18 (if they can afford the tuition and other fees) and they will have to make their own decisions – and will be subject to a wide array of people and pressures – in all aspects of life in this environment.

It is about loosening the grip slowly and imperceptibly in the same way as a child grows physically and mentally each day. In order to achieve this delicate balance it is important to maintain communication with your child and to know your child's peer group and interests. Children need their parents most physically as babies; however they need them most emotionally as teenagers. Parents generally spend very little time with their teenage children and yet this is a time when their children need them most. Peer pressure and the culture of 'the West' presents parents as an embarrassment to their teenaged children and this way of thinking is adopted by most teenagers. It is therefore no easy task to resist this pressure and it cannot be achieved by suddenly demonstrating interest in your children's friends and activities on their 13th birthday. Nothing magical happens when a child turns thirteen; however something strange occurs in the minds of parent and child.

One of the most apparent mistakes that increasing numbers of Afrikan parents are making with their children is in their differential treatment of the sexes and in their willingness to allow our teenage boys to roam wild; in the apparent belief that they are less at risk than teenage girls. However all the statistics would; if anything, point in the opposite direction and indicate that the Afrikan male is becoming an endangered species and that if your child is out on street in the early hours of the morning (when most shootings and other deadly encounters take place) he is at high risk.

It is sometimes said – often unfairly, but sometimes accurately – that Black mothers raise their daughters and love their sons. This saying is alluding to the fact that too many of our boys are allowed to avoid household chores and routines which are imposed upon girls. Our boys are crying out for structure, routine and boundaries and so are our girls. In particular, our boys need pro-social adult male leadership and example. If it is not provided they may seek out anti-social adult male leadership and example. It is only the desperate nature of the situation facing our boys that is diverting our attention away from the crisis facing Afrikan girls, in all the areas (crime and criminality, educational achievement, work and poverty, mental and physical illness) highlighted for the Afrikan male together with other issues such as teenage conceptions, male violence and sexual abuse, self harm etc.

Don't give in to the ways of others who do not have you and your child's best interests at heart. Listen to the words of those who do have you and your child's best interests at heart and have demonstrated some competence in the field of parenting.

18-24

If you think that your job as a parent is done when your child hits eighteen; think again. You may have laid the foundations, built the walls and roof, laid the floors, put in the fixtures and fittings, and decorated, however without a tiled – or similarly covered – roof a house is not complete and is dangerously exposed to the elements.

In my previous book I made reference to the Afrikan Life Cycle and how in many Afrikan cultures one was not considered an adult until one reached the age of 25. The period between the ages of 13-24 was considered a period of Adulthood Training. Adulthood was (is) a serious business for Afrikans and was not granted automatically. One had to prove oneself in order to be considered an adult. In 'Western' societies adulthood is reduced to a physiological/chronological process which runs the danger of producing adult males and females as opposed to men and women. The road to adulthood should be a physical, intellectual, emotional and spiritual (PIES) journey and our job as parents is to direct, guide and facilitate that journey.

In a 'Westernised' cultural context the role of the parent when the child is aged 18-24 will be almost wholly advisory, however this should not prevent one from being an active advisor and intervening positively in your child's life. If you have built a strong relationship with your child they will listen and invariably take your advice and the mistakes that they will inevitably make will not be too disastrous.

Two areas where purposeful parental input is absolutely vital are relationships and finance. The vast majority of young Afrikans already are; or will become, sexually active during this period in their life. The need to assist young adults to make healthy (physical, spiritual and emotional) sexual choices is vital. Hopefully parents will have raised their children to see sex as more than just a physical act and hence to select a sexual partner using criteria that extend beyond the purely physical. However, peer pressure is a powerful pressure, for good or ill and parents need to be able to speak openly to their children – always remembering how you were when you were 18!

One of the best things you can do for your child is to provide them with a sound and fundamental understanding of money and wealth creation. The general level of financial illiteracy amongst adults is worrying, but amongst Afrikans in the UK – and no doubts other parts of the world – it is shocking. As an example, the average person in the UK is more likely to get divorced than to change their mortgage provider. This is like throwing money down the drain. I have changed my mortgage provider three times in the last four years and my latest change in August 2005 saved me nearly £100 per month. That is a saving of £1200 per year for what was effectively a few hours work. Unless you can earn more than £1200 for less than half a day's work then you need to be looking at simple ways like this of saving money. Even if we can't leave a huge nest egg for our children we can provide them with the knowledge to avoid making our mistakes and to build a secure financial future.

Recommendations for Parents

The following recommendations are taken from a brief paper produced by Paul Obinna Wilson-Eme, one of the leading Afrikan-centred thinkers in the UK. Paul is a qualified teacher who taught in Mosside, Manchester for more than a decade and has also taught in South London. Working alongside his friend, Lance Lewis, Paul was the creative force behind the highly acclaimed 'Education of The Black Child' conferences held in Manchester which were attended by some of the leading Afrocentric scholars in the world. Paul has been working with our children, young adults and adults for many years and can just as accurately be described as a scholarly activist as an activist scholar.

Media

1. Gain more understanding of media influences.
2. Lower the 'volume' in the home. (i.e. one media source at a time!)
3. Let children see you reading and doing things with them you expect them to do.
4. Watch and listen to the media with them and discuss the content so that they form opinions along with you (reasoning/argument).
5. Be aware of 'Soap Opera' problem solving and 'Chat Show' social manners from yourself and them.
6. Put a cover on the television so that there has to be a positive action before switching it on.

Language

1. Invest in an extensive dictionary (with Etymology).
2. Build up your own understanding of words and use them wisely and in context (vocabulary or Nommo).
3. Correct yourself if you make an error in front of your children.
4. Apologise if you drop a 'cuss'.
5. Listen out and correct Grammar to help your children select the correct language code for the context.

Culture

1. Balance the discipline holistically. Remember 'the word'.
2. Stop the use of 'nothing' as a denial word.
3. Encourage the leaving of the bad spirit at the door! "Lef it inna de street"!
4. Immediately correct negative Non Verbal Communication. i.e. 'Cut Eye' and 'Kissing Teeth' and be aware if this is what you do.
5. Do not treat the child as though they are 'size' to lessen your responsibility to them. Show and build the '3 R's' in them (Reasoning, Respect and Responsibility).

General

Seek to understand and teach the wisdoms of the 2 P's (Proverbs and Parables).

Read the works of Amos Wilson, Jawanza Kunjufu, Paul Hill Jr., Na'im Akbar, Mary C. Lewis and Nathan and Julia Hare and apply the theories.

One of the issues Paul Obinna Wilson-Eme often talks about during his workshops/seminars is emotional literacy and that great ancestor Amos Wilson (1987) set out systematically how powerfully negative emotions such as frustration – which he saw as endemic to the 'Black Condition' in the US and Afrikan world – can affect an Afrikan's ability to parent effectively. I have partially reproduced a table setting out these effects below:

Table 6

Parental Frustration Symptoms	Parental Attitudes and Childrearing Practices
Powerlessness	Lack of interest in maintaining control over child, feels powerless to effectively control child s destiny,
Inability to Delay Gratification	Tends to act with hostility towards child when it is perceived as a hindrance to parental pleasure,
Apathy	Fails to take deep interest in child s development, neglect of child s mental, physical and emotional wellbeing,
Denial of Worthiness of Social Goals	Not interested in being a socially acceptable model for child to imitate,
Fatalism	Believes the child s growth and development is a matter of luck, believes that deliberate efforts in child-rearing are futile,
Low Achievement Motivation	Not highly motivated to achieve optimal circumstances for self development and the child s development, does not motivate the child to achieve,
Ego-restrictiveness	Parental self is the main source of interest, the child is secondary, the home is not child-centred, takes little interest in the child as an individual,
High Interest in Diversive Activities	Interested mainly in pastime activities, not problem-solving activities, which leads to child neglect, only interested in playing with or distracting the child as a means of dealing with its problems,
Unrealistic Striving	Parental unrealistic striving alienates self and child, leaves inadequate time for proper child-rearing, teaches child to pursue goals beyond its inherent, acquired, and attainable talents, powers and means, .

Source: *The Developmental Psychology of the Black Child Amos N. Wilson (1987) pgs 57-59*

The best way to heal the child is to heal the parent and there is an urgent need for Afrocentric adult re-education programmes. Whilst there has been a lot of attention paid to Afrocentric teaching content the important issue of Afrocentric pedagogical method and practice is sometimes overlooked. Whilst she does not go the full Afrocentric nine yards Dr Margaret Shaw provides some useful tips for those people engaged in teaching Afrikan-American adults and which could no doubt be transferred to teaching Afrikans in other parts of the world.

Vol. 1, No.3
1993
Professional Tips for Adult and Continuing Educators

TIPS ON TEACHING AFRICAN-AMERICAN ADULTS

by

Margaret Shaw, Ed. D. Pennsylvania State University

These tips focus on teaching African-American adults from a cultural perspective. This teaching approach includes all the basic objectives of adult education but with a slightly different emphasis so that learning activities will have increased meaning for African-American adults. Teaching from a cultural perspective pays attention to the subject matter as for any adult student; however, the subject matter is contextualized to have meaning for the African-American adult. Teaching from a cultural perspective also pays attention to the developed knowledge structures, perceptual patterns, and the preferred processes of learning within that culture. It also pays attention to teachers and their cultural perceptual patterns as well as their effects on the teaching/learning process. Following are some tips for students, curriculum specialists, and teachers that may lead to better services for African-American adults.

Tip #1. Teachers should encourage students to interpret their own world through the students' two ways of knowing: Afrocentric and Eurocentric.

African-Americans grow up in a distinct culture that shapes their cognitive development and impacts the way they behave in an academic setting. African-Americans have two ways of knowing: an African-American and a European-American way within a largely Eurocentric culture. From their home cultural context, many African-Americans are taught an Afrocentric way of thinking and living: thus the development of the Afrocentric eye. From the larger societal perspective, they are taught the Eurocentric perspective and develop ways of knowing from the Eurocentric eye. African-Americans have learned both within and outside their own culture everyday negotiating strategies to regulate their movement and grasp meaning between the cultures. These strategies are called LENS (learning everyday negotiating strategies). They look through their LENS with two eyes at every situation. This two-ness is well documented in the literature. LENS serves as the perceptual filter through which their world is viewed and structured. The dualism provides a keen awareness that permits them to examine, evaluate, and interpret situations critically and quickly. The constant shifting between cultures creates a shrewd sense of skill and precision in perceiving the two worlds in depth, both singly and jointly. Many times it becomes critical that African-Americans hold and utilize the two worldviews simultaneously.

LENS focuses on the two worlds that African-Americans see – the world which acknowledges their presence and possibilities, and the other world which views African-Americans as maladjusted facsimiles of the European-American culture. African-Americans focus on ethnocentric orientations that increase their vision and society's orientations that limit their vision. To the degree that one lives in an overtly racist and oppressive system, one will have developed LENS.

The Eurocentric environment of schools forces the development of a Eurocentric eye as well as an Afrocentric eye. This dualistic experience influences the development of a unique pattern of learning characterized as "learning-to-learn-to-live." This pattern creates a critical perspective that is not merely an intellectual process. It is about a process of coming to believe in the possibility of a variety of experiences, a variety of ways of understanding the world, a variety of frameworks of operation without imposing, consciously or unconsciously, a notion of norm.

How does this process look in action? First, the teacher dis-empowers oneself and therefore gives students the opportunity to empower themselves by becoming the authority in their own voice. It shows students that there are multiple frameworks for learning in the classroom.

Tip #2. Teachers must have methods and approaches that allow African-American adults to examine and question not only the instructor but the textbook or the "official knowledge" for validity and utility.

Official knowledge is what is written in textbooks, and it may be different from what students have been taught. Many African-Americans are suspicious of official knowledge when the educational encounter is between the dominant educational system and those whose history, traditions, and assumptions have been ignored and often denigrated. If people don't feel empowered they must, as students, feel as though they are in control of their learning. Respect for what they can contribute as well as what they wish to learn is essential to their education. It is an opportunity to take part in knowledge production generated out of their own culture. For example, one group of students might question the content validity of a history textbook. In response to this, they could write their own history books.

Tip #3. Teachers must recognize that African-American adult learners are capable of complex learning in the classroom and should design learning activities that evoke and challenge these abilities.

Researchers argue that complex thinking can be observed in the streets among students who drop out, but seldom has this complex thinking been captured in the classroom. In order to use this process in the classroom, teachers must first understand how such complex thinking and learning operates. Secondly, teachers must begin helping students use their everyday critical thinking and learning strategies within the classroom environment. For example, drop-outs on the street learn rap songs quickly. Why? They understand the rhythm and beat because it is important to them. Teachers can build a classroom activity around rap music by asking students to develop their own music within the context of the planned lessons.

Tip #4. Teachers should emphasize practical application.
Teachers who experience the most success are those who illustrate new concepts or broad generalizations by using life experiences drawn from the learners. In addition, the transfer of learning and the ability to maintain that learning suggests that learners plan and rehearse application of concepts within their daily contexts. For example, for many urban African-Americans, illustrations related to using a currency exchange may be more appropriate than illustrations using banking and checkbook operations.

Tip #5. Teachers should use experiential learning methods.
Many African-American teachers have found that experiential learning strategies provide greater success than other methods. Strategies that tap the experiences of the adult learners include group discussion, the case method, the critical-incident process, simulation exercises, role playing, skill-practice exercises, field projects, action projects, laboratory methods, demonstration seminars, work conferences, counseling, and community development.

Tip #6. Teachers should look at their own culture and understand how their perceptual patterns operate within the classroom and their impact on the teaching and learning process.
In viewing African-American students through an outside culture lens, European-American teachers may have a distorted image of their students, even though it may be masked by the cloak of professionalism or be unintentional.

We must take into consideration the teacher's attitudes, beliefs, expectations and values about the academic strengths of African-American adult students. Teachers need help in looking at how their beliefs, values and behavioral styles affect their students. Training programs that take teachers beyond superficial intellectual discussions about cultural differences, racial relationships and Black history are necessary. Teachers should participate in both formal and informal learning experiences that are focused on racism and other social issues. Formal learning experiences consist of structured events such as workshops, presentations, oral histories, and other explications of traditions through storytelling, sensitivity groups, and focused group sessions. Teachers need to take a deeper look at themselves as persons, how they communicate, how they judge and value others, how students perceive them, and most importantly, how these human characteristics affect the development of the students' learning. By looking at one's own biases, teachers can build more constructive relationships with African-American students.

Professional Tips for Adult and Continuing Educators is published by the American Association for Adult and Continuing Education. Permission is granted to reproduce the contents of Tips.

The MisEducation of Afrikan Children in Nottingham – A Case Study

"One of the most tragic beliefs widely shared by Blacks throughout the world is that White-controlled educational institutions – regardless of whether they are elementary schools or universities – will educate our children. Faith continues to prevail in spite of overwhelming evidence which disputes this belief. Blacks continue to ignore the irrefutable truth that, in a racist social system, all institutions will reflect, protect, and sustain values that are consistent with racism. This should not be considered surprising or profound since all institutions serve to perpetuate the social theory of the group which created them. Therefore in any social system established by Whites, the institutions will reflect racism." (Wright 1984: 31)

This is the genius that was Bobby Wright describing institutional racism in a far more profound and meaningful way than Lord Macpherson (author of the Stephen Lawrence enquiry report) or any of his Caucasian legal predecessors ever have; or could.

Introduction

It seems to me that there still remains, a nagging, unspoken question mark – in the very deepest recesses of the average Afrikan's psyche – as to the intellectual capability of Afrikan people. That is to say, just as Afrikans proclaimed 'We are Black and We are Proud' as an antidote to our feelings of lack of racial self-worth, just as we proclaimed 'My nose is broad, my hair is curly, my lips are thick, my skin is black and I am beautiful' as an antidote to the reality of the self-hatred many Afrikans felt about the way they looked (see next chapter), so we talk about our genius stemming from the genes-in-us as a defence against the internalisation of racist stereotypes that place us at the bottom of a Caucasian conceived human intellectual ladder.

Many of our people, children as well as adults, believe in our intellectual inferiority, of that I have no doubt. Observe our people's behaviour and aspirations, as opposed to their more self-conscious comments and you will see how widespread this phenomenon is. Slogans and chants will not change this inferiority complex, just as they will not make most of us like the way we look in comparison to Caucasians. We have to act our way out of these mental prisons. We have to tackle our demons head on and slay them.

There is actually ample evidence of the precocity of Afrikan children. Amos Wilson provides useful coverage of this topic in his excellent book 'The Developmental Psychology of the Black Child' (1987) where he recounts how Caucasian researchers who went to Uganda in the 1950's, seeking no doubt to reinforce their 'deficit model' of Afrikan intellectual development, were stunned to see how much more advanced in gross motor skills (skills of movement and co-ordination) and cognitive recognition skills (ability to think and perceive) Ugandan infants were in comparison to their European-American counterparts.

Nottingham – Afrikans in the Educational Abyss

I have lived in Nottingham since 1991 and have become increasingly involved in issues relating to the exclusion from school and educational achievement of Afrikan children in this city since around 1997. I am currently a member of the Afrikan Education Forum, an umbrella organisation bringing together several voluntary sector organisations as well as Afrikan teachers and parents. The group has two strands to its work, firstly to set up an independent Afrikan school in Nottingham and secondly to influence the policies of the Nottingham City Council Education Department and other statutory bodies that have an impact upon the educational experience of Afrikan children in Nottingham.

After many decades of Afrikan people in Nottingham shouting and fighting for educational justice, both the Education Department and Local Strategic Partnership (a city wide strategic umbrella partnership set up with a mandate from central government to tackle inequality) have made the educational achievement of Black children one of their strategic priorities. We will let time be the judge as to their commitment and success in tackling this longstanding problem; however I thought it would be useful to provide the background to our children's performance in Nottingham schools to highlight the disastrous overall effect White Education has on Black minds.

There follows a document produced by the One City Partnership Nottingham (OCPN) the Local Strategic Partnership for the city of Nottingham. This document is one of a series that are referred to as 'Action From Facts' documents and are designed to summarise the key issues related to issues that the partnership has decided to prioritise for action. Take a read and pay particular attention to the graphs which clearly highlight the deterioration in our children's educational performance as they pass through the school system. I have interspersed my own comments, which are highlighted in bold, where appropriate.

The Fresh Start logo below is indicative of the fact that just like a failing school that is shut and re-opens with a new name, the OCPN was failing and was rebadged and relaunched under the Fresh Start logo.

FRESH START
Nottingham

Neighbourhood Renewal Floor Target

Between 2002 and 2006 the proportion of those aged 16 who get qualifications equivalent to 5 GCSEs at grades A*-C rises by 2 percentage points each year on average at least 25% of pupils in all schools achieving this standard*

EDUCATIONAL ATTAINMENT – FOCUS ON BLACK BOYS

How Are Black Boys Performing Against The Floor Target
Nottingham reflects the national picture of negative outcomes for Black boy pupils by the time they reach Key Stage 4 (GCSEs). The most recent national GCSE figures confirm this fact, with 37.5% of Black Caribbean pupils and 43.3% of Black African pupils achieving 5 or more GCSEs with C grades or better, compared to the national average of 52.3%. In Nottingham the figures for the most recent year, 2004, are as follows:

Table 7 – Key Stage 4 achievement by Ethnicity

Ethnic Description	Number of Pupils	% Achieving 5+ A*-C
Caribbean	61	23
White And Black Caribbean	39	12.8
Other Black Background	39	15.4
African	11	45.5
White and Black African	10	20
City Total — All Ethnic Backgrounds Male Pupils	1368	35.2

The table above shows that only one group of Black boys, those of African background, achieved a score higher than the city average and none of the groups achieved a score comparable to the national average. This low level of achievement was not reflected in the scores

297

of boys from other ethnic minority backgrounds. For example, boys from Indian backgrounds scored 70%, those from Bangladeshi backgrounds 66.7% and those from Pakistani Backgrounds 53.9%.

The figures for 2004 reflect the general trend in Nottingham. The table below shows the trend line for different ethnic groups' performance in Nottingham over the last five years.

Graph (i) – Comparison of boys' attainment of 5+ GCSE at A*-C

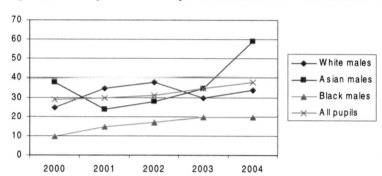

This demonstrates that whilst there is a steady upward trend in improvement for black boys, from 2001 it has been slower than for boys from Asian backgrounds and that overall achievement remains well below that of all other pupils.

Performance Across the Range of Key Stages

Of importance to note is that the performance of Black Caribbean and Black Other pupils at the first monitored key stage is higher than for all other ethnic groups (***This reinforces the point made by Amos Wilson in his book 'The Developmental Psychology of the Black Child' [1987] regarding the precocity of Afrikan children.*** The decline in performance over the school career of these pupils is therefore more severe than for any other group of pupils. The graph below illustrates attainment of Nottingham pupils compared to the national average in 2003 across all key stages.

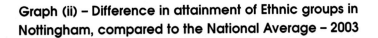

Graph (ii) – Difference in attainment of Ethnic groups in Nottingham, compared to the National Average – 2003

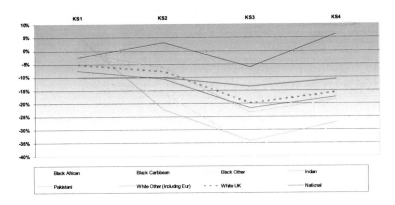

The importance of this graph, in a Nottingham context, is that this is the first cohort that has gone through the whole of their secondary schooling under the management of Nottingham City LEA and for whom progress can be tracked and trends analysed. In future years it will be possible to track performance of pupils as individuals and groups and trends for gender and ethnicity will be far more apparent. *The real importance of this graph is that it highlights that despite experiencing disproportionate poverty, single parent households, poor housing and living environments Afrikan/Dual heritage children come to school equipped to learn. It is the education system that is underachieving not Afrikan/Dual Heritage children.*

As can be seen all groups of pupils suffer a drop in performance between Key Stages 1 and 3, with a rally in performance for Key Stage 4. It is commonly acknowledged that the transition period between leaving primary school and the first couple of years of secondary schooling (Key Stages 2 –3) is marked by a decline in relative academic performance for all pupils. The inference that could be drawn from the very marked decline in the performance of some black pupils between Key Stages 1 and 2, is however, that the problems that result in overall poor performance of black boys in GCSE results are already manifest between the ages of 7 and 11. It would therefore suggest that early interventions (i.e. at the upper

299

primary level – age 7+) are necessary to sustain the educational performance of black boys. The scale of the issue is significant as Nottingham has the largest Black primary population outside of London.

What else do we know?

During the last 12 months the City Council's Children and Young People Standing Panel has been undertaking a scrutiny review of the attainment of BME pupils. It is due to publish its full set of recommendations imminently. A number of these focus specifically on factors which they consider impact on the attainment of black boys. The review has drawn upon a wide range of quantitative and qualitative evidence sources, including "expert" witnesses, parents, those responsible for providing supplementary schooling and young BME people. There are a number of issues that are consistently identified across all the evidence sources. These are:

- Exclusions are a serious issue and the numbers of Black boys excluded, both officially and in less obvious ways, far exceeds that of white children
- A disproportionately high number of Black children were discriminated against by being selected to study for lower level qualifications.(known as "Tiering")
- Racism in schools is not crude or obvious – it is often well intentioned but misguided decisions by teachers thinking they are doing the best by their pupils. Cultural awareness needs to be an on-going developmental issue for teachers
- Schools need to foster the development of positive relationships between pupils, teachers and parents

Exclusions

Whilst the levels of permanent exclusions are reducing (1.7 per 1000 this year compared to 2.3 per 1000 last year), Black pupils in Nottingham have experienced disproportionately high levels of permanent exclusions from 2001 to 2004 from Nottingham City schools. (See graph below). There are also significant levels of exclusion of City resident pupils from County schools, also disproportionately affecting Black pupils.

Graph (iii) – Permanent Exclusions (rate per 1000) from 2001-2004 (Nottingham)

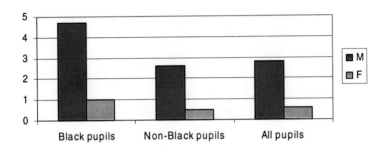

What further information is required?
The extent to which 'tiering' limits the levels of attainment of Black boys at GCSE need further investigation.

The impact of voluntary groups, including supplementary schools, and how to maximise their value for Black boys

Good Practice Example
A case study of a primary school in Birmingham published by the Neighbourhood Renewal Unit highlights a number of issues that are of relevance to this discussion. The school identified the same tailoring off of achievement during the 7-11 age range amongst Black pupils, as is evident in the Nottingham data, but has been able to reverse this decline, to the extent that Black Caribbean pupils leave the school as the highest achievers.

According to the case study success was underpinned by the strength of the links between the school and the community. "The school ensured mutual respect between teachers and pupils, involved parents, set clear targets and celebrated success" It states that:

- Parents and the community should:
- Have high expectations of children and support their education;
- Establish a positive two-way relationship with the school
- Try to find ways to assist in school
- Consider standing for PTA or Board of Governors
- Communicate with the school if you see problems, either with the way your children are receiving education or in the school's ethos or understanding of cultural issues

The School should:

- Have high expectations of all children
- Encourage parental input and links with the community
- Have clear anti-racism and positive non discrimination polices
- Ensure that all children and parents are aware of these policies and abide by them
- Employ staff who will support the ethos of the school
- Set targets for academic and personal involvement
- Have a consistent all-school approach

Both school and community should:

- Adopt a consistent approach. If attitudes to attainment, behaviour, attendance, diversity are consistent between home and school, the children are bound to benefit.
- Taken from "High attainment levels for Black Caribbean pupils in a Birmingham junior school" – renewal.net Case Study 2004

At the end of the day, whilst exemplifying laudable sentiments, the above example of good practice is simply one of the small number of exceptions that prove the rule, as cogently expressed by Bobby E Wright at the beginning of this section. White Education does not work for Black children irrespective of whether it equips them to get

5 A*-C grades at GCSE, since education is about far more than the narrow instrumental process of passing examinations.

Our children need an education that equips them with the Afrikan Virtues (see 'Living the Afrikan Virtues' chapter in part IV) and our oppressors will never do that.

Are you willing to do for Black girls and boys what you have done for White girls?

This was the challenge I and a colleague, Sonia Davis, from the Afrikan Education Forum put before the Headteachers conference organised by the Nottingham City Council Education Department in 2005. It was an explicit recognition of the remarkable turnaround in the educational achievement of Caucasian girls as compared to Caucasian boys over the past twenty years in the UK. This conference was focusing upon the achievement of Black children and used to discuss the Draft Black Achievement Strategy. The Education Department has significantly improved its collection and analysis of data, however the most significant thing is that the more data they collect and present, the more it tells us what we already know, namely that the longer Black children stay in their miseducation system the more their educational performance deteriorates.

At the time of writing this chapter (September 2005) Nottingham City Council had been working on a 'Black Achievement Strategy' for well over a year. The Strategy is now on its twentieth draft and after some initial engagement of Black community organisations, via the Afrikan Education Forum (see below); there has been an almost total disengagement from the process of community consultation, let alone community participation. What was most instructive during the few months of engagement with the Afrikan Education Forum (AEF) was the fact that the initial drafts of the strategy did not identify racism as a central causal factor in our children's poor educational performance. After strong protests from the Forum this omission was supposedly rectified, however it was a telling indictment of the view of Caucasian educationalists regarding their role in our children's miseducation.

This grim determination, of the vast majority of Caucasian

educationalists, to cling to the 'conventional' (a euphemism for Eurocentric) explanatory paradigm with regard to the 'underachievement' of Black children, remains one of the most interesting aspects of the debate in Nottingham – and no doubt nationally – about our children's educational performance. This paradigm places the blame squarely upon the shoulders of the children themselves, their feckless single parents, the wider Black community and lastly, but by no means least, 'Black street culture'. In this world it is the anti-intellectual, anti-learning cultural environment that Black children are raised in that is the cause of the problem and against which brave and heroic Caucasian teachers are forced to battle every day.

As with every good lie there is a germ of truth within the foregoing explanation. The truth is that the Black family is in crisis. The truth is that children raised in single parent households are more likely to live in poverty. The truth is that you will find many Black children who say they dislike or even hate school – although this is very different to hating learning. The truth is that there is a sordid, grimy, nihilistic Black sub-culture that is promoted by Caucasian owned record, film, radio and Television companies and presented as if it is the embodiment of 'Black Culture'.

The questions which advocates of this proposition do not ask, let alone investigate include:

- Why has the Black family disintegrated so rapidly (this book provides an explanation in earlier chapters)?
- Is there any evidence that Black children enter school with a negative attitude to education?
- How did Black musical genres such as Reggae in the 1970's and Hip Hop in the early 1980's which had strong political and Black nationalistic overtones become subverted and transformed into dancehall, dominated by gun songs and slackness and rap music dominated by gangsterism and booty?
- Why were Black children performing so badly – and being classified as ESN (Educationally Sub-Normal), as opposed to the current SEN (Special Education Needs) – in the UK

education system between the late 1940's and early 1980's even when most were living in stable two parent households, when our music still had a high proportion of consciousness, and our parents came from a culture in which education was highly prized?

- Given all of the trials and tribulations of Black people, how do they explain the fact that Black children outperform all other groups at key Stage 1 (not just in Nottingham but in many other cities)? If their parents are not interested in education, if they are more likely to live in poverty and if they are nurtured in a negative Black culture how on Earth do they achieve this miracle? Are they genetically superior?

Of course whilst Caucasians can come up with all sorts of damning explanations for the educational failure of our children they would not even conceive of asking the last of the questions listed above given the 'deficit model' into which they, and us, have been socialised. It is not Black children that are underachieving it is Caucasian schools that are underachieving and this is an extremely important change in approach and emphasis that Afrikan people must adopt in engaging with the Caucasian educational establishment.

The Caucasian paradigm has little explanatory power since it is rooted in White Supremacy. The current explanation focuses upon Afrikan cultural inferiority as opposed to the traditional Afrikan genetic inferiority, however both concepts have the same meaning, White Supremacy is natural.

As mentioned earlier I am a member of the Afrikan Education Forum in Nottingham which is an umbrella organisation bringing together groups that provide educational services to Afrikan children, as well as Afrikan teachers and interested individuals. This group is working towards the creation of an Afrikan school in Nottingham which is the only real answer to creating sane, conscious, high-achieving Afrikan-centred children.

Blue Skies For Afrikans

Black Beauty in The Eye of the White Beholder or, When Black Became Beautiful

It is a cliché and yet truism to say that if you do not love yourself, no one else will love you and if you do not have self-respect no one else will respect you. The question of the Afrikan relationship with self is the focus of this chapter and within that the notion of female beauty and desirability. Some of the earlier chapters in this section highlighted the deeply troubled and self-negating beauty concept of many Afrikans, both worldwide and continental. In this chapter we intend to probe a little deeper and explore the highly damaging consequences of chasing the rainbow of a universalised Caucasian beauty standard.

This chapter was catalysed by a three part television programme broadcast on BBC2 during March 2004 which was entitled 'When Black Became Beautiful'. Needless to say it was another assault on the Afrikan psyche dressed up as liberal, progressive film-making, however it was nonetheless fascinating to observe the unconscious belief in their superiority of the Caucasian film-makers and contributors and the absolute buy-in to the Caucasian cultural paradigm – in this case a universal beauty aesthetic whose idealised physical characteristics just happens to occur most frequently amongst Caucasians – of the Afrikan contributors.

The title of the programme itself is a simple but incredibly instructive starting point. 'When Black Became Beautiful'. Embedded is a presumption and an unanswered question. The presumption and embedded statement is that at some point Black was Ugly. The logical question which follows is, Who has; or had, the power to change that aesthetic judgement? The answer to this question is the rationale that underpinned the three programmes, namely that Caucasians are the final arbiters – as well as the benchmark – of beauty and it was in the seeking and gaining of Caucasian acceptance that Black Became Beautiful.

Let us be clear, this programme did not chart any fundamental change or realignment of the universalised Caucasian beauty ideal. What it depicted was the process by which Afrikan women who most closely approximated to the idealised Caucasian phenotype were allowed to participate more fully in the Caucasian beauty industry. Throughout the programme the benchmark and milestones for this acceptance and 'progress' was a series of 'firsts' in which Afrikan women who were the first to do this or first to do that in the beauty industry were celebrated as pioneers, changing the face of the beauty industry and wider society.

The most noticeable of these firsts was when Helen Williams, an Afrikan-American woman, became the first Afrikan model to be featured upon the front cover of Vogue magazine. It was rather sad to hear an Afrikan-American former beauty queen and model enthusing how Helen Williams was "..so beautiful. She looked like a White girl who was Chocolate Brown." One of the Caucasian commentators who was involved with Vogue at the time of this 'first' noted how Helen Williams had 'conventional features' and was not 'exotic'. This type of language was used by the Caucasian commentators throughout the programme to highlight differences between Caucasian and Afrikan models and to emphasise the type of attributes required of Afrikan models who wanted to gain acceptance to the higher echelons of the industry.

Similarly, it was interesting to note that the same Caucasian commentator who noted Helen Williams' 'conventional features' could not bring herself to use the word 'beautiful' to describe Ms Williams – she used the term 'good looking' – whilst she had no such reluctance when referring to Caucasian models of the same era.

The series of programmes commenced by going back to the 1920's and 1930's when the Afrikan-American performer Josephine Baker was at the height of her fame. They contrasted favourably the more 'progressive' and accepting French attitude to Ms Baker with the hostility of Caucasians in the USA, with their segregation of audiences and social and legal restrictions placed upon Afrikan-Americans. Now whilst they never took the time to explore the wider social, economic, historical and psychological reasons which might explain this difference, they also did not probe very deeply into the nature of this acceptance.

Whilst in France it was quite commonplace for Ms Baker to perform as a bare breasted 'Afrikan native'. Whilst a famous Caucasian actress baring her breasts would have scandalised Paris – and would no doubt have been banned toute suite – this was seen as acceptable from a member of a primitive group. Her acceptance was the condescending acceptance given to an Afrikan stranger. Similarly, Muhammad Ali was warmly embraced by the British public even whilst he was castigated as a Black racist in the US. If he had been a British Afrikan denouncing white supremacy in the UK he would have become a hate figure in Britain. Compare the vastly differing reaction of British Caucasians to Lennox Lewis and Frank Bruno (at least up until the point that Bruno was accused of domestic violence by his Caucasian wife and admitted to a mental institution with severe depression).

Josephine Baker did find greater freedom and tolerance in Paris; however that is only because the French did not perceive themselves as having a 'Black problem' at the time. With a significantly increased Afrikan population you would have seen an increased level of hostility in France (as you see nowadays) in line with the population theory I set out in my previous work (Grant 2003). Ms Baker did all the things that were necessary to gain acceptance from the French public. She frequently expressed her gratitude, she married a Caucasian man (acceptable for a star), she played stereotypical stage roles that reinforced the Caucasian sense of superiority and she bleached her skin to try to look like and gain acceptance from Caucasians.

So the presentation of the story of Josephine Baker set the tone for the rest of the programmes. The programme makers went on to describe the experience of Dorothy Towles, a very light skinned Afrikan-American model, who also went to Paris and caused 'a sensation' when she dyed her hair blonde. In the programme Ms Towles described how from that point on her career took off.

This was the explicit tone and rationale of the programme. Afrikans desperate for acceptance by Caucasians and prepared to go the extra mile to receive this cultural blessing. We were told how Berry Gordon, founder of Motown record company, repackaged the White Beauty Ideal and sold it back to the White public and that this was 'pure genius'. This was presented as part of how Afrikans took what they needed from the White Beauty Standard, adapted it and "made it their own". Perhaps the epitome of this mimickery and repackaging of the White Beauty Ideal was Diana Ross. Ms Ross and the other Supremes wore the obligatory wigs – Afrikan-American male artists would chemically straighten their hair – however Ms Ross has gone further and subjected her skin to the type of skin lightening agents used by Michael Jackson – although she has shunned the type of radical cosmetic surgery he has undertaken – and if you compare pictures of her from the 1960's and today you can see the dramatic lightening of her skin that has taken place.

As highlighted in earlier chapters in this book this type of psychology and behaviour leads Afrikans in the USA and worldwide down a psychological cul-de-sac where the physical attributes that are most valued are those which are least frequently found amongst Afrikan people (Staples in Hare and Hare 1989). Naturally the product of this anti-Afrikan value system is the development of a deep and abiding sense of self-hatred which manifests itself most acutely amongst dark skinned Afrikan women, since women represent the symbols of beauty of any ethnic/racial group, whilst dark skinned Afrikan women are furthest removed from this self-hating Afrikan beauty ideal.

There is no clearer and sadder depiction of this self-hatred than in the following two adverts which were taken from the ironically titled UK publication 'Black Hair and Beauty' in the Dec 2004/Jan 2005 edition. The irony is no doubt lost on the Negroes who publish this magazine and actually believe that their various representations of Afrikan women make some positive contribution to our people's sense of self worth. Look at the following adverts and judge for yourself.

Makes you feel proud doesn't it. You too can heal the wounds of time!

This is the 21st century version of Negro/Nigger beauty. What is more disturbing? The fact that thousands of Afrikan women buy this magazine and obviously either support the use of these products (the manufacturers produce these products to satisfy a demand), do not care enough about this gross insult to boycott the magazine or complain, or that the Afrikans who publish this magazine care so little about their people that they will accept these types of adverts which I am sure they are aware can only do damage to the Afrikan psyche.

Having read an article about the editors of all the 'premiere' Black publications, including Black Hair and Beauty, the equally ironically titled 'Pride' magazine, The Voice newspaper etc. in which it was noted that they all have Caucasian partners, I am not surprised by anything that emanates out of the world of Negro publishing.

When you look at the 'After' picture in the advert above it is obvious to me that it is only the effects of the 'functional mental illness' that I wrote about in my previous book (Grant 2003), and which I believe to be rampant in the Afrikan community, that allows seemingly sane people to consider such self-abuse as beauty treatment. It is funny, but until I read this advert I did not realise that my dark elbows and knees were as a result of hyperpigmentation!

It is not just the Swiss cashing in on this vibrant and ever growing market in self-hatred. Many of these skin bleaching products are manufactured in Nigeria and exported all over West Afrika as well as further afield. Here in Nottingham, where I live, you see Jamaican women in particular, but by no means exclusively, sporting the unmistakeably ghastly pinky bleached face look with accompanying naturally dark skinned hands and feet. Zombie would a fraid a dem.

Of course one has only to watch any music video to see that the *Brown paper bag rule* of Black beauty – which states that a Black woman should be no darker than those ubiquitous US brown paper shopping bags and that her hair should blow in the wind – is still in full effect. This is the more subtle, yet insidious, side of Afrikan self hatred.

I recall sitting in a barber's shop in May 2005 and overhearing a conversation between two Jamaican sisters – one of whom had the unmistakeably raw pink face look of a bleacher. They were discussing skin bleaching, in that strangely matter of fact manner that I still cannot get used to, and one sister noted how during a visit to Kentish Town in London she had gone into a hairdresser's shop and seen a Black woman who was so pale you could hardly tell she was Black. The narrator went on to note how she looked "pretty pretty" and how she got a shock when the woman opened her mouth and she realised that she was 'an Afrikan'. "Me couldn't believe it. Me tell yu de ooman look pretty." She went on to note how the woman's pale face did not have any of the pink blotches which are commonly associated with skin bleaching and how she felt that the bleaching agents actually worked better on darker skin. Their conversation moved on to the general topic of continental Afrikans whom they both agreed were 'some dangerous people' who were prone to human sacrifice and other demonic acts.

When you sit and listen to some of our people it is a salutary lesson in reality. Whilst we Afrocentrics are talking about the glories of Kemet and other such nostalgia, many of our people are mired in a level of ignorance and self-hatred that is perhaps deeper than that manifested during the enslavement period.

Just for the record. The active ingredient in most of these skin bleaching agents is the compound hydroquinone. The maximum recommended 'dose' in the UK is 1% by volume. After suffering a bad bout of chicken pox in my early twenties I was prescribed a product called 'Fade Out', by my doctor to apply to the areas of most severe scarring on my face resulting from the chicken pox. I can remember checking the label and noting it had 1% hydroquinone by volume. I also remember that my doctor advised me to use it for no more than six weeks. It is worth noting that some of the skin bleaching agents produced in Nigeria and other countries have up to 5% hydroquinone by volume.

Hydroquinone is a carcinogen – like many other chemical compounds – and even at the 1% level should be considered dangerous. When you think of the prolonged and liberal use of these products by Afrikan women one can only dread to think of the health problems that they are storing up for themselves.

I suppose it is like the Caucasian woman who when warned of the dangers of skin cancer associated with sunbathing commented 'well at least I will be a good looking corpse'. For too many Afrikan women the prize of light skin is obviously worth risking cancer for.

We are *functionally mentally ill* (Grant 2003) and the worst thing is that most of us don't even know it.

Take a look at the following pictures to see images of the 'White Beauty' so many of our women consciously and unconsciously strive for.

Pamela Anderson – Before and After

Goldie Hawn – Before and After

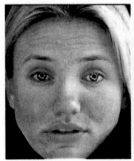

Cameron Diaz – Before and After

This is the mirage that Black Women are chasing. A Caucasian beauty standard that does not even exist amongst Caucasians. Women who get their beauty out of a jar and increasingly from a surgeon's scalpel are presented as the epitome of womanhood. Virtually all the top female Hollywood stars – and many of the male stars – for that matter, have had plastic surgery. You can go back to Marilyn Monroe who was the archetypal 'Blonde Bombshell' who had a nose and chin job and even male stars such as James Stewart, who did not trade on his looks, had plastic surgery. These are early examples of stars who went under the knife to give nature a helping hand.

The images of 'perfect' models in magazines and other publications have all been air brushed to remove bodily 'flaws' – such as cellulite – that are incompatible with the myth being sold to hapless consumers. This is a fake world; full of fake beauty and the 'beauty' industry is a compelling example of this fraudulent culture designed to make people feel inadequate in every way.

The most ironic thing is that Caucasian women are trapped in their own beauty ideal. A survey in 2004 asked British women "what part of your body do you most dislike". The Welsh came out top of the self-hatred chart with 30% of Welsh women replying "all of it" in response to this question.

Take a look at the picture (a few pages overleaf) entitled 'The vanity, the vanity' taken from the Guardian. It is a reproduction of a photograph published in Vanity Fair magazine. This is an example of the type of subliminal communication that attacks the Afrikan psyche. The picture is all the more effective because it appears so stark and in your face that it is easy to miss the deeply White Supremacist messages layered within it.

The photograph appeared in the March 2005 'Hollywood' edition of Vanity Fair and was produced to promote the 2005 Oscars. The photograph reproduced in this book appeared over three pages within the body of the magazine with only a section of it, featuring three of the blonde Caucasian actresses; Uma Thurman, Cate Blanchett and Kate Winslett, appearing on the front cover. The photograph is a beautifully crafted tribute to white supremacy and patriarchy.

The 'second string' posers whose portion of the photograph appeared folded behind the cover picture in the magazine – that featured the three aforementioned actresses – are Claire Danes, Scarlett Johansson, Rosario Dawson and Ziyi Zhang. At the bottom of the 'beauty' hierarchy come Kerry Washington (the Afrikan), Kate Bosworth and Sienna Miller whose photograph was buried in the midst of pages advertising handbags and perfume.

It is always a moot point as to whether this type of carefully crafted hierarchy reflects a conscious attempt to reinforce the values and beliefs of the prevailing social order or is unconsciously put together by people who instinctively recreate the prevailing values and mores of their culture. Even placing some of the non-Caucasian models in the middle category does not hide the clear racial hierarchy at work.

The Guardian journalist Tanya Gold in an article previewing the appearance of this photograph in Vanity Fair is quite clear on this issue. ..."Rosario Dawson, 25 the first of three strategically placed ethnic minority representatives (remember VF, like the Oscars, is a global marketing phenomenon these days: they are present but not too prominent) has done controversial for the shot. She is actually smiling – well, a little." (Tanya Gold, Guardian: 02/02/05: 4). Of course Ms Gold reveals the nature of her own indoctrination in suggesting that in a global market non-Caucasians who comprise over 90% of the world's population represent ethnic minorities. The over-representation (7 out of 10) and positioning of the white models – the Caucasian women occupy all the front positions and strategically encircle the three non-Caucasian models – reinforces the prevailing racial and social hierarchy.

This photograph also represents the continued subordination of women in service of a crude Caucasian male sexual fantasy. In analysing the cover shot Tanya Gold says the following,

"On the first rung of the paper podium Kate, 29, Cate 35, and Uma, 35, mug ferociously for the camera lens, trying to ease each other out of the viewers' eye in a nightmare of expensively dressed passive aggression. Uma has her hand resting on her neck and stretches out lasciviously in a parody of post-sexual languor. Cate has chosen to fling out her arms and toss her hair as if she's been caught on board a ship in a gale. She too is doing the repulsive yearning thing, which should only be done in secret, with a lover. Kate is arching her back and flinging her hand across her crotch, with enormous "No, don't fuck her – fuck me" eyes. And these three are the talented ones." Ms Golding finishes off her article with the sad conclusion that .."Leibovitz's cover is simply a casting couch, a homage to the blowjob values of 1950's Hollywood. To watch 10 beautiful women (of which at least four are talented) bicker for the lens' attention like tarts in an upper class brothel is dispiriting." (Tanya Gold, Guardian: 02/02/05: 4)

There are two striking – to my eyes at least – features of the photograph that go without mention by Ms Gold, perhaps because they are taken for granted. The first is the representation of female beauty within the literally narrow confines of a very thin Caucasoid body shape. The second is the fact that all of the Caucasian women in the photograph are blonde. This would be quite remarkable if it were not so predictable. You need to remember that such pictures are not constructed to represent true diversity, they are constructed from a cultural psyche that uses the veneer of diversity – as represented by the non-Caucasians – to hammer home its arrogant message of Caucasian Supremacy – as represented by the blondes.

The assault on the Afrikan mind and self-image is relentless and manifests itself in every form of human activity. If we learn to critically analyse the media we actually reduce the harm inflicted by such images as their intent becomes clear and we then consciously defend our emotional selves against these forms of cultural imperialism.

There is a real benefit associated with being seen as physically attractive in this and most societies. A recent article in the METRO newspaper on Monday July 7th 2005 highlighted the point.

"LOSING pounds in weight is the best way to get the other sort of pounds rolling into your bank account, according to a study. Dieters usually end up richer than those who stay fat. White women whose body mass index dropped by ten points saw their incomes leap by £6,500. Black women increased their wealth by £3,000 and white

men earned £7,000 more. But black men's incomes were unaffected. The results show that a one unit increase in a person's BMI led to a £740 loss in wealth. This may be because overweight people are discriminated against at work and do not earn as much, Jay Zagorsky of Ohio State University told Economics and Human Biology journal." (Metro 15/07/05 : 15)

Just goes to show, in a sizeist world even a slim brother can't get an even break!

The vanity, the vanity

EXCLUSIVELY FOR VANITY FAIR BY ANNIE LEIBOVITZ

Hair Today, Gone Tomorrow

'Under processed hair there is a processed mind'

Hair. Is there a more potent, powerful, physiological symbol of how Afrikan women feel about themselves? Is there any other part of the Afrikan woman's body that is subject to as much financial expenditure, female discussion and causes as much personal angst as Hair? This is dangerous territory for a brother to step into; however step forward we must since the Afrikan male plays a significant role in shaping the way Afrikan women feel about their hair as part of their beauty self-concept.

"… few things generate more anger and passion among black women than their hair. Some black critics say that black women are in a frenzied search to shed the ancient racist shame and stigma of "nappy hair" = "bad hair" by aping white beauty standards. Others say that, like many non-black women, black women are hopeless captives of America's fashion and beauty industry, which is geared to making them more attractive and pleasing to men. Many black women counter this by saying that they are merely seeking their own identity or to look better.

They are all right. But the great hair obsession among many black women reflects the still deep and compelling need by African-Americans to identify with and accept America's values and standards. The beauty care industry has skillfully fed that compulsion with fantasies of physical glitter and social glamour and turned them into mammoth profits. Hair care product manufacturers have sold many black women on the notion that their hair is the path to self-esteem, success, and sexual allure. A century ago the legendary Madame CJ Walker built a multi-million dollar empire on the premise that black women want to look like white women and that "good hair" is the key to independence and prosperity.

"Elegance, spiced with Southern flavor begins with a mane awash in a light golden blond shade."

The Afro or natural hair look of the 1960's and the braid craze of the 1990's are touted as examples of black women rejecting white beauty standards. They aren't. The Afro style was short lived, always more a chic fad than a revolution in black consciousness, and was tied to style and fashion trends. Today's braided look is even more tightly tied to style and fashion trends with none of the pretensions of the black pride of the 1960's. Even many black women who sport the bald look are fixated on matching the proper clothes, make-up and ear rings with the style. Most soon tire of these hair fads and retreat back to the straightening comb, fashion braids/extensions or a perm.

The great hair obsession is driven by the painful need of many African-Americans to conform to the dominant values of American society. And beauty, fashion and hairstyles are the most popular and perverse expressions of those values. .....many African-Americans still believe the fiction that good hair makes you, and nappy hair doesn't."

Earl Ofari Hutchinson (1998 Afrocentric News *"The Crisis in Black and Black"*)

Hair has always had great significance for Afrikan people. For example the ancient Nubians used to braid their hair prior to warfare, however that deep cultural meaning has now given way to an equally deep, but far less healthy, psychological meaning.

Hutchinson concisely summarises many of the pertinent issues in relation to Afrikan women and their relationship with their hair, although there is one key point that he overlooks and that is the convenience explanation for hair straightening and the wearing of weaves/wigs.

The convenience explanation, which is probably the most often cited reason why Afrikan women say they chemically straighten/attach false hair to their heads is centred around the notion that Afrikan women's increasingly busy and hectic lives mean that they do not have the time to mess around with natural hairstyles and that the only, or primary reason, they straighten their hair is for reasons of convenience.

Now, on the face of it, this argument appears convincing, however as we know when analysing and decoding our behaviour it is very rare for Afrikan adults to openly express feelings of racial self-loathing, even when these feelings are consciously felt or experienced. Hence even the most extreme example of such self-hatred, Michael Jackson, can make a record in which he says "It does not matter if you are Black or White" without the slightest hint of irony let alone embarrassment.

There is a test for the convenience explanation. If the chemical straightening of Afrikan women's hair was primarily a practical response to their busy lives, as opposed to a psychological response to their denigrated feminine status, then Afrikan women who chose not to use chemicals to straighten their hair would receive no adverse reaction from Afrikan women who use hair straightening products and/or wigs, weaves etc. However this seems not to be the case. Most of the Afrikan women I know who choose to keep their hair natural report reactions ranging from mild disapproval to outright hostility, ridicule and contempt. If it was all a question of convenience, surely the only response they would receive would be 'how do you find the time to do your hair?'

I know one sister who when she 'went natural' and cut her hair was greeted with shock and dismay by her mother and sisters. I am absolutely convinced that if she had greeted them in a full length blonde wig she would have received a more enthusiastic, supportive response. It was so sad that one of her sisters was actually suffering significant hair loss at the time – as a result of the peroxide based chemicals used in hair straighteners – but refused to even give her hair a break to recover from this chemical attack, such was her addiction to the idea of straight hair. Ironically, she was the family member most hostile to her sibling 'going natural'.

Similarly, I can recall when I worked in schools there was an Afrikan girl who was called 'toast' and other insults by some of the little self-hating Negroes who my generation are raising up, due to her lovely dark skin. When she had her hair chemically straightened another girl said to her by way of a compliment 'your hair looks decent now'. Of course she still continued to be insulted by her schoolmates based upon her dark complexion.

Just to show that this behaviour crosses all age ranges, I can remember a sister who previously had her hair natural and never received any compliments from other Afrikan women (and only a few Caucasians) coming into work one day with her hair freshly straightened and walking into a positive hailstorm of compliments. 'Hey sexy lady' and so on and so forth. After such positive affirmation you could hardly blame her for clinging on tightly to her 'Dark and Lovely' products. I guess the decoding is *Not too Dark (Afrikan) if you want to be Lovely*.

Another example of this deepseated madness was related to me by a friend one lunchtime. He told me of an Afrikan woman in her thirties who works in an environment where she has contact with Afrikan adolescents. This woman has some deep psychological problems, not the least of which are her hair issues. She wears a sumptuous weave and has taken the decision to tell her colleagues and young service users that it is her own hair. One day my friend – who has not let on that he knows she wears a weave – casually commented upon the changed colour and appearance of her hair and was told she had dyed her hair and had undergone some other styling treatments at the hairdressers.

As is normally the case, lies catch up with you. One day this young woman was preening 'her hair' a bit too vigorously when a large clump of the weave dropped out of her head and onto the office floor. One of her stunned colleagues could think of no other response than to pick the offending article up from the floor and hand it back to the owner with the comment "I think this belongs to you." To add insult to injury this sister has had to endure the recurring complaints of the cleaner about how her hair is always clogging up his vacuum cleaner! I was not surprised to hear that this woman manifests other forms of strange and reactionary behaviour since her steadfast refusal to acknowledge that she wears a weave – as much as the fact that she wears a weave – is symptomatic of a deep and abiding self-hatred.

It is incredible to me, but sadly true that it actually takes courage for an Afrikan woman to walk in this world with her own hair, and nothing but her hair (including chemical straightners), so help her ancestors. Of course, a few years ago we had the short hair fad amongst Afrikan women over 40 – which seemed to emanate from the US – but this usually involved the application of chemicals and dyeing the hair a golden/rust colour. Fads come and go but hostility to Afrikan hair remains unchanged.

What I want to know is why don't Afrikans who say they believe in God consider this chemical attack an act of blasphemy? Religious people tell me their God is perfect. Omnipotent, Omniscient, Ubiquitous. Seems to have everything this geezer (because of course God is a Man if they adopt the religion of their oppressor), seems perfect, except it seems like he can't do hair for Afrikans properly! Seems to have messed up big time there. Well, you can't have it both ways. Either your God is perfect and therefore his/her creation is perfect and therefore Afrikan hair is as it should be and the problem is within your mind. Or, your God is not perfect and therefore his/her creation is not perfect and therefore it is fine to correct his/her big mistakes, so roll out the peroxide and horse hair!

Am I being a little harsh? Perhaps, especially since the psychological pressure to 'lighten and lengthen' Afrikan hair is everywhere. Afrikan girls as young as four or five are expressing detestation for their hair. If they were saying they hated their skin colour we would see it as a major problem (I hope), however I guess it is difficult for many Afrikan mothers to speak authoritatively against such sentiments from their daughters since we all know that Practice is better than Precept, ...Psyche!

It is said that 'Blondes have more fun' and even Caucasian women who dye their hair blonde report increased male sexual attention. So what chance for the Afrikan woman with her benighted 'nappy' or 'knotty' hair. Even Afrikan girls as young as three or four are now having the horse hair fixed to their manes. Why on earth Afrikan mothers are tying extensions into their young daughters' hair I cannot understand. For whose benefit? I have noticed that mothers have a greater tendency to impose these extensions on their very young daughters when their children have naturally short hair so I can only presume it is a projection of the mother's own feelings about Afrikan hair onto their children.

Having your hair chemically straightened used to be a sort of anti-

Afrikan rite of passage for Afrikan young women. You can forget that nowadays, the peroxide or horse hair can't wait 'til adolescence. Needs those young Afrikan scalps.

It is an irony that one of the main preoccupations that Afrikan women have regarding hair, namely hair length, is undermined by the application of these chemical agents to the hair. The hair straightening process, whether by the application of chemical agents or heat (as in the hot iron that was used by Afrikan women in the UK when I was a child) involves the disruption of the chemical structure of the hair and weakening or breaking of chemical bonds within the hair's structure. This is one of the reasons why so many women who use these chemicals experience their hair breaking, split ends, the occurrence of small bald spots and the tell tale chemically induced receding hairline. Chemically treated hair is weaker than well maintained natural hair and has a greater tendency to break.

Of course the amazing thing about nature is its resilience and despite the chemical attack, those chemical bonds keep reforming, those curls keep recurling and the dreaded Afrikan 'regrowth' keeps growing and reappearing. You don't beat nature, you simply keep it at bay – if you try to fight it – as the citizenry of New Orleans found to their cost.

As a general rule of thumb anything that has to be applied to the skin or hair using gloves – as is the case with these peroxide based straightening agents, is not doing you, your hair, or indeed your brain and the rest of your body any good. Remember, your hair is alive and connected to your scalp. Your skin is the largest organ you have and is porous to chemicals. What you put on your skin is absorbed into your body. Not in the same concentration as if ingested orally, however it is ingested nonetheless.

So the trade off is hair texture and straightness, for hair length, and health. It would appear that (European) hair texture and straightness are the most important characteristics of hair for Afrikan women and so the peroxide flows and the Afrikan pounds and dollars flow into predominantly European hands.

The Price of 'Beauty'

There follows an article that was contained in an email I received highlighting the possible serious long-term damage that many of the 'hair care' products sold to Afrikan women can cause and which reinforces the points made above about the ingestion of chemicals through the scalp and skin in general.

Lifestyles Report...Hair scare
by Debbie Norrell

At least two months ago WPXI contacted me to do an interview about ingredients in hair care products used by African-Americans possibly leading to breast cancer. I was selected because I am a 15-year breast cancer survivor. I agreed to do the interview. However at the end of the taping I didn't know anything more about the study than before the cameras started rolling.

Recently WAMO news anchor and New Pittsburgh Courier freelance writer Allegra Battle did a story on this same subject and it was a feature on the May 9, 5 p.m. KDKA news. But at the end of these stories we still did not have a list of the products. Battle gave me the list that didn't make her feature during a recent visit I made to the WAMO studios promoting the Pittsburgh Race for the Cure. So many of my friends have seen the stories on television or read about this issue in the paper and they want to know which products to be concerned about. However I wanted to give you more so I went to the Internet and looked for articles from the Center for Environmental Oncology and found one entitled: Why Healthy People Get Cancer: Center Examines Environmental Suspects (update spring 2005).

The article stated, one of the immediate research priorities of the new center is the puzzling phenomenon of breast cancer in African-Americans under the age of 40, who have nearly twice as much breast cancer as do white women. The center will work with Silent Spring Institute, a Massachusetts based cancer institute, to identify suspect contaminants and ingredients in hair care products and other personal products regularly used by African-American young women and their mothers.

More recently, attention has turned to estrogenic compounds in hair care products used by Black women as a possible explanation for higher cancer rates in this population. I've started to carry copies of the list in my purse but we're going to share it with you right here. The list simply says: The following is a list of products that have previously been found to contain hormones:

> Placenta Shampoo
> Queen Helene Placenta cream hair conditioner
> Placenta revitalizing shampoo
> Perm Repair with placenta
> Proline Perm Repair with placenta
> Hormone hair food Jojoba oil
> Triple action super grow
> Supreme Vita-Gro
> Luster's Sure Glo Hormone
> B & B Super Gro
> Lekair natural Super Glo
> Lekair Hormone hair treatment with Vitamin E
> Isoplus Hormone hair treatment with Quinine
> Fermodyl with Placenta hair conditioner
> Supreme Vita-Gro with allantoin and estrogen plus TEA-COCO
> Hask Placenta Hair conditioner
> Nu Skin body smoother and
> Nu Skin Enhancer.

The majority of these products contain placental extract, placenta, hormones or estrogen. As early as 1983 Dr. Devra Davis (epidemiologist and director of the Center for Environmental oncology, part of the University of Pittsburgh Cancer Institute) and co-researcher Leon Bradlow advanced the theory that xenoestrogens, synthetic estrogen imitators, were a possible cause of breast cancer. Davis also says, "most cases of breast cancer are not born, but made and the more hormones a woman is exposed to in her lifetime, the greater her risk of breast cancer." We need to be more cautious of the products that we use on our hair and our bodies and demand that more information about our health is shared.

Ladies and gentlemen beware.
(Email the columnist at debbienorrell.com.)

It is truly frightening isn't it to think that we have fifteen year old 'breast cancer survivors'.

Seke Toure said that 'the culture of your oppressor can never set you free'. Culture is about values and similarly the beauty standard of your oppressor is part of their culture and equally will never set us free.

Sisters, can you find the courage to resist. Why be a second rate pseudo-Caucasian when you can be a first class Afrikan Queen?

PART IV

BLUE SKIES FOR AFRIKANS

Blue Skies for Afrikans – Reframing Our Minds

Introduction
Well, you are on the final lap of this book now. Hopefully you will feel that we have travelled far together, however remember the *race* is won or lost on the final lap. I have tried to set the scene and context for our domination by Caucasians (part I), help the reader to understand the necessity to make a choice, to stand for Afrikan liberation or for White Supremacy (part II). Remember, if you stand in the middle of the road you will get run over. I have identified creating effective intra-racial relationships as the central and necessary component for transforming our position in the world (part III). All human transactions, be they emotional, political, economic, legal, spiritual, physical etc are based upon people relationships.

The first three parts of this book were designed to give you a good idea of the lay of the land. To highlight the barren or precipitous terrain to be avoided, to guide you through economic swamps and emotional quagmires, to draw a mental picture of the world we live in and to set out the choice we face plainly before you: *'To be Afrikan or not to be Afrikan, that is the question'*. What then is your answer? Perhaps you have a legitimate question still nagging at the back of your mind, what is it to be an Afrikan? If this is where you are at I hope this book, together with my previous work, has at least provided you with a map and a compass and pointed you in the right direction. We are Afrikans who need to become *The Afrikan*.

This final part has been the most difficult to write. Not as many people as you may think know the right questions to ask, but even less can provide any of the answers, so I qualify this section by saying that this is what I think, believe and in some cases know to be the answers to some of our questions. Some of the answers and lessons are also woven into the proceeding chapters since it is in the telling of the story that the lessons become apparent.

So many of us are always on about '*keeping it real*' and yet this has quickly become just another rhetorical cliché. The world of Afrocentrism is no different, lots of clichés, lots of chants, lots of Afrocentric versions of keeping it real and yet full of all the same pettiness and emotional frailties as in the *non-conscious* world we love to criticise and berate. I am no longer surprised at the lack of warmth, friendliness, support and sometimes just plain good manners that I often encounter in the world of Afro-centrism. Very often the label tells you very little about the person wearing it. Many Afrocentrics need to fix up personally, just like the rest of our people.

The story is always about change and transformation which is the goal of rites of passage, to transform a person from one psychological state into another. It is the process of *de-seasoning* the Afrikan psyche. I was once asked to come up with a personal motto and I put forward '*Every day do your best and every day make your best better*'. How many of us can honestly say that we do this most days of our lives?

Afrika needs some lifetime personal best performances from all of us to part those grey clouds and to reveal those Blue Skies for Afrikans.

Understanding Different Explanations for the Condition of Afrikans in the World Today

*White Supremacy (Racism) is not just about prejudice/hostility towards another group of people. It is a cognitive paradigm, a worldview; underpinned by the need of those people who classify themselves as White for **POWER AND CONTROL** over those they classify as non-White. (Ani 1996)*

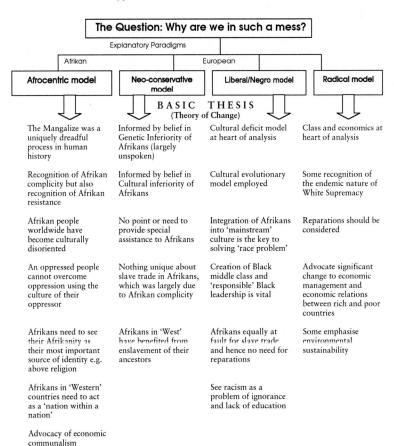

The Question: Why are we in such a mess?			
Explanatory Paradigms			
Afrikan		European	
Afrocentric model	**Neo-conservative model**	**Liberal/Negro model**	**Radical model**
		BASIC THESIS (Theory of Change)	
The Mangalize was a uniquely dreadful process in human history	Informed by belief in Genetic Inferiority of Afrikans (largely unspoken)	Cultural deficit model at heart of analysis	Class and economics at heart of analysis
Recognition of Afrikan complicity but also recognition of Afrikan resistance	Informed by belief in Cultural inferiority of Afrikans	Cultural evolutionary model employed	Some recognition of the endemic nature of White Supremacy
Afrikan people worldwide have become culturally disoriented	No point or need to provide special assistance to Afrikans	Integration of Afrikans into 'mainstream' culture is the key to solving 'race problem'	Reparations should be considered
An oppressed people cannot overcome oppression using the culture of their oppressor	Nothing unique about slave trade in Afrikans, which was largely due to Afrikan complicity	Creation of Black middle class and 'responsible' Black leadership is vital	Advocate significant change to economic management and economic relations between rich and poor countries
Afrikans need to see their Afrikanity as their most important source of identity e.g. above religion	Afrikans in 'West' have benefited from enslavement of their ancestors	Afrikans equally at fault for slave trade and hence no need for reparations	Some emphasise environmental sustainability
Afrikans in 'Western' countries need to act as a 'nation within a nation'		See racism as a problem of ignorance and lack of education	
Advocacy of economic communalism			

335

APPROACH FLOWING FROM THESIS

⬇	⬇	⬇	⬇
Adoption of Afrikan value systems, e.g. Ma'at, Nguzo Saba	Survival of the fittest, Individualism	Integration of Afrikans is key	Encourage Afrikans to join fully in overthrow of existing system to create new system based on 'universal' (Caucasian) values
Need to overthrow not refine or ameliorate White Supremacy	Minimal social welfare system	Mixed relationships are good and accurate barometer of race relations	Rejection of 'race based' action
Rejection of Individualism. 'I am because we are'. Do for self together (self reliance)	Assimilation of Afrikans is key	Need to create Black middle class through positive action/affirmative action	One world internationalist perspective from Caucasian cultural model
Need for limited, controlled centred contact with Caucasians/Caucasian culture	No special measures or initiatives for any group apart from vested interests	Encourage Afrikans to Blackenise Caucasian culture e.g. feminism	
Need for independent Afrikan schools	Blame Afrikans for the 'failure' to achieve and compete	Try to moderate worst effects of capitalism	
Strong emphasis on history but not enough on economics and contemporary politics			

RESULTS FLOWING FROM APPROACH

⬇	⬇	⬇	⬇
Overall, jury still out. Afrocentrism has failed to capture hearts and minds of critical mass of Afrikans	Increased economic marginalisation and disenfranchisement of Afrikans where these policies have been enacted e.g. Reagan/Bush years in USA	Rapid growth in Black middle class helped by affirmative action/positive action programmes	European culture spread by stealth
Made big impact on way Afrikans view their history	Creation of social conditions in which the victim is blamed for their circumstances	Huge increase in mixed relationships (where Afrikans are a minority in society)	Decrease in income inequality and other forms of inequality
Big impact on publishing and created 'Black Books' movement	Accelerated disintegration of the Afrikan family	Strong drive to depersonalise and institutionalise notions of racism i.e. its all about systems and structures and not people	Less overt discrimination against Afrikans
Lots of small isolated successes	Negro collaborators turn on and lead attack upon Afrikan poor	Strong emphasis on presenting Afrikan faces up front e.g. in media, without change to anti-Afrikan content	Attack by vested interest groups in retaliation for stopping the spread of economic exploitation by transnational corporations

Failure to date to establish firm roots in Afrika and influence direction of state policies	Removal of all special programmes to assist Afrikans	Afrikan imprisonment increases rapidly as well as incarceration in mental health institutions	Difficulty in marrying equality with efficient economic management
Failure to create significant wealth and asset base	Increase in cultural nihilism in society and amongst Afrikans in particular	Emphasis on Black street culture as cause of problems in Afrikan community and hence efforts focus on integrating Afrikans into Caucasian middle class culture	Caucasians still predominate in leadership positions
Failure to address bread and butter issues of the Afrikan masses who are generally uninterested in ancient Afrikan history	Increased economic and social division in society and amongst Afrikans in particular. Rapid growth in income inequality	Europeans maintain control of all key economic and social institutions	Afrikan physical and mental health is better than in other Caucasian societies
	Afrikan imprisonment increases rapidly as well as incarceration in mental health institutions		
	Europeans maintain control of all key economic and social institutions		

The foregoing information is designed to achieve two things. Firstly, to exemplify how our worldview will unconsciously direct our actions – and hence to some extent the results arising from those actions – our rationale for taking any particular course of action and our explanation as to why those actions led to the particular outcome achieved. Whatever the outcome our explanation/rationalisation of the end result will always serve to justify and reinforce our worldview. In the exceptional cases where our explanation does not serve this end these are times when people experience a severe crisis of confidence, awakening or epiphany and psychologically are able to make the jump from one paradigm to another. Changing one's socio-political worldview is a bit like changing one's religion and often involves tremendous psycho-emotional upheaval and can result in the severing of relationships with family and friends.

In the foregoing framework I have described the failings of Afrocentrism in what may seem to be fairly harsh terms for one who professes allegiance to this cause. However I am of the view that whilst the truth hurts the truth will set us free and there are too many

Afrikans using the words and theories of Afrocentrism for intellectual masturbation, safe in the knowledge that they will never be called upon to implement these ideas in their personal lives or the public realm. Afrocentrism calls for changes in thoughts, words and deeds. Afrocentrism calls for both a social and personal morality. Afrocentrism calls for right conduct. Afrocentrism calls for risk, commitment and sacrifice. If we cannot acknowledge our individual and collective failings we will never find the will to succeed.

Afrocentrics need to bring forth a more sharply focused economic and political manifesto for change reinforced by the practical implementation of the ideas suggested at a family, local, regional, national and international level. If we cannot get the ideas to work we need to question the ideas as well as the implementation. If the patient is not getting better either the diagnosis is wrong or the treatment is wrong. We need practical life sustaining Afrocentrism.

Chess as a Metaphor for the battle against White Supremacy

- White vs. Black

- The Objective is to Checkmate the King

- White always makes the first, offensive move

- The Queen is the most powerful piece on the Board

- In order to win Black must effectively co-ordinate the movement of all pieces, to firstly repel the White attack and secondly launch an effective counterattack

- It is essential that the Black King and Queen work together in harmony and that the Black King keeps his eyes on his Black Queen

- The most vulnerable pieces on the Board are the pawns (children), they are in the front line of the battle, however they can wreak havoc if provided with sufficient protection to be developed effectively

- Sometimes pawns are sacrificed in chess. Is the reward for the sacrifice sufficient?

- You either play for the Black side or the White side, you cannot play for both or avoid the contest

Standing on Our Cultural Feet

Q.   What are the key cultural determinants of racial/ethnic success?

A.   Countries/Racial/ethnic groups that exercise significant self-deterministic intent and power in the world demonstrate two key common cultural hallmarks:

1.   The use of an indigenous language in their education system and institutional life.

2.   They practice an indigenous religion/spiritual system.

Table 8 – The relationship between language, religion and power

Country	Institutional Language	Dominant Religion	World Power Level
Nigeria	English	Islam	Low
South Africa	English/Afrikaans	Christianity	Low
Ghana	English	Christianity	Very Low
Jamaica	English	Christianity	Very Low
China	Mandarin	None (Confuscianist philosophy)	High
Japan	Japanese	Shintoism	Med/High
South Korea	Korean	Christianity	Medium
India	Hindi/English	Hinduism	Med/High
USA	English	Christianity	Very High
Germany	German	Christianity	High/Med
U.K.	English	Christianity	High/Med
France	French	Christianity	High/Med
Italy	Italian	Christianity	Med/High

Language and religion are the two legs of culture used in the race of life (Biko 1998). As you can see from the table above most Afrikan countries don't have a leg to stand on. Or put another way, we have as much chance of competing on the world stage in our current state as a one legged man in an arse kicking contest. These are issues that will not be solved in my lifetime but must be constantly pushed to the fore if we are ever to have a realistic hope of digging our way out of this mess we are in.

You may be surprised to see countries such as Japan and Germany with a lower power rating than China even though their per capita income is far higher; however there are a few points to note. Firstly, China may have lots of very poor people, however it has economic scale and its economy is already bigger than Germany's and about to surpass Japan's. Secondly, and crucially, China has nuclear weapons and the freedom to develop whatever weapons technology it likes. Both Germany and Japan have been in the doghouse since their crimes in the Second European War on the World. Since that time they have both had external and internally imposed controls on their military development.

Forget the crap about nuclear non-proliferation. If the Caucasian has weapons we need weapons that are just as deadly. As Frederick Douglass said, "The only argument that satisfies man is power."

In a similar vein Professor Wade Nobles tells us that,

"Power is the ability to define reality and have other people respond to that definition as if it were their own."

Reality is born out of a people's perception and conception of the world around them, which in turn is born out of their culture. If a people accept another people's culture, they accept their conception of reality and in turn cede them power. This power can then be turned against them. This is why the most powerful countries in the world – and those with the greatest potential to acquire power – stand on two cultural legs.

Nana Kuntu, who is also known as Del Jones speaks to the dilemma facing many of our people in dealing with the reality of what enslaved us and what made us susceptible to enslavement.

"If we truly knew and felt the slave experience we would divorce ourselves from everything that delivered those experiences to us, whether they were social, economic or religious. How could these creations be good for us if they came with and helped cause and maintained slavery. The answer is clear, we still have a slave mentality, world view and relationship with this white supremacist system. Being super consumers is not freedom."

Del Jones
Showdown (2005)

Of course many of our people are happy being super consumers. Happy to close their mental eyes and shut out the ugliness all around them. Happy to pretend that being part of a degraded and disrespected people is of no consequence to them, who after all is simply an individual who just happens to be Black.

Until Afrikan people understand and take on board the reality of inter-group rivalry and competition there is no hope of substantive change. If you go into a pit bull's cage yu had better ready fi fight.

Isn't it about time (for freedom)?

Managing Your Time and Effort
One of the truisms of life is that 'If it is important enough you will find the time'. Afrikans, myself included, are forever complaining about how busy we are and yet seem to have little idea about how to address this perennial problem. Following the publication of my first book; friends and acquaintances often asked me how I found the time to write a book. The simple response was that most of the writing was done between 10pm-12am at night. The more important realisation was that it was the motivation and determination that provided the energy that allowed me to work at a time when I was often tired after a long day at work – and very often community group evening meetings following work.

So motivation and desire increases one's capacity to undertake work, however there are only 24 hours in each day, and with work, eating, washing, sleeping etc. there is a finite limit to the time one can free up for all the demands that are made upon your time. The more fundamental question is how we earn our living. Most of us spend most of our working lives working for institutions, companies or individuals that do not have the best interests of Afrikan people at heart. I touched upon some of these issues in an earlier chapter in this book entitled *Working for 'The Man'*.

This chapter is about cutting your existing cloth accordingly. How can you look at your existing commitments, lifestyle and approach to getting things done and find ways of increasing your personal effectiveness. There follows some tips and advice to assist you in this process.

1. *Time is Money*
    Time is scarce and has to be managed. You don't spend time you have to invest it. There is an "opportunity cost" to all decisions you make. N.B You can save money but you can't save time.

2. *Focus on Critical Activities*
    80:20 Principle (Pareto's Principle)
    Critical Few vs. Trivial Many
    Spend 80% of your time on the critical 20% of activities that will yield 80% of critical results. Most people spend a disproportionate amount of time on trivial activity.

Diagram (v) – Relationship between Critical Few and Trivial Many

3. *Learn How to Procrastinate*
    Procrastinate on the 80% of activities that yield 20% of results. Do not put off Critical Activities. Critical activities are those which contribute towards achieving your strategic goals.

4. *Throw Away your 'To Do' List*
    Getting things done is not the same as getting the right things done. 80% of things on your To Do list are Trivial. Create a 'Critical Task List'. Split a page of paper and put the Critical Activities at the Top, Trivial at the Bottom. Spend 80% of the time working on those activities at the top. Do things at the bottom when you need a break.

5. *Reward Yourself for Doing the Right Things*
    The things that get rewarded get done.

6. *Do FTF – Feared Things First. Not Fast, First, or Fun Things First*
    E.g. make that difficult call first. You will get an energy boost
    when you overcome these fears.

7. *Do a Daily Power Hour*
    "Plans are nothing. Planning is everything" Gen. Eisenhower
    Plan each day. Spend 15 minutes each morning planning.

8. *Exercise*
    Exercise is good for the mind and body. However everything in
    moderation. If you feel pain during exercise you should stop or
    reduce the intensity of the activity. The only people who need to
    push themselves through the pain barrier are competitive athletes.

9. *Layer Activities*
    Use waiting time productively e.g. on a bus, in a taxi, driving or
    on a train. You can listen to a talking book in your car; write a
    report on the train.

10. *Set Specific Goals in Life and Work*
    Write a Life Plan / Work Plan and review it regularly. What gets
    measured gets done.

11. *Engage in Scattered Focus*
    Focus and then scatter. Focus and then scatter. Broaden your field
    of perceptual vision. Sometimes those lifechanging opportunities
    can be sighted in your area of peripheral vision. As they say feel
    the fear and do it anyway. Try out lots of different activities and
    avenues until you find what you are supposed to be doing.

12. *Delegate*
    Delegation is to time what leverage is to money. Delegate the
    80% routine activities. If you have no one to delegate to then

delegate routine/trivial tasks to your 'low time' i.e. the time of day when you know you are least productive. Critical tasks for critical time, trivial tasks for trivial time.

13. Do it Now
Procrastination is suicide by instalments.

14. Do a four quadrant test each day
At the end of each day write activities into one of the four quadrants.

Diagram (vi) – Four sector task analysis

Routine Tasks	Unexpected
Other People's Tasks	Dreams Goals Targets

How much of your day at work, or life outside of work, do you spend addressing tasks related to each quadrant? If you are like most people you will spend a lot of time on routine tasks and very little working towards your dreams, goals and big targets. Monitor yourself for a week and see how you use your time. If you don't like the results of the analysis, you need to make some changes.

15. Learn to Say No!
This is one of the hardest but most important lessons to learn and do.

16. Handle Paper Only once
Delegate, Do It, File It, or Throw It Away

17. Do It Wrong the First Time!
If it is worth doing it's worth doing badly! Fail your way to success. Or.. Ready, Fire, Aim. The conditions will never be perfect to tackle a big task, so make a start with the imperfect and shape excellence out of imperfection.

18. Blitzing
Every hour on the hour 'blitz' for 10 minutes on an intense activity.

19. Return and Review
Review the day at the end of each day.

20. Challenge Yourself Daily
Creativity dramatically increases as a deadline approaches.

21. Practise the speed of going slow
Work on all areas of your life to stay in balance.

Being
Brain
Body
Time
People
Money

Use the tips above and you can start to create the time to build the future you want and the future our people need.

Much of the material in this chapter has been adapted from the work of Robert G. Allen on his Compact Disc Audio Book 'Multiple Streams of Income: How to Generate A lifetime of Unlimited Wealth' produced by the Enlightened Millionaire Institute.

Black Consumption –
From Bling to Wealth Creation

In terms of economic development many of us have been fooled by the mirage of Black Economic progress that has been spun to us, particularly in terms of Afrikans in the US. Now, whilst there are many individual examples of Afrikans accumulating wealth in the US, when one looks at the overall picture it is still bleak and gives pause for thought.

In terms of earnings, at the end of the 19th Century Afrikan-Americans median income was 57% of that of European-Americans. By the mid sixties the figure was still 57%, by the 1980's it had risen to the dizzy heights of 61% and by the beginning of the 21st Century it was back down to under 60%.

In terms of wealth an article on the Afrocentric Experience website highlighted a significant increase in Afrikan-American wealth, however this was from a very low base.

Boosted by a rising rate of home ownership, the net wealth of the typical African-American household increased from $5,919 in 1989 to $19,010 in 2001, according to Federal Reserve (news – web sites) data analyzed by the Consumer Federation of America, a nonprofit advocacy group.

That increase of 221 percent far outstrips the 33 percent increase posted by all U.S. households during the same period, the Consumer Federation noted. But black households still lagged far behind the nationwide median average of $86,100 in 2001, the group said.

Despite the persistent gap in net wealth – defined as financial and property assets minus mortgages and other debts – the increase is significant as it shows that more black families are following good financial habits, said Stephen Brobeck, executive director of the Consumer Federation.

"We do not believe that a greater than 200 percent increase in black families' wealth is trivial," Brobeck said.

Much of that increase in wealth was due to a rise in home ownership, which increased from 42 percent in 1990 to 48 percent in 2003, said Vada Hill, chief marketing officer of Fannie Mae, the giant mortgage-finance company. The nationwide home-ownership rate is 68 percent.

Home ownership is especially important because on the whole, black families have had lower incomes and smaller inheritances with which to build wealth, Brobeck and Hill said, and tend to invest less in the financial markets.

"This is an audience that is pretty conservative about investment, pretty risk averse," Hill said.

Source: *The Afrocentric Experience*

In an article that appeared in *USA Today* magazine entitled 'Tough Choices for Tough Times' (2004) writer Yolanda Young highlights some of the poor financial choices that contribute to Afrikan-American economic stagnation.

"These are tough economic times, especially for African-Americans, for whom the unemployment rate is more than 10%. Alarmingly, rather than belt-tightening, the response has been to spend more. In many poor neighborhoods, one is likely to notice satellite dishes and expensive new cars. According to Target Market, a company that tracks black consumer spending, blacks spend a significant amount of their income on depreciable products. In 2002, the year the economy nose-dived; we spent $22.9 billion on clothes, $3.2 billion on electronics and $11.6 billion on furniture to put into homes that, in many cases, were rented.

Among our favorite purchases are cars and liquor. Blacks make up only 12% of the U.S. population, yet account for 30% of the country's Scotch consumption. Detroit, which is 80% black, is the world's No. 1 market for Cognac. So impressed was Lincoln with the $46.7 billion that blacks spent on cars that the auto maker commissioned Sean "P. Diddy" Combs, the entertainment and fashion mogul, to design a limited-edition Navigator replete with six plasma screens, three DVD players and a Sony PlayStation 2.

The only area where blacks seem to be cutting back on spending is books; total purchases have gone from a high of $356 million in 2000 to $303 million in 2002. This shortsighted behavior, motivated by a desire for instant gratification and social acceptance, comes at the expense of our future. The National Urban League's "State of Black America 2004" report found that fewer than 50% of black families owned their homes compared with more than 70% of whites.

According to published reports, the Ariel Mutual Funds/Charles Schwab 2003 Black Investor Survey found that when comparing households where blacks and whites had roughly the same household incomes, whites saved nearly 20% more each month for retirement, and 30% of African-Americans earning $100,000 a year had less than $5,000 in retirement savings. While 79% of whites invest in the stock market, only 61% of African-Americans do.

Certainly, higher rates of unemployment, income disparity and credit discrimination are financial impediments to the economic vitality of blacks, but so are our consumer tastes. By finding the courage to change our spending habits, we might be surprised at how far the $631 billion we now earn might take us."

Ms Young's article emphasises that whatever the level of discrimination experienced by us, at the end of the day we need to change our individual and collective behaviour if we are to change our economic position. As the Afrikan saying goes

'Once you conquer the enemy within, the enemy outside can do you no harm.'

Whilst Ms Young is correct in describing our people's spending patterns as shortsighted we need to develop a clearer understanding of what might be some of the root causes of this self and group retarding behaviour.

It is well known that many people who have low self-esteem or who are experiencing stress or other life difficulties will find refuge in food and this phenomenon is known as *comfort eating*, where food is used to meet a psychological as opposed to physiological need. Similarly, it is also a well established fact that some people engage in reckless spending at times when they are feeling 'blue' or depressed. This type of behaviour is often referred to as *retail therapy* where the acquisition of consumer goods is used to anaesthetise psychological pain. Of course the pain is only dulled temporarily and very soon some more therapy is required. These types of behaviour can be described as self-deluding psychological distraction techniques, which are doomed to failure since they do not help the person to address the real and underlying cause of their emotional pain.

What I am suggesting is that Afrikan-Americans and no doubt Afrikans in many other parts of the world are engaging in mass retail therapy, purchasing huge quantities of *conspicuous consumer items* in order to send a message to the world that they/we are successful and have the material trappings of wealth. Of course, none of this self-deluding behaviour fools us or anyone else and so the pain continuously needs to be dulled by further bouts of consumption.

There is no quick fix to our financial problems. They can only be overcome by the implementation of sound financial principles and facing our personal and collective angst over how others see us. When we concern ourselves with addressing how we see ourselves we will be in psychological shape to transform our current situation.

I have listed below some tips I came across for personal financial management which I hope you find useful.

Black Enterprise Magazine Declaration of Financial Empowerment:

From this day forward, I will declare my vigilant and lifelong commitment to financial empowerment. I pledge the following:

1. To save and invest 10% to 15% of my after-tax income

2. To be a proactive and informed investor

3. To be a disciplined and knowledgeable consumer

4. To measure my personal wealth by net worth, not income

5. To engage in sound budget, credit and tax management practices

6. To teach business and financial principles to my children

7. To use a portion of my personal wealth to strengthen my community.

8. To support the creation and growth of profitable, competitive Black-owned enterprises

9. To maximize my earning power through a commitment to career development, technological literacy and professional excellence

10. To ensure that my wealth is passed on to future generations

TODAY IS THE DAY I MADE THE CHANGE!!!!!!!!!

If we just follow these 10 points, who knows how far we can go?

The following chapter provides the reader with a practical example of the type of long-term concerted, co-operative, financial activities that we need to engage in to transform our current situation.

ABDF Re-visited
By Mark Dunwell

It has been 2 years since Paul Grant first introduced you to the ABDF Limited in his first book 'Niggers, Negroes, Black People and Afrikans' (2003). He told you about the progress the organisation had (or had not) made in its lifetime. It now rests with me to bring you up to date with where we are now. Nine years as one of the elected Directors charged with running the organisation gives me the opportunity to offer an informed view of the success, failures and lessons to be learned in this community business endeavour. The health warning that must accompany these words is that they represent my view and not necessarily the view of ABDF Ltd. the organisation. These reflective words are offered as self-help and help to others who are, or are looking to; tread a similar path for our community's economic well being.

Where are we now?
At the time of writing this piece (August 2005) ABDF Ltd. has 57 members across 8 cities and we manage 2 rental properties. For those of you who have read Niggers, Negroes, Black People and Afrikans (and if you have not you should) you may recall that in 2003 we had 49 members and were managing 2 rental properties. Not much progress there some might say. This may be true but when put into the context of our initial 5-year plan (Jan 2002 – Dec 2006) we can see we are not far adrift from where we planned to be. We had modest targets, which were the following:

- 70 members by the end of year 5
- Purchase 3 properties for equity growth and rental income by

the end of year 5
- To remain financially stable with positive cashflow throughout the five year period

With respect to the targets above; 70 members by the end of year 5 is achievable, it is unlikely that we will purchase 3 properties by the end of year 5 and we have remained financially stable and now generate profit. Any business plan has to be adaptable for ever-changing business circumstances. Our reduction from 3 to 2 properties is largely due to the massive rise in property prices through the life of the plan and our failure to strike while the iron was hot!

How did we get there?

Our ambitions at first glance appear modest and seem to lack the audacity of an organisation with its sights set on national and international development. It serves us well to remember that all journeys start with a single step. Our prudent start is informed by the many failed – as well as the relative dearth of – attempts to build self-reliant (economical and political) Afrikan organisations in the UK. Paul covered some of the seemingly endless reasons for our failures in his first book and hopefully provided some solutions to overcome the high failure rate. The ABDF is about overcoming these reasons and building an institutional organisation capable of bridging generations. With this in mind, whether the reasoning was sound or not, the initial business plan was based on the following premises:

- The organisation must grow with stability, build **trust** and above all must survive and thrive.
- Initially without full-time human resource we need to grow the membership at a rate that is manageable with the resource available. Individual member's interests need to be transparent and secure to build **trust**.
- Our initial business venture must be low risk to minimise the risk of failure so that we can build **trust**.
- Initially without full-time human resource to run the business

we need to undertake business investment that requires minimal day-to-day management.

In our case building **trust** was reliant on commitment; goodwill of members and a sense of *meaningful progression* (even if it appears slow). Paul previously spoke of what academics call 'social capital'. For a community enterprise it is your foundation and from where we are coming from it takes longer to build than you think.

Above are some of the planned reasons that our rate of progression has frustrated some of our members, not least the author of this book! The many unplanned and unforeseen reasons for that slow progression are the lessons we must learn from.

Barriers to meaningful progression

When we started the Afrikan Business Development Fund one of the most difficult processes was getting people involved in defining what the organisation's purpose would be and creating a vision for our future. Bringing together individual ideas and perspectives into a cohesive vision is always a difficult process. The main areas that make this a difficult process in our community are:

- Cultural perspective
- Spiritual (religious) perspective
- Political perspective
- Community perspective
- Individual perspective
- Motivation (or lack of = apathy)

It was a process that was crucial as the whole principle of defining our future, determining our future and building self-reliance is built on it. As we approach the end of our current 5 year plan the main challenge that faces our organisation right now is mobilising our members to take part in the process of continually defining our future – the next 5, 10... years. Ironically we are victims of one of our successes. Right now we have all the above factors to contend with

(with more people) and we are more heavily afflicted with the disease of apathy. By engendering a degree of trust it appears we are not motivated to get involved. At this point you have to ask the question was the process at the genesis of our organisation thorough enough?

Many doers NOT Mighty leaders

Often times we can wonder in awe at the achievements of some of our great ancestors, such as Harriet Tubman or Marcus Garvey. How did these great people inspire and mobilise so many and achieve such mighty things under seemingly impenetrable circumstances? In part the answer lies in the question. The circumstances were clear and unquestionably desperate and so great things came out of great necessity. Nevertheless they were extraordinary people. Most of us are ordinary (even if talented) by comparison. Far too often we hear complaints of the lack of leadership in our communities followed by desperate praise of heroes and sheroes. We need lots more doers not leaders. Without doers there are no leaders. From a membership of 57 we do not have enough doers that actively contribute to the organisation moving forward. There is an apathy, which I would define as *the 'gap' between what you do relative to what you can do*. For sure the majority of us are guilty, some more than others. There are various things you can do in a group such as the ABDF ranging from significant to virtually no time commitment. The following list outlines some of these things but is by no means exhaustive:

- Standing as a Director (elected office)
- Becoming a member of a sub-committee
- Participate in property management
- Providing skills and expertise in research or miscellaneous duties
- Recruiting effective members
- Contributing to shaping the future of the organisation (meetings, phone, e-mail, letter etc.)
- Attending meetings
- Turning up on time for meetings

- Giving apologies for non-attendance at meetings
- Attending social events
- Reading minutes of meetings
- Making contact to take part in decision making processes
- Providing up to date contact details

It is often said that these things that I describe are true of all types of organisations in all communities. This may be true but to what degree I do not know, however, what should concern us is our condition relative to other communities. We are in worse shape and therefore need to deal with apathy with a more determined and ruthless attitude.

The reasons why levels of involvement are low could circumnavigate the globe twice. The fact is if you are not doing – you are doing nothing (for something you value). It is at this point that you must question your motivation.

What have you done for ME/your community lately?

'I am because we are' is the Afrikan philosophy of self relative to community. This philosophy stems from communal spirit, teaching and action. Simply put it means if it's good for me it should be good for the community and if it's good for the community it should be good for me. All over the world our Afrikan rootedness has been dampened down and tampered with. The societies we live in totally contradict this philosophy. Consequently, matching Afrikan philosophy with Afrikan action is not as easy as it sounds. I was told by a hardworking, frustrated member of the ABDF that they feel like they are working for a charity – time, money and effort in, with not much return. A community enterprise, such as the ABDF, is sold on the benefits to the community as a whole and the benefits to the individual. The philosophical principle is alluring, but the practical reality is much more demanding (on a few). By definition an enterprise that benefits you and the wider community requires you to invest more. The potential returns are far greater than any other kind of investment you could make, but those returns are not calculated in purely financial terms. We are talking 'social capital' worth more than its weight in gold. Words like these are sometimes lost on the frustrated few. The lesson to learn here is striking the right balance between philosophical ideals for community needs and visions of the future with the pragmatic needs of individuals in the here and now.

Solutions for barriers to meaningful progression

In this section we ask ourselves the following, what have we learnt from our experience to date that we can carry forward and share with others looking to tread a similar path? We need to apply the principles of Sankofa (looking back to go forward) to achieve 'meaningful progression'. This is important as we live in a society and culture that believes in 'progress for progress' sake' with no means of going back.

Lesson 1: Acorn to Oak

If you start a journey and your plotted course is 1° degree out by the time you reach your desired location you can be several miles off course. This principle holds true for organisations plotting a journey. You need to be absolutely clear on where you are taking your organisation. I am convinced our process in the beginning of defining purpose and vision and defining a course for the ABDF was the correct one, although it seemed to be painfully slow. What was not as thorough as it should have been was the process of checking whether members coming on board were absolutely clear of the path. Failing to do this creates a number of problems.

- You are constantly re-visiting the same discussions.
- The organisation will progress at the rate of the slowest member i.e. the chain is only as strong as the weakest link.
- As the organisation grows this problem can only get bigger.

Solution

Every member of the ABDF is a valuable member that has willingly decided to join this organisation and take this journey. The choices that need to be made are around where an individual is located on their personal journey in life and how does that fit with the path the ABDF is taking. Where an individual's path and the ABDF path become coincident is not the same for everyone. It is advisable to start with a small group of 'single-minded serious individuals' that have the ability to not self destruct. An unshakeable foundation is the best start you can have. This would not please some people because in the first instance the rate of progress would probably be slower; however, in the long run this single action will save you a lot of time. Make no mistake a project such as this is a long-term venture. For the ABDF Ltd. this lesson means that we should not be afraid to go backwards to go forward again.

Lesson 2: Business does not run on good will
Community Enterprises are associated with words like co-operation, support, unity and assistance, but too often we misinterpret and take advantage of these positive words and translate them into the word 'free'. In the early days of ABDF we often had a debate on whether members should be paid for the services they provided for the organisation. The decision was taken not to pay any members for services provided, mainly based on the reasoning that the organisation could not afford it in its infancy and as a Community Enterprise, members should be willing to 'give'. At the time the argument seemed reasonably innocuous, but on hindsight we were busy planting the seeds of psychological walking sticks. What do you think you get free from business entrepreneurs like Richard Branson of Virgin or Bill Gates of Microsoft?

Business costs and the major currency you expend is commitment. The currency of commitment is made up of finance, time and creativity/skill, all of which are interchangeable in the business world.

Diagram (vii) – Commitment Triangle

All the business clichés tell you what you need to know. 'Speculate to accumulate', means you need to invest before you get a return. Time is money', speaks for itself. By ABDF members providing services for free we build a number of psychological barriers that require breaking down.

The true cost/commitment (finance, time and creativity/skill) of running a business is masked. Sheltering ourselves from what is truly required to succeed is not a good starting point. If you cannot afford to do something then you should not do it. This principle teaches us to cut our cloth accordingly. A lesson we need to learn as individuals as well as organisations.

Goodwill does not engender accountability and responsibility. It is more difficult to demand or expect high performance from a person (ABDF member, elected officer or supporter of ABDF) that provides a service to the organisation for free. There is not enough *pull* for progress from the leadership within the ABDF, which hinders development.

You value something that costs more than something that you get for free. If you pay for a product or service you are far more likely to be demanding. The membership of the ABDF is not demanding. A demanding membership would *push* the organisation to progress.

Solution
The future of the ABDF Ltd. should be built on the true cost of running the business. That way the organisation (members) will

understand the true value of the organisation and the level of commitment needed to succeed. This has major implications for future structures and strategies designed to further develop the organisation.

Conclusion

The shareholders of the ABDF have travelled a long way together, however just as in the case of the struggle for Afrikan liberation the journey has just begun. The ABDF was never designed to be a get rich quick scheme – which is probably why membership has grown slowly – it is more of a get financially independent very slowly scheme. Similarly, the struggle for Afrikan liberation was always bound to be a get liberated very slowly venture. I think that many ABDF members are realising that a major and fundamental part of the ABDF's mission and success has been in increasing the financial literacy and awareness of its shareholders. This has catalysed many members to embark upon their own personal financial ventures, many of which they may have hesitated to participate in were it not for the support, advice and above all example of other ABDF shareholders.

During this chapter I have heavily emphasised the centrality of building trust when it comes to developing an organisation such as ABDF Ltd that is asking Afrikans to invest their money collectively. It is a cliché that we do not trust each other, but nonetheless often true. It is also true that in general Caucasians do not trust one another which is why they have spent so much of their legal history refining the law of contract and why they invest so much time and effort into anti-fraud measures. This still does not stop them investing in their own financial institutions and it should not stop us. The key is to enact practical measures that create reassurance whilst working on ways to strengthen the emotional and psychological bonds within your organisation.

I hope that this review of the progress of ABDF Ltd contained within this chapter has been useful to you and look forward to the opportunity to share further news of our accelerated growth and development whenever Paul publishes his next book.

The Long Run to Freedom

"Speed determines the outcome of battle. A great army strikes like lightning and devastates like a thunderbolt."
Shaka Zulu quoted in 'Emperor Shaka the Great' by Mazisi Kunene

During the war between the Zulus and the British in the 19th Century for control of much of the territory that is now known as South Africa, there were many famous battles and acts of great courage by the Zulu warriors were commonplace. I was watching a television programme which examined one of these battles (my apologies that I have not been able to identify the name of the battle) and the Caucasian South African presenter, who I must say was unusually fair to the Zulu, was describing the battle scene and praising the extraordinary courage of the Afrikan warriors.

The British had set up their encampment and were faced by the Zulu who were some 800 metres or so away on the brow of a small hill. The Zulus were armed with shields and spears and the British soldiers had rifles. There was no circuitous way to get closer to the British position before mounting a charge. The Zulu commander was faced with no option other than to order his warriors to run into the British guns. Now it must be remembered that this was no act of suicide or madness, it was a decision based upon the circumstances.

So the Zulu warriors were given the order to advance and summoned their courage for the assault. They ran just over 800 metres across open savannah towards the British riflemen. Imagine how you would have felt if you were one of the warriors standing in the front rows. Many of us would no doubt have been running to the toilet or asking if there were any brown trousers we could put on!

These brave Afrikans began their run in the face of death. They could not run too quickly or they would be too fatigued to fight effectively when they finally came upon the enemy and they could not run too slowly or they would all be picked off by the British rifles before they could engage them in hand to hand combat. It is interesting that some of the senior Zulu commanders ran in the frontline to give heart and courage to their warriors. The run would take the Zulus around three minutes. Three minutes to think about fighting, living and dieing.

The British waited, and waited. Their soldiers did not commence firing until the Zulu warriors were within around 200-300 metres away but when they did open fire it was almost impossible to miss the onrushing wall of Afrikan courage that confronted them. Zulus fell by the dozen, the score, the hundreds, eventually thousands, however they got there, they got there. They got there tired but determined and wreaked a bloody vengeance upon the British, overwhelming the camp and lowering the Union Jack flag.

This was one of many great battles won by the Zulu, however the war was eventually lost. Shaka was betrayed by some of those close to him and with the loss of their inspirational leader the Zulu were defeated. Many years later it must have made the great Zulu chief turn in his grave to see one of his lineage, Chief Mangasutu Buthelezi, turn weaselling collaborator as he worked hand in glove with the Afrikaner apartheid regime of President P.W. Botha to undermine the ANC and catalyse a tribal conflict that had never previously existed. All so that he could maintain his personal power as a Chief of slaves. The legacy of the incredible violence instigated by the South African government and Buthelezi's Inkatha party still lives today in a 'free' South Africa that has one of the highest crime rates in the world and where whilst Black income – which was already at poverty levels – is falling, White income is rising.

What lessons can we glean from the Zulu victory I have described above? Well, there are some obvious conclusions that can be drawn. Firstly, Afrikans will need to summon up tremendous courage, belief and unity to defeat the Caucasian army. Secondly, there will be many casualties along the way (too many to count), however this should not deter us given the enormous daily losses we are suffering at present. Thirdly, we must learn to take orders from our (competent) leaders. Fourthly, we require courageous leaders who are prepared to stand in the frontline with the troops. Finally, love and prayers will not defeat our enemies, a well planned military strategy and appropriate military technology will give them the choice of either backing off or dying.

We are going to have to learn to be more coldhearted with our enemies and to save our love for those who love us. Xenophilia is wasted upon Xenophobes.

I will finish this chapter with a quote from the incomparable Marcus Mosiah Garvey which sets out the cost of liberation which the Zulu warriors described above were well aware of.

"...Any sane man, race or nation that desires freedom must first of all think in terms of blood. Why, even the Heavenly Father tells us that "without the shedding of blood there can be no remission of sins?" Then how in the name of God, with history before us, do we expect to redeem Africa without preparing ourselves-some of us to die."

Marcus Mosiah Garvey cited in 'The Philosophy and Opinions of Marcus Garvey: Or, Africa for the Africans' (Garvey 1986: 11)

Living The Afrikan Virtues

Introduction

In his highly acclaimed book Stolen Legacy (1954) George G.M. James identified the soul attributes that the Kemetic neophyte (trainee for priesthood) was required to manifest. The process of training for the Kemetic priesthood makes our idea of education and commitment to learning look shallow and half hearted. The first stage took seven years to move from neophyte to the lowest level of priesthood, however in total there were seven stages each lasting seven years. By the time you completed this type of training you would be a master, perfectly in tune with your mind, body and spirit.

Let us look at these virtues and see what they could mean for us in our everyday lives and how they can – if implemented diligently and with commitment – help us to 'fix up' for want of a better phrase.

The Ten Afrikan Virtues

1. Control of Thought

This is probably the toughest of all the virtues to master. How can one control one's thoughts? This is not about filtering out negative thoughts, this is about training the mind to generate the correct thoughts. As I highlighted in the earlier chapter on 'Working for The Man' our values determine our thoughts and our thoughts determine our actions, however we can engage in psycho-cultural reverse engineering. That is to say if we can identify those areas where we experience cognitive dissonance i.e. where what we say and what we do is in contradiction, then we can begin to change our behaviour and by so doing we begin to reprogramme our brain computer and transform our real values. Many of us operate from a rhetorical basis as opposed to a practical, operational basis. That is to say too many people talk the talk but don't walk the walk. These people cannot control their thoughts since they are operating from a basis of psychological disharmony. Think right to act right, Act right to think right.

2. *Control of Action*

Naturally this virtue links intimately to the previous one. If you can establish control of thought then control of action should not prove a problem. One of the aspects of action that too many people overlook is speech. As I was advised when growing up 'once the words are out you can't recall them'. Too many people speak in haste and repent at leisure (if at all). A constant theme in Afrikan tradition is that of 'Nommo' or the power of the word. To emphasise this point regarding the power of the word Professor Maulana tells us in the introduction to his book 'Selections From THE HUSIA..' that "The title of this text, *The Husia*, is taken from two ancient Egyptian words which signify the two divine powers by which Ra (Ptah) created the world, i.e. *Hu*, authoritative utterance and *Sia*, exceptional insight." (Karenga 1989: xiv)

Afrikans more than anyone should know the power of the word and yet so many of us are so cavalier and careless with our words, tossing them to the wind like so much confetti, casually unaware of the whirlwind of fury misplaced words can galvanise. To rephrase a saying from my childhood,.... Sticks and stones may break your bones but words can wound more deeply. If we have control of thought and control of speech then other forms of action should be controlled and purposive. An oppressed people cannot afford the luxury of ill-discipline and yet we seem to have an increasing number of ill-disciplined adults raising ill-disciplined children. There is no longer time for excuses such as 'I didn't mean it'. If you didn't mean it why did you do it? We need to eliminate words such as hopefully, perhaps, try, maybe etc. from our vocabulary and remember! You either will or you won't, do or you don't.

3. *Steadfastness of Purpose*

What is your purpose in life? It can seem almost, but not quite as daunting as the question, What is the Meaning of Life? In a very real and substantive way one could write a whole book on this subject, exploring all sorts of philosophical and esoteric ideas; however for our purposes we will try to limit our discussion to some practical and concrete ideas. In my previous book (Grant 2003) I put forward the proposition that the concept and principles of Ma'at offer a basis for living that is broad enough to achieve widespread buy in from most Afrikans, irrespective of religious affiliation, and yet clear and specific enough to provide a sound framework for living. The seven cardinal principles of MA'AT are:

TRUTH [honesty], RIGHTEOUSNESS [compassion, piety, faith, integrity], JUSTICE [fairness, equity], HARMONY [respect for the natural environment and laws of nature], BALANCE [gender equality] (GOOD) ORDER [self-discipline, consideration for others, social structure], RECIPROCITY [do unto others as you would have them do unto you].

I have put into brackets some examples of the social manifestations of these principles to highlight that these ideas are about real action to be taken by real people like me and you. So the struggle for Afrikan liberation takes on life and higher meaning in the context of reinstituting MA'AT and overturning ISFET (Chaos and Disorder [White Supremacy]). So, no matter who and where we are, our age, gender, socio-economic status etc. we can all find purpose and meaning in bringing these principles to life through our thoughts, words and deeds.

4. *Identification with Spiritual Life or the Higher Ideals*

This virtue links to virtue 6 below 'Evidence of a Call to Spiritual Orders'. It is about the development of a spiritual life and adherence to a set of ideas which embody fundamental principles regarding what it is to live a good life e.g. Principles of Ma'at. It is about placing one's life within a broader context both historically and cosmically i.e. seeing the connection between yourself, those who have gone before and those who have yet to come as well as recognising your connection with creation as embodied in the Afrikan principle of consubstantiation, the idea that everything in the universe is connected and comes from the same source.

5. Evidence of Mission in Life

Mission links to purpose. In exploring the third virtue we identified the principles of MA'AT as providing a framework from which we could all find purpose in our lives. In terms of manifesting evidence of mission in life I will use the struggle against White Supremacy and the metaphor of war to bring clarity to this subject. If we conceptualise our condition as being at war – perhaps more accurately under attack – then we can recognise ourselves as part of a great – if disorganised – army.

As with any army there will be commanders/generals and all ranks beneath. There will be specialists and generalists, but everyone will have a purpose. Some will be in the infantry taking the flak in the frontline and experiencing the highest casualty rates, others will specialise in covert operations working behind enemy lines, whilst still others will work in logistics, medical services etc. and other essential support services. However, whatever your role everyone has a vital role to play if the war is to be won.

Therefore your mission is to be an effective warrior or soldier. We may each battle in different ways, operate on different terrain, utilise different weapons (resources), however we must all fight to the end. You must identify your role in the army in order to carry out your purpose which will be how you fulfil your mission which is to contribute to the reinstatement of Ma'at.

6. Evidence of a call to Spiritual Orders

As mentioned earlier, the ten Afrikan virtues represented those qualities the neophyte priest in Kemet was expected to manifest. Since we are not all looking to enter the priesthood we perhaps need to reinterpret this virtue as 'Evidence of Spiritual Development'. This virtue does not require adherence to any particular religion or belief system but rather the desire for, and manifestation of, a greater interest in the metaphysical over the material and the ability to translate that into action that represents right conduct.

7. Freedom from Resentment (under persecution or wrong)

On the face of it this is a tough one. Perhaps the toughest. How do we interpret this virtue? How do I interpret this virtue given all I have written in the preceding pages about the war against White Supremacy? How can we demonstrate freedom from resentment under persecution or wrong, and more to the point why should we?

My take on this virtue is that it is a warning against the effects of prolonged bitterness and resentment. I do not think it is an advocation to 'Love Thine Enemy' or 'Turn the other Cheek'. It is a health warning, physical, mental and spiritual. It is a warning against the corrosive effects that certain emotional states can have upon one's well being, even if it is understandable to experience these feelings when wronged. It is also important for us to understand that this virtue is not suggesting that one should endure persecution without complaint. We have a duty to reinstate Ma'at and hence to fight for Justice. This is something the ANC forgot with their Truth and Reconciliation Commission in South Africa which did not seek or deliver Justice and hence perpetuated the wrong committed against Afrikan people.

The test is to avoid both self-pity and resentment whilst engaging in the battle for liberation.

8. *Confidence in the power of Master (as Teacher)*

"When the pupil is ready, the master will appear." (James 1954: 31). As I mentioned in my previous book (Grant 2003) I have had the great fortune of learning directly from three master teachers or

Walimu. These are Mwalimu Aina Anku Ra (George ben Anthony), Paul Obinna Wilson-Eme and Martin Glynn. Each has taught me in their own unique and special way. I say I have been lucky, however it goes beyond luck. If there is any credit due to me it is for having the sense to recognise these Master teachers when they appeared before me and drinking deeply from there respective fonts of knowledge. Many people are presented with great opportunities to learn and study from those who have greater wisdom and knowledge, however many reject these chances due to pride and ego. Sometimes your Master teacher will be your mother or father, sometimes a friend, most of the time they will not be consciously teaching you, however you need to be consciously learning. Use every day as a learning opportunity and remember that you can learn something from everyone you meet. The key is to decipher the lesson to be learnt.

9. *Confidence in one's ability to Learn*
   The talk in education over the past ten years and more has all been about lifelong learning. Learning from the womb to the tomb. There is a push to emphasise that education does not begin and end at the school gates and anyone who has had involvement with education in the UK – and no doubt the same is true in many other parts of the world – would recognise that much of what passes for education is little more than regurgatative training. Teaching children to spew forth information as opposed to assisting in the process of acquiring knowledge.

   The formal education system systematically devalues, deskills, demotivates and destroys the confidence in their ability to learn of the majority of Afrikan children who pass through its institutions. This is the reason why many Afrikan children only retain their confidence to learn in a narrow and stereotypical range of activities which the dominant Caucasian culture has prescribed as acceptable for Afrikans to excel in, namely, singing/rapping, dancing, particular sports and other forms of entertaining. From having a 360 degree learning field of vision at birth the Afrikan child is reduced down to a 36 degree learning field of vision. The 10% confident 90% unconfident Afrikan child becomes the 10% confident 90% unconfident Afrikan adult. When W.E.B. DuBois spoke of the 'talented tenth' of Afrikan-Americans he was wrong. These were probably the 10% of Afrikan-Americans who had obtained some small degree of opportunity to break free of the intellectual shackles placed upon them by their Caucasian oppressors and were grabbing every opportunity for learning with both hands. Most people have some form of talent in some field, however most do not discover this talent, do not pursue it or give up the pursuit when discouraged. Afrikans have more barriers and discouragements placed in our path, which is why so many of our people are failing to fulfil their gifts.

We need to push ourselves further and harder to unleash the potential within.

10. Readiness or preparedness for Initiation

This attribute links directly to the need for, and processes of, rites of passage. There are five main rites of passage in Afrikan culture which are associated with birth, adolescence, marriage, eldership and death. The rite that most people are familiar with is the rite of adolescence. This rite is the often unrecognised basis for many of the support programmes aimed at Afrikan – and non-Afrikan – adolescents. However, increasingly we see community groups explicitly and consciously linking their programmes to the rites of passage concept and model. In the UK the New Initiatives project has been carrying out such work for many years and in Nottingham a group I am involved with Brother to Brother launched a rites of passage programme in late 2005. Rites of passage programmes have been well established in the USA for many years and of course in Afrika we have rites of passage still surviving in its original undiluted form.

The basic rites of passage model is shown below.

Diagram (viii) – Rites of Passage conceptual model

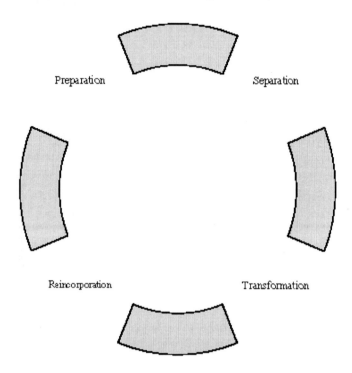

Preparation

Separation

Reincorporation

Transformation

In the Afrikan cultural system a young person would spend the whole of their life in preparation for each of the various stages of initiation that they would undertake and therefore none of the ideas described here would be of surprise to them although the concepts would no doubt be articulated differently. For those of us in 'the West' it is about trying to learn about that which we have lost due to the Mangalize (see glossary) and reclaiming, recapturing and contextualising these processes for ourselves and our children. In other words, what does it mean to us in the time, space and place we occupy.

We once knew how to prepare ourselves for initiation and change. We are now remembering and in remembering, re-membering, putting the Afrikan mind, body and soul back together as Auset did when she re-membered Ausar.

Amos Wilson sets out in clear terms the challenge facing Afrikan men (and much of this applies to Afrikan women) in preparing our young and indeed ourselves for adulthood.

"Within the context and confines of White male dominance and racism however, the failure of 'mature' Afrikan American males to assume full responsibility for educating and training Afrikan American boys and adolescents for productive manhood — their failure to take economic and political control of their national communities; to aggressively move in and capture economic territory, real estate, health and other economic institutions in the larger society and the world so as to alleviate and prevent the conditions of which we speak in this volume; their failure to learn of the realities of power and of power relations between groups and nations; to prepare for the defense of Afrikan peoples against their current and future enemies; their willingness to continue their dependence on the largesse of White males; to submit to the dominance of White males in America and the world; their apparent inability, lack of will or courage to form a nation-within-a-nation and to set as one of their ultimate goals the collapse of White male power advantages; their relative powerlessness to transform the social and economic misfortunes of the Afrikan American community and of the Pan-Afrikan community — glaringly reveal their inadequate preparation for assuming the responsibilities of Afrikan manhood, whether they may be classified as prosocial or antisocial, responsible or irresponsible."

Amos N. Wilson
Understanding Black Adolescent Male Violence (1991)

Endnote

It is very common to hear Afrikan youngsters using the phrase 'Yu get meh' and I suppose that would be the question I would ask you the reader at the end of this book. Did you get where I was coming from? Did this work have meaning and relevance to you and your experience and understanding of the world around you?

I have tried to set out the nature of the challenge placed before us in order to assist each reader to play their part in banishing the storm clouds that seem to hover over an all too often bleak and desolate Afrikan economic, social and cultural landscape. Which way to go? For us, like water, the path of least resistance seems so tempting and alluring.

Even those of us who are not struggling are tired of the struggle. As an elder often reminds me... "Yes, it's hard. That's why they call it a struggle"! However, I know I get tired of being part of a 'disorganised truth up against an organised lie'. Just like you I would like to see transformational change in my lifetime. I yearn to see our people free, our babies happy and fed, our elders healthy and content, our sisters loved in the arms of brothers, our brothers happy to love a sister, our resources back under Afrikan control, the Earth respected and repaired, our ancestors remembered and venerated, the Creator known through an Afrikan mind and heart. This is my dream; however a dream without a plan is like trying to catch smoke in your hands. It can't work.

So, enough dreaming and more planning. We need to ask ourselves a few simple questions:

> How do I contribute to the uplift of Afrikan people?
> Could I do what I currently do better?
> What more could I do to contribute to the uplift of Afrikan people?

Are the things I think, say and do congruent with Afrikan cultural values?

How can we improve Afrikan cultural practice?

All these questions must be asked if we are to move ahead constructively. We cannot put Afrikan culture in a glass cabinet like some museum piece, untouchable, unchanging, decaying. Our culture must adapt, reform and reshape just as the geophysical landscape, adapts, reforms and reshapes in response to the environment. However in order to be able to undertake this cultural renewal we have to find out what we lost in the first place in order to identify that which must be reclaimed and that which must be discarded. This is no easy task. It is the 'New Sankofa' The Sankofa bird looking in all directions simultaneously as we not only go back to fetch that which we have lost, but move ahead creating new cultural manifestations to meet our needs in the world today.

Are you up for it? This book is one contribution I can make towards achieving this goal. Tiny in the wider scheme of things, but big for me. And so it will be for most us, tiny steps for individual Afrikans put together equates to huge strides for us all. Put together a billion tiny steps and you have transformational change.

It requires a leap of faith. So, let's all leap together.

Bibliography

Afrika, L. (1998) Afrikan Holistic Health: your guide to health and well-being, Brooklyn, New York: A & B Book Publishers Group

Akbar, N. (2003) Visions for Black Men, Tallahassee, FL.: Mind Productions & Associates, Inc.

Amadiume, I. (2001) REINVENTING Africa: MATRIARCHY, RELIGION & CULTURE, London: Zed Books

Andrews, G.R. (1980) The Afro-Argentines of Buenos Aires 1800-1900, Wisconsin: University of Wisconsin

Ani, M. (1996) YURUGU: AN AFRICAN-CENTERED CULTURAL CRITIQUE OF EUROPEAN CULTURAL THOUGHT AND BEHAVIOR, Trenton, NJ: Africa World Press

Baruti, K.B. (2003) HOMOSEXUALITY AND THE EFFEMINZATION OF AFRIKAN MALES, Atlanta, Georgia: Akoben House

Baruti, K.B. (2004) ASAFO: A WARRIOR'S GUIDE TO MANHOOD, Atlanta, Georgia: Akoben House

Biko, F. (1998) Speech at Ancestors Memorial Day, Birmingham and other speeches

Black Hair and Beauty Magazine Dec 2004/Jan 2005

Blum, W. (2003) ROGUE STATE, London: Zed Books

Budu-Acquah, K. (1960) Ghana, The Morning After, Self-published in London

Carruthers, J.H. (1999) Intellectual Warfare, Chicago: Third World Press

Carruthers, J.H & Karenga, M. (eds) (1986) KEMET AND THE AFRICAN WORLDVIEW, Los Angeles, California: University of Sankore Press

Chomsky, N. (1996) World Orders Old and New, New York: Columbia University

Clarke, J.H. (1998) Christopher Columbus and the Afrikan Holocaust: Slavery and the Rise of European Capitalism, New York: A & B Publisher Group

Diop, C.A. (1989) THE CULTURAL UNITY OF BLACK AFRICA: The

Domains of Matriarchy and Patriarchy in Classical Antiquity, London: Karnak House

Do Nascimento, A. (1979) BRAZIL MIXTURE OR MASSACRE?: Essays in the Genocide of a Black People, Dover, Mass: The Majority Press

Evans, M. (1995) in Moore, Sanders and Moore eds. The Relationship of Childrearing Practices to Chaos and Change in the African American Family, African Presence in the Americas, Trenton, NJ.: Africa World Press

Faal, S. (13 July 2005) www.rense.com

Garvey, A.J. (1986) editor. THE PHILOSOPHY AND OPINIONS OF MARCUS GARVEY: Or, Africa for the Africans, Dover, Mass.: The Majority Press

Grant, P. (2003) Niggers, Negroes, Black People and Afrikans, Nottingham, United Kingdom: Navig8or Press

Golding, W. (1969) Lord of the Flies, London: Faber and Faber Limited

Griffiths, P. (2003) The Economist's Tale: A Consultant Encounters Hunger and the World Bank, London: Zed Books

Guardian Newspaper, 28 April 2004, London and Manchester, Guardian Newspapers Ltd.

Guardian Newspaper, 19 January 2005, London and Manchester, Guardian Newspapers Ltd.

Guardian Newspaper, 18 July 2005, London and Manchester, Guardian Newspapers Ltd.

Hare, N. and Hare, J. eds. (1989) CRISIS IN BLACK SEXUAL POLITICS, San Francisco, Cal: BLACK THINK TANK

Hare, N. and Hare, J. (1993) The Endangered Black Family: Coping with the Unisexualisation and Coming Extinction of the Black Race, San Francisco, CA,: BLACK THINK TANK

James, George G.M. (1954) STOLEN LEGACY: Greek Philosophy Is Stolen Egyptian Philosophy, Trenton, New Jersey: Africa World Press, Inc.

Jones, D. (2005) SHOWDOWN, Philadelphia: Del Jones Books n' Music, Inc.

Karenga, M. (1984) SELECTIONS FROM THE HUSIA: SACRED WISDOM OF ANCIENT EGYPT, Los Angeles, Cal: The University of Sankore Press

Karenga, M. 'The Black Male/Female Connerction' in Hare, N. and Hare, J. (Eds) (1989) CRISIS IN BLACK SEXUAL POLITICS, San Francisco, Cal: BLACK THINK TANK

Klein, N. 02 February 2005 Guardian Newspaper, London and Manchester, Guardian Newspapers Ltd.

Kunene, M. (1979) Emperor Shaka the Great, London: Heinemann

Ligali African History Newsletter March 2005

Madhubuti, H. (1991) BLACK MEN: Obsolete, Single, Dangerous, Chicago, IL: Third World Press

Martin, T. (1993) THE JEWISH ONSLAUGHT: Despatches from the Wellesley Battlefront, Dover, Mass: THE MAJORITY PRESS

Morrone, F.C. (1995) *LOS NEGROS EN EL EJÉRCITO: DECLINACIÓN DEMOGRÁFICA Y DISOLUCIÓN,* Argentina: Centro Editor de America Latina

Nation of Islam (1994) The Secret Relationship Between Blacks and Jews, Boston, MA.: Historical Research Department, Nation of Islam

New Internationalist Magazine March 2004, Vol. 10, Issue 11

Nobles, W.W. (1990's) Education of the Black Child Conference, Manchester

One City Partnership Nottingham, (2005) Action From Facts: Educational Attainment, Focus on Black Boys, (Unpublished)

Pachecho, R. (1997) Florida, Florida State University

Persaud, R. (2004) Why Black Men Love White Women: An Explicit Excursion in Sexual Politics, Brooklyn, New York: D & R Publishing

Polya, G. (2005) www.countercurrents.org

Observer Newspaper 17th July 2005

Olivelle, P. (2004) THE LAW CODE OF MANU, Oxford: Oxford University Press

Ramirez, L.O. (ed) (2004) Mexican Jaguar: For Honor and Glory

Redfield, J. (1994) THE CELESTINE PROPHECY: AN ADVENTURE, London: Bantam Books

Rotello, S. 3rd February 1998, Los Angeles Times

Scott, J.W. (1989) in Hare, N. and Hare, J. (Eds) (1989) CRISIS IN BLACK SEXUAL POLITICS, San Francisco, Cal: BLACK THINK TANK

Shaw, M. (1993) Vol. No.3 Professional Tips for Adult and Continuing Education, Tips on Teaching African-American Adults, Pensylvania: Pensylvania State University

Staples, R. (1989) 'Beauty and the Beast: The Importance of Physical Attractiveness in the Black Community' in Hare, N. and Hare, J. (Eds)

(1989) CRISIS IN BLACK SEXUAL POLITICS, San Francisco, Cal: BLACK THINK TANK

St Clair, J. Grand Theft Pentagon (awaiting publication)

T'Shaka, O. (2004) Press Release promoting 'The Integration Trap The Generation Gap'

United Kingdom Census 2001

Vallely, P. (2005) Independent Newspaper, 09 September 2005, Independent News & Media (UK) Ltd.

Welsing, F.C. (1991) The ISIS PAPERS: THE KEYS TO THE COLORS, Chicago, IL.: Third World Press

Wilson-Eme, P.O. Recommendations for Parents, Unpublished

Wright, B.E. (1984) THE PSYCHOPATHIC RACIAL PERSONALITY: AND OTHER ESSAYS, Chicago: Third World Press

Wilson, A.N. (1987) The Developmental Psychology of The Black Child, New York: Africana Research Publications

Wilson, A.N. (1991) Understanding Black Adolescent Male Violence: Its Remediation and Prevention, New York: AFRIKAN WORLD INFOSYSTEMS

Wilson, A.N. (1998) BluePrint for BLACK POWER, New York: AFRIKAN WORLD INFOSYSTEMS

www.blacksandjews.com

www.blink.org.uk

www.countercurrents.org.

www.maafa.org

www.renewal.net High attainment levels for Black Caribbean pupils in a Birmingham junior school (2004)

www.washingtonpost.com

www.wsws.org

Young, Y. (2004) 'Tough Choices for Tough Times' USA Today, first appeared on www.womeninthelife.com/articles/commoncents/toughchoices

Zagorsky, J. in Metro Newspaper 15 July 2005, London

About The Author

Paul Ifayomi Grant was born in Edmonton, North London in 1966, the second of three children. He was (mis)educated in Edmonton, Enfield and Leicester up until the age of 22. He has worked in a variety of roles in the Midlands, including running his own recruitment consultancy business, working in prisons and with ex-offenders as an Employment/Training Adviser, working as a Training & Development Manager, as a Community Safety Consultant and as the Deputy Chief Executive for a regeneration programme where his responsibilities included: overall programme delivery, Human Resources, Equalities, Social Procurement and Community Elections.

In February 2006 Paul returned to self-employment and founded Navigation Consulting Ltd a management consultancy through which he conducts social research and organisational development activities. In January 2007 he launched an Empowerment Coaching service which assists individuals to fulfil their potential, be it in their professional, personal or financial sphere of life.

He is an active member of the Afrikan community in Nottingham and is involved in a number of community groups, most notably: Nubian Link a community education group, ABDF Ltd (formerly Afrikan Business Development Fund) a community economic development company which he conceived and co-founded, Chair and co-founder of the Nottingham Black Families in Education Parent Support Group which provides educational advocacy and support, and a founder member of Brother ll Brother, an Afrikan men's group developing and delivering rites of passage programmes. Paul also helped to create the Empower Group, a support group for Afrikans working in mentoring, which over time has transformed to become a group of friends who support each other on their life journeys.

Paul is the son of Orinthea and Reuben Grant. He is married to a beautiful Afrikan queen Beverley and they have two lovely children Jawanza Kwesi and Abiba Ashia Orinthea. He has an elder brother Nigel and a younger sister Tracey.

To contact the author please email him at: ifayomi@ntlworld.com or telephone him on 0770 3004813. You can also visit his website www.houseofknowledge.org.uk where you can read his essays, buy his books, CDs/DVDs and register to receive his free e-newsletter 'The Navig8or'.

Other Books by Paul Ifayomi Grant

Niggers, Negroes, Black People & Afrikans

Saving Our Sons (DVD also available)

Sankofa The Wise Man and his Amazing Friends

Forthcoming Titles:

Why Willie Lynch Must Die

A Celebration of Black Love

My Special Time

No More Ifs, Buts and Maybes - The Practical Guide to Ethical Success